Qur'ānic Stories

Edinburgh Studies in Classical Arabic Literature
Series Editors: Wen-chin Ouyang and Julia Bray

This series departs from conventional writing on Classical Arabic Literature. It integrates into its terms of enquiry both cultural and literary theory and the historical contexts and conceptual categories that shaped individual writers or works of literature. Its approach provides a forum for path-breaking research which has yet to exert an impact on the scholarship. The purpose of the series is to open up new vistas on an intellectual and imaginative tradition that has repeatedly contributed to world cultures and has the continued capacity to stimulate new thinking.

Books in the series include:

Qur'ānic Stories: God, Revelation and the Audience
Leyla Ozgur Alhassen

The Reader in al-Jāhiz: The Epistolary Rhetoric of an Arabic Prose Master
Thomas Hefter

Recognition in the Arabic Narrative Tradition: Discovery, Deliverance and Delusion
Philip F. Kennedy

Counsel for Kings: Wisdom and Politics in Tenth-Century Iran
Volume I: The Naṣīḥat al-mulūk of Pseudo Māwardī: Contexts and Themes
Louise Marlow

Counsel for Kings: Wisdom and Politics in Tenth-Century Iran
Volume II: The Naṣīḥat al-mulūk of Pseudo Māwardī: Texts, Sources and Authorities
Louise Marlow

Al-Jāhiz, the Quibbler: Equivocations in Kitab al-Ḥayawan and Beyond
Jeannie Miller

Al-Jāḥiẓ: In Praise of Books
James E. Montgomery

Al-Jāḥiẓ: In Censure of Books
James E. Montgomery

Ḥikāyat Abī al-Qāsim: A Literary Banquet
Emily Selove

edinburghuniversitypress.com/series/escal

Qur’ānic Stories

God, Revelation and the Audience

Leyla Ozgur Alhassen

EDINBURGH
University Press

Edinburgh University Press is one of the leading university presses in the UK. We publish academic books and journals in our selected subject areas across the humanities and social sciences, combining cutting-edge scholarship with high editorial and production values to produce academic works of lasting importance. For more information visit our website: edinburghuniversitypress.com

Edinburgh University Press Ltd
The Tun – Holyrood Road
12 (2f) Jackson's Entry
Edinburgh EH8 8PJ

First published in hardback by Edinburgh University Press 2021

Typeset in 11/15 Adobe Garamond by
Servis Filmsetting Ltd, Stockport, Cheshire,
printed and bound by CPI Group (UK) Ltd,
Croydon, CR0 4YY

A CIP record for this book is available from the British Library

ISBN 978 1 4744 8317 9 (hardback)
ISBN 978 1 4744 8318 6 (paperback)
ISBN 978 1 4744 8320 9 (webready PDF)
ISBN 978 1 4744 8319 3 (epub)

Contents

Figures and Tables

Acknowledgements

I am grateful to the series editors Wen-chin Ouyang and Julia Bray, as well as the reviewers of this book, whose feedback has drastically improved it. They, along with Nicola Ramsey, Emma Rees and Kirsty Woods, made this a smooth and transparent editing and publishing process. Many thanks to the Department of Near Eastern Studies at the University of California, Berkeley, as well as to Asad Ahmed, Robert Alter, Charles Hirschkind, Margaret Larkin and the late Saba Mahmood for our discussions on my research. I began my journey of studying Arabic literature at the University of California, Los Angeles, with Michael Cooperson, who helped me develop and refine my thoughts for this book with his knowledgeable, detailed and insightful guidance. Immense gratitude goes to him and the rest of my dissertation committee members for their support in this process: Carol Bakhos, Lowell Gallagher and Nouri Gana. Thanks are also due to Kecia Ali, Sarra Tlili, Asad Ahmed and Michael Cooperson for sharing publishing and professional advice. The completion of this book was partially funded by a National Endowment for the Humanities Summer Stipend. I am also grateful to have received a Sultan Fellowship from the Center for Middle Eastern Studies, University of California, Berkeley. Many thanks to Arielle Tonkin for expanding my mind by exploring beauty and justice together. It is a blessing to have such an enlightening and encouraging friend. I am grateful to the artist, Salma Arastu, for sharing her artwork depicting Qur'ānic verse 20:46 for the cover of this book. I have been repeatedly struck by the generosity with the gifts of time and thought that my colleagues and friends have given me by reading and commenting on drafts of this book, and in conversations about my research.

I thank my parents, Necva and Mehmet Ozgur, for their support and love. They have been my number-one supporters and were always eager to hear about and discuss my research. My husband, Fares Alhassen, helped me manage my time and encouraged me to finish this book. My appreciation and love go to my entire family. I hope that my children will one day read this book and benefit from it.

I dedicate this book to my parents, my children and to my dear friend, Angeles Flores, who taught me that love, learning and knowledge can all be intricately connected.

1

Introduction: A Narratological and Rhetorical Approach to Qur'ānic Stories

In *Sūrat Āl 'Imrān* we read about a woman dedicating the child in her womb to God (3:35). Here, a story begins with a dialogue, but the readers are not told that this is a woman to whom they should pay close attention, nor that the woman is pregnant, nor even her name. Instead, the readers overhear her prayer to God and from her prayer can infer certain things. With this story, the audience realises their lack of knowledge and that they know things only if and when the narrator chooses to relate them.

In response to such reading experiences, this book adopts a literary approach to the Qur'ān[1] and analyses the structure, rhetorical devices, narratological features, semantic devices, themes and audience reception as evidenced in scholarly exegesis (*tafsīr*). For example, Chapter 3 on *Surat Maryam* employs a structural analysis, looking at verse length and echoing phrases in order to demonstrate how the structure changes from a focus on family relationships to a relationship with God. This approach centres on the relationship between narrator and audience, and how the text aims for a response from its audience. One may notice, for example, in *Sūrat al-Qaṣaṣ* a selective presenting and withholding of information in which readers are given new and exclusive information about Mūsā's marriage, balanced by incomplete descriptions of a contract that he enters and, later, the location of his conversation with God. This is a narrative technique that keeps listeners and readers of the Qur'ān in the dark and makes them wonder about certain things; the narrator makes it very clear that what we know about this story is what God tells us. Here, it is useful to look at the reception of Qur'ānic stories in the context of Qur'ānic commentary: commentators try to supply the missing details about which the text makes one curious – such as the exact number of the years that Mūsā agrees to work for his father-in-law and the reasons why readers are told that it may be eight or ten years, but not the exact number.

This study examines the interaction of the text with the audience. First and foremost, it is important to mention that the Qur'ān is a text that is not only read, but also heard and recited. When I refer to the audience of the Qur'ān as the audience or readers, this may be considered a shorthand term that also includes the reciters and listeners of the Qur'ān. Who exactly is this audience? It is not a reader approaching the text from a historical standpoint – such a reader would probably look to other sources to draw comparisons and to ask questions about the text different from the present concerns. Neither is it a hostile or polemical reader – such a reader might dismiss narrative techniques when feeling challenged by them. Rather, it is an analytical believer who also has a sense of literary or artistic appreciation – a believer who can read a text knowing that it has resonated (and continues to do so) with millions of people who belong to the same community of the faithful, who will wonder and try to understand what the text does and how it works to achieve such results. The commentators whose works I analyse as examples of readers encountering the text hail from both modern and classical *tafsīr* traditions. They provide multiple loci for looking at the Qur'ān as a dialogue between God – the ultimate narrator in and of the Qur'ān – and the audience.

It is worth taking a moment to consider the Qur'ānic references to God as reflected in the present study. In the Qur'ān, God or Allah is referred to in the third person masculine singular *huwa* and the first person plural *naḥnu* (which is usually explained as reflecting God's majesty). At the same time, Allah is not considered to be gendered in Islamic theology. Accordingly, I refer to God as God or He, and I have reduced my use of the pronoun in order to keep gendered reference to a minimum.

The Qur'ān itself describes its audience (for example, 2:2 and 2:26) and addresses them by using the second person singular and plural.[2] The second person singular sometimes specifically addresses the Prophet Muḥammad (see, for example, 5:41, 5:67, 8:64, 8:65, 8:70, 9:73, 33:1, 33:28, 33:45, 33:50, 33:59, 60:12, 65:1, 66:1, 66:9, 73:1 and 74:1). There are also second person singular addresses that do not specifically mention the Prophet. We see this, for instance, with the word '*qul*,' 'say', that initiates some verses (112:1,

113:1, 114:1 and more). Commentators and translators tend to interpret this 'you' as a direct address to the Prophet Muḥammad; yet, it can also be fruitfully analysed as a direct address to the reader.[3] The Qur'ān uses the plural to address all people (2:21, 2:168, 2:172, 2:178 and many more), other beings (55:31), specific faiths (4:47), those who believe (2:104, 2:153, 4:19, 4:29, 4:43 and many more), those who disbelieve (66:7) and messengers (23:51).

In this work I juxtapose scholarship from different socio-historical contexts in order to explore the performative dimensions of the Qur'ānic narrative. While many scholars of the Qur'ān focus on its historical dimensions – its development, its canonisation and the history of its interpretation – and while some assert that it cannot be studied as literature since it uses a limited number of narrative strategies, I approach the Qur'ān as a dynamic literary, religious and performative text. Accordingly, the following pages will discuss the text in reference to theories from Qur'ānic Studies, structuralism, rhetoric and narratology.[4] Narrative is an integral feature of the Qur'ān, and a narratological and rhetorical approach can contribute new insights to our understanding of the canonised text and how it utilises stories to further theological messages. It is hoped that this book will complement already existing historical and comparative studies[5] by offering a text-focused narrative analysis.

Key narrative features of Qur'ānic stories will be discussed: how characters and dialogues are portrayed, what themes are repeated, what verbal echoes and conceptual links are present, what structure is established and what theological beliefs are strengthened by these narrative choices. Some otherwise puzzling narrative features can be seen as instances in which God, as the narrator, centres Himself while putting the audience in their place, thus rendering the act of reading an interaction between God and the readers.

My analysis is structured around the concept of *tawḥīd*, or the oneness of God, as presented in the Qur'ān.[6] The Qur'ān is a theocentric text, and narrative choices are made to achieve the strongest possible theocentric impact. Hence, God is central in the content and style of Qur'ānic stories; narrative choices serve to highlight God, God's omnipotence and God's omniscience. We can look at the Qur'ān as a union of the temporal with the eternal.[7] For instance, Michael Sells writes about boundary moments in the Qur'ān and investigates how 'the structures of language (with temporality built into them) are transformed through contact with a realm beyond temporality'.[8]

While Sells focuses only on specific boundary moments, reading the entire Qur'ānic text as the meeting or joining of the eternal with the temporal presents a useful approach.

Here, I am interested in 'the impact, intended or actual, of a text on its audience or recipients'.[9] Rather than making claims about the Qur'ān's intentions, I extract and elaborate upon narrative choices that have a logic of their own and reflect the theological message that over the centuries has found resonance amongst listeners, readers and interpreters, in order to come to a better understanding of 'the power that the text has exerted on generations of Muslims'.[10] Given its nature as a performance text, in the present context the Qur'ān is to be considered as an event, a performance, a relationship and an act of revelation. The Qur'ān is an interaction between the speaker who establishes God's ethos and the audience.[11] In a manner most relevant to this context, Ulrika Martensson explains Aristotelian rhetorical concepts thus: 'In classical rhetoric, a speaker has three means to persuade the audience: His own moral character (ethos), the emotional state of the listener (pathos), and the argument (logos).'[12] Jane Dammen McAuliffe writes that the relationship between reader and Qur'ānic text is a dynamic one: 'The reader/hearer is changed through the event and brings that transformed consciousness back to the text in an ever-adjusting series of reciprocally transformative exchanges'.[13] The reading process, then, is an active one: 'The rhetorical affectivity of the Qur'ān challenges any notion of receptive passivity, any sense that hearing or reading it can be a matter of the mere conveyance of meaning'.[14]

Wayne Booth also provides relevant ways to think about the relationship between the Qur'ānic narrator, text and audience. One may think about the way in which readers feel about talented narrators: We may 'surrender ourselves to the great authors and allow our judgment to merge completely with theirs'.[15] There can also be a 'growing intimacy between the narrator and the reader'.[16] Regarding the relationship that the text develops between reader and narrator, one may moreover add the sense of awe that the Qur'ānic reader feels for the omniscient narrator. Booth writes that narrators 'succeed by persuading the reader to accept them as living oracles. They are reliable guides not only to the world of the novels in which they appear but also to the moral truths of the world outside the book'.[17] This notion works beautifully as an image of God appropriate for the Qur'ān, a book that presents itself as a source of Truth.

We can find many layers of narration in Qur'ānic stories. Drawing on Seymour Chatman's presentation of Gerald Prince's frame transmission, as well as Gerard Genette's distinction between stories and narrative discourse, one may then peel back these layers of narrative discourse, of which there exist three: Within the first layer, God as narrator addresses the audience. In the second layer, God the narrator addresses the Prophet Muḥammad. Within the second layer is embedded a third layer, featuring God as a character interacting with other characters. The model of layers (Figure 1.1) is particularly useful when analysing Qur'ānic stories, as it helps to maintain a clear perspective about the various interactions between God, the characters and the audience.[18]

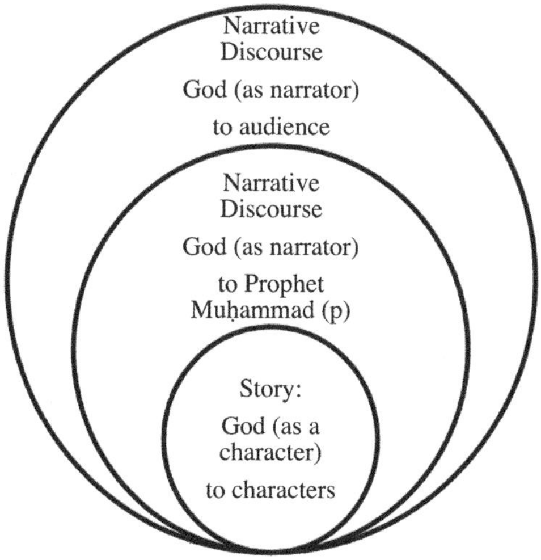

Figure 1.1 Qur'ānic narrative discourse and story

Furthermore, it is possible to discern auto-intertextual patterns in which an image, a word or a phrase connects one Qur'ānic story to another. In the context of Qur'ānic Studies, my work is inspired by Anthony H. Johns,[19] M. A. S. Abdel Haleem[20] and, more particularly, Toshihiko Izutsu who investigates the ways in which semantic echoes based on root letters connect verses in and across suras, and how these connections develop meaning.[21] I am equally indebted to Biblical Studies, and especially the works of Robert

Alter, which demonstrate how to analyse stories within their larger contexts, as well as in terms of their connections to other stories.[22] Alter examines semantic echoes based on root letters and discusses repetition in themes, both of which constitute elements of the present study.[23] In Qur'ānic commentary (*tafsīr*), this type of intertextual approach can be found under the term *tafsīr al-Qur'ān bi-l-Qur'ān*.

This work centres around the dynamic relationship between God, the Qur'ān, Qur'ānic commentary, the characters in Qur'ānic stories and the audience, as exemplified by the living traditions of *tafsīr* around the world. I use commentaries on and translations of the Qur'ān as examples of readers' understanding of the text. *Tafsīr* provides a context to see whether it is merely my own perspective – resulting from everything that makes me who I am, that makes me ask, understand and read in particular ways – or whether other readers have seen the text in the same way. In other words, I engage in conversation with *tafsīr*, in an approach to secondary sources that is reminiscent of Khaled Abou El Fadl's *Conference of the Books*.[24] My goal here is not to present a historical or comparative study, a literature review, history or survey of *tafsīr*. Neither do I look at its historical progression, or at how common or influential an interpretation may be. Rather, I bring *tafsīr* into the conversation because it is a record of how some audiences approached, understood and read the text.

We will encounter the commentaries of al-Tustarī (d. 283/896), al-Ṭabarī (d. 310/923), al-Zamakhsharī (d. 538/1144), al-Ṭabrisī (d. 548/1153), al-Jalālayn (d. 863/1459 and 911/1505), al-Thaʿālibī (d. 875/1471), Abū al-Suʿūd (d. 951/1544 CE), Sayyid Quṭb (d. 1387/1966) and Muḥammad al-Ghazālī (d. 1417/1996). I also refer to the comments of Muhammad Asad (d. 1412/1992) in his translation of the Qur'ān, as he uses various commentaries, including those of al-Baghawī ((d. 516/1122), al-Zamakhsharī (d. 538/1144) and al-Rāzī (d. 605/1209). These nine commentators illustrate some of the many possible reactions to the stories, employing various exegetical approaches and representing different time-periods. In addition, *tafsīr* can lend insight into a variety of topics such as occasions of revelation, a community's commentaries on certain verses and linguistic issues concerning those verses.

Given the great number of *tafsīr*, no attempt has been made to be comprehensive, whether in terms of location, time-period, or exegetical position. I use Qur'ānic commentary as a lens through which to see some of the many ways in which Qur'ānic verses can be used, interpreted and disputed. While some of these commentators count amongst the earliest (al-Tustarī), others are modern (Sayyid Quṭb). Al-Ṭabarī uses interpretation through transmitted material; al-Ṭabrisī presents a Shi'i commentary; al-Tustarī offers Sufi perspectives; and al-Zamakhsharī's commentary focuses on the rhetorical aspects of the Qur'ān. I analyse these commentators' interactions with the text, the questions that the text pushes them to ask and answer, and the evidence that they provide or that they fail to provide, thus contributing to our overall understanding of *tafsīr*. The commentaries serve as examples of readers' responses to the text, an encapsulation of the interaction of the Qur'ān with its readers and listeners; therefore, they can further our understanding of Qur'ānic narrative workings. This approach to commentaries in itself constitutes an argument that no one or no group of *tafsīr* is authoritative; rather, it is a way of resisting authoritarian, simplistic or hegemonic approaches to *tafsīr* and the Qur'ān. The point is their variety, in a horizontal expanse, and not their hierarchy.

Within this general framework, I examine stories that represent some of the variety and depth of Qur'ānic narrative technique. *Sūrat Yūsuf* figures here because it is unlike many other Qur'ānic narratives in that it consists of one isolated and lengthy iteration of the story of Yūsuf. The sections from *Sūrat Āl 'Imrān* and *Sūrat Maryam* form a pair, showing several repeated elements, as well as other elements that are not repeated. I chose *Surat Ṭā Hā* because it is a lengthy telling of Mūsā's story and because Mūsā's stories are the ones most frequently told in the Qur'ān. This is paired with *Sūrat al-Qaṣaṣ* because, like the previous pair, these two suras show ways in which the Qur'ān makes use of repetition. Alternatively, one may have compiled and analysed the stories of characters in the Qur'ān, but such a choice would have resulted in rewriting the stories. Mirroring this book's structure around the Qur'ānic stories' structure is more conducive to understanding them as they stand. In the end, the choice fell on stories that in different ways resisted contemporary expectations of how stories should be told, on stories that are told frequently and on stories that illustrate instances of repetition and intratextuality. Although this is not a comparative study, it is worth noting that the characters and stories from the Qur'ān under study here also appear in the Bible and the Torah.

Throughout, I will discuss the overarching questions of how Qur'ānic stories withhold knowledge, create consonance and forge connections, especially in *Sūrat Āl 'Imrān*, *Sūrat Maryam*, *Sūrat Yūsuf* and *Sūrat al-Qaṣaṣ*. We will explore the ways in which the text withholds from the audience information concerning signs and secrets, non-narrative verses, evidence, judgment and remorse, as well as the ways in which it provides new mysteries. In *Sūrat Āl 'Imrān*, one may also notice the withholding of control. This elucidates how the Qur'ān uses stories and narration to demonstrate and instil in its readers a belief in God's omniscience and omnipotence. God knows all and shows this to the audience by withholding certain things from them.

Although the narrator asserts God's power and control through narrative technique, we also see what I call the 'creation of consonance' in *Sūrat Āl 'Imrān*, *Sūrat Ṭaha* and *Sūrat al-Qaṣaṣ*. The creation of consonance presents a useful concept to discuss the Qur'ānic narrative strategy to build a relationship between various elements of the text: God, revelation and the audience. The word 'creating' is intended to bring to mind the Creator, who is the Qur'ānic narrator and author. This usage in and of itself argues that the Qur'ān's style goes hand in hand with the beliefs about God that it emphasises. Its narrative choices work to further beliefs about God and people's relationships with God.

The last overarching question concerns the ways in which the Qur'ān makes connections through semantic echoes (in *Sūrat Maryam*, *Sūrat Ṭaha* and *Sūrat al-Qaṣaṣ*). I explore how the Qur'ān uses semantic echoes to establish structure and to make intratextual allusions. These allusions occur within a story, between various parts of the same suras and with other suras. The semantic echoes connect verses throughout the Qur'ān in intricate webs; they complicate themes and comment on stories. By using intratextual connections, the Qur'ān rewards the attentive audience member who reads and listens carefully, notices echoing words or phrases and then traces them to other parts of the text, comparing them with each other and reflecting on them.

Each chapter employs a different analytical approach and focuses on a different theme. This will enable me to elucidate key features of specific stories, while also examining the breadth of the literary techniques in Qur'ānic stories.

Knowledge, Control and Consonance in *Sūrat Āl 'Imrān* 3:33–62

This chapter focuses on the story of Maryam, Maryam's mother, 'Īsā and Zakariyyā in *Sūrat Āl 'Imrān*, 3:33–62. This Qur'ānic narrative puts the readers – including Qur'ānic commentators – and characters in their place, by emphasising God's knowledge and control, as well as the readers' and characters' deficiency in both. This is achieved by cryptic explanations within the story, such as Maryam's words about provisions she has received, mostly unexplained leaps across time and portrayals of dialogues that do not fit our conceptions of historical reality. At the same time, the story comforts the audience by developing a consonance between the readers and the characters, and even the readers and God, while also including echoes that signal to the audience that they can understand more of the story if they read more of it in other passages within the Qur'ān. Based on these notions, this chapter will explain some otherwise puzzling stylistic choices.

God, Families and Secrets in the Story of *Sūrat Maryam* 19:1–58

The subsequent chapter concerns a story in *Sūrat Maryam*, 19:1–58, which includes some of the same characters as the previous story, as well as an iteration of the story in *Āl 'Imrān*. I focus on the story's structure, showing that, although it begins with the themes of God and family, the latter becomes less prominent and is eventually replaced by the theme of God and faith. Thus, God the narrator not only makes Himself central to the family, but God makes Himself replace the family. I then trace connections between this story and the sura's other parts that comment on it. At the same time, by contrasting the characters' secrets with God's secrets, the narrator once again reinforces God's privileged and omniscient position, while we further develop our understanding of the reader's place. In addition, I analyse examples from the *tafsīr* that demonstrate how readers notice and respond to the narrative portrayal of isolation and secrecy in the story.[25]

Evidence, Judgment and Remorse in *Surat Yūsuf*

The chapter on the story of Yūsuf takes at hand this lengthy, detailed story that features only one single iteration in the Qur'ān. I focus on the way in which God centres Himself in that story, specifically by showing through the narrative style that all that matters is God's forgiveness, truth and judgment; human notions of evidence, guilt and remorse are insignificant. By concentrating on these prominent themes, we further advance our understanding of God the narrator in the Qur'ān. Also part of the discussion are the points at which commentators struggle with these themes presented in the story; we sometimes see commentators supplying details that are not in the Qur'ān and thereby witness how the text has pushed them into a position of curiosity or puzzlement.

Merging Words and Making Connections in *Sūrat Ṭaha*

Sūrat Ṭaha, which discusses Mūsā at length, constitutes the vantage point for the next chapter. Here, I explore the ways in which the narrator shapes the perceptions and norms of the readers through the narrative style, while making them work. This approach is inspired by Wayne Booth's scholarship on different types of narrators and the narrator's interaction with the reader. I discuss examples of this interaction based on the following three categories: God the narrator confirming His own words, God the narrator confirming good people's words and semantic connections. In this context, God appears as an omniscient and reliable narrator who sometimes withholds information from readers or makes them work hard by using subtle language. This chapter also discusses several examples of how commentators fill in the gaps within the Qur'ānic story.

Sūrat al-Qaṣaṣ and its Audience

In this chapter, I examine the story of Mūsā in *Sūrat al-Qaṣaṣ*. Albeit another lengthy iteration of Mūsā's story, it includes details that do not figure in *Sūrat Ṭaha*. This discussion utilises an intratextual approach in order to gain insight into how Qur'ānic verses can explain each other. The Qur'ān is an oral and a recited text and, therefore, any intratextual references are striking. Here, I focus on the way in which the narrator provides new and sometimes exclusive details, while also presenting new mysteries. In addition, we see allusions to other stories and verses in the Qur'ān. Through these narrative devices, the narrator sometimes makes the reader a privileged one (again, a concept inspired by Booth); yet, these are balanced by mysteries meant to keep the audience in their place. At the same time, the narrator rewards hard-working and attentive readers who continue to engage with the text, who thus understand more and consequently notice references to other stories within the Qur'ān. Furthermore, I discuss commentators' reactions to these mysteries.

In its entirety, this book aims to contribute to discussions on scripture, the Qur'ān as literature, Qur'ānic stories, Qur'ānic commentary and Qur'ānic literary style, while also offering an introduction to Qur'ānic narrative and to some of the ways in which the Qur'ān interacts with its readers. Qur'ānic stories present features that can deepen our understanding of Arabic literature and of stories in general. Although the present research does not directly address the questions of whether there exists narrative in the Qur'ān or whether the Qur'ān features a coherent structure, it implies (and presents evidence for) both.[26] Discussing irony in *Sūrat Yūsuf*, Mustansir Mir – who has played a critical role in the literary analysis of the Qur'ān – argues that irony may also be found in other places in the Qur'ān and that readers may not understand or misunderstand it,[27] simply because they are not reading the text from a literary perspective. Mir expands this point:

> . . . it is doubtful whether the theology of the text can be fully comprehended in disregard of its literary dimension. In a wider sense, therefore, [my work] may be taken as a plea for studying the Qur'ān as literature not only for the sake of cultivating a largely ignored area of Qur'ānic studies, but also for the sake of developing a better understanding of the content of the Qur'ān.[28]

Hence, this study lends insight into the Qur'ānic message itself, by examining intersections of language, interpretation, ambiguity, power, control, authority and knowledge through the lens of Qur'ānic stories. Throughout the Qur'ānic text, God the narrator shows that He can do as He wills, in regard to the characters, the readers as readers and the readers as actual people. God chooses to reveal what He wills to whom He wills, in the manner that He wills. Thus, both narrative style and content in the Qur'ān encourage readers to believe in one omnipotent, omniscient God and to know their own place in relation to God.

Notes

1. I have chosen to use the translation of the Qur'ān by M. A. S. Abdel Haleem as a convenient vantage point for discussion. Where other translations are used, this will be clearly indicated. Abdel Haleem, *The Qur'ān: English Translation and Parallel Arabic Text.*
2. For more on Qur'ānic addressees, see Hoffmann, 'Agnostic Poetics in the Qur'ān' 43–5.
3. See, for example, Ozgur Alhassen, 'You Were Not There'; Saleh, *Classical Tafsīr Tradition* 113; Yazicioglu, *Understanding the Qur'ānic Miracle Stories* 165 (in reference to Saleh, *Classical Tafsīr Traditions* 119); Morris 204. Similarly, Anthony Johns mentions in *Surat Yūsuf* that, although Yūsuf begins by addressing his prison-mates in the dual form, 'then using the plural, he turns to the world outside the story' (12:39–40). Johns, 'Joseph in the Qur'ān' 33.
4. For more on a literary approach to the Qur'ān, see Ernst 8–9, 11.
5. For examples, see Angelika Neuwirth, Michael Pregill and Gabriel Said Reynolds. Their research questions are of a historical nature, such as who the Qur'ān's audience was, how it changed and why. Moreover, they employ a comparative methodology, looking at the Torah and various Biblical sources in comparison to the Qur'ān.
6. Al-Ghazālī 333; Ben Abdeljelil 14.
7. See Kazmi 202; Neuwirth, 'Qur'ān and History' 16; Klar 7; Wahyudi 19; Laude 159.
8. Sells, 'A Literary Approach to the Hymnic Sūras of the Qur'ān' 4.
9. Zebiri 95–6, 104, 111. See also: Kermani, *God Is Beautiful* 69, 73.
10. Zebiri 115.
11. Ozgur Alhassen, 'You Were Not There' 69.
12. Martensson 381.
13. McAuliffe, 'Text and Textuality' 68.
14. McAuliffe, 'Text and Textuality' 70.
15. Booth 213.
16. Booth 216.
17. Booth 221.
18. Morris includes a model specifically for *Sūrat Yūsuf*: 'Frame NARRATOR; Divine "WE"; ACTORS; INNER "ASIDES."' Morris 205.

19. For example: Johns, 'Narrative, Intertext and Allusion in the Qur'anic Presentation of Job' 2, 22 and 23.
20. For example: Abdel Haleem, 'Qur'anic "*jihād*"' 147, 156 and 163.
21. Izutsu, *God and Man in the Qur'an* and *The Structure of Ethical Terms in the Quran.*
22. Alter, 'Sodom as Nexus' 38.
23. Alter, *The Art of Biblical Narrative* 95–6.
24. Abou El Fadl, *Conference of the Books.*
25. Parts of this chapter have been previously published in Ozgur Alhassen, 'A Structural Analysis of *Sūrat Maryam* Q. 19:1–58.'
26. For discussions on coherence in the Qur'ān, see Mir, *Coherence in the Qur'ān*; Cuypers, *The Banquet*; Ernst; El-Awa, *Textual Relations in the Qur'ān*; and Robinson, *Discovering the Qur'an.*
27. Mir, 'Irony in the Qur'an' 185.
28. Ibid.

2

Knowledge, Control and Consonance in *Sūrat Āl ʿImrān* 3:33–62

I. Introduction

Sūrat Āl ʿImrān 3:33–62 contains a story in which God is portrayed as saying 'Be' and it is. Maryam questions how she could possibly have a child, and she is told: '"This is how God creates what He will: when He has ordained something, He only says, 'Be', and it is"' (3:47). There follows a verse comparing the creation of ʿĪsā to the creation of Ādam: 'In God's eyes Jesus is just like Adam: He created him from dust, said to him, "Be", and he was' (3:59). Thus, we see God creating as He wills, with God saying 'Be' and it is, *kun fa-yakūn*. When examining the entire story in verses 3:33–62, one finds that the Qur'ānic narrative style serves to embody this image of God the narrator as omnipotent and omniscient.[1] Several stylistic choices that are otherwise puzzling can be explained by this idea; thus, the style in this story serves to put both the audience and the narrator/God in their place.

First, an overview of the verses in the sura is in order. The sura begins with disconnected letters, which are not to be recited as a word; their meaning is unknown. Here, the letters are: 'Alif Lam Mim' (3:1).[2] Then the sura mentions God's revelation of the Qur'ān and previous books. A verse states that 'nothing on earth or in heaven is hidden from God' (3:5), which stands in contrast to the discussion of the limited human knowledge that will follow. The readers are told that God 'shapes you all in the womb as He pleases' (3:6), which can be considered a comment on the story that is to come, of Maryam's mother being pregnant with her. Then follows a verse that mentions clear and ambiguous verses in the Qur'ān, once again striking in a story that itself harbours many ambiguities:

> 3:7 it is He who has sent this Scripture down to you [Prophet]. Some of its verses are definite in meaning – these are the cornerstone of the Scripture – and others are ambiguous. The perverse at heart eagerly pursue the ambiguities in their attempt to make trouble and to pin down a specific meaning of their own: only God knows the true meaning. Those firmly grounded in knowledge say, 'We believe in it: it is all from our Lord' – only those with real perception will take heed.

According to this verse, God, and possibly a few people, know the true meaning of the Qur'ān. While Abdel Haleem's translation says that 'only God knows the true meaning', this could be taken to mean 'only God and those firmly grounded in knowledge know the true meaning'. The idea of ambiguity in the text plays a prominent role in this chapter. Connected to this, this verse contains the idea of knowledge, which is relevant for the following discussion. In particular, there are 'those firmly grounded in knowledge' (*al-rāsikhūna fi-l-'ilm*) and 'those with real perception' (*ūlū-l-albāb*). It is ambiguous whether these are the same or different people; if they are different, perhaps this reflects different levels or ways of knowing. Karen Bauer explores different locations of knowledge and feeling in the words used in the Qur'ān for the heart and mind—*qalb*, *ṣadr*, *fu'ād* and *lubb*.[3] Perhaps these different locations for knowledge can result in different types of knowledge. Moreover, Carl Ernst writes about the gendered language in verse 3:6–7 and how it seems to be reflected in the story – prefaced with the word 'wombs', *al-arḥām*, in 3:6, then through the phrase '*hunna umm al-kitāb*', which is translated above as 'these are the cornerstone of the Scripture', but could instead be translated as 'these are the mother of the book'.[4] While this gendered language is an important topic, this chapter will focus on other themes of the story and the sura.

In the next verse, faithful readers are told to pray for God's constant guidance (3:8). While there may be some ambiguities in the text, there is no doubt about Judgment Day (3:9). Wealth and children are of no benefit in the hereafter (3:10), although children will feature in the story to come. Fir'awn and his people are mentioned (3:11). We see contrasts between this life and the next (3:12–15), and a description of those who believe (3:16–17). Then one reads that 'God bears witness that there is no god but Him', and

'True Religion, in God's eyes, is *islam*: [devotion to Him alone]' (3:18–9). People are told to have faith, told about faith and disbelief, and punishment and reward (3:20–6). God causes night and day, which are like life and death (3:27). God knows what we reveal or conceal (3:29), and everything that people do is revealed (3:30) – this again seems to connect to narrative techniques in the story to come. People should love God and follow the Prophet (3:31–2).

Then comes the story that serves as the focus of this chapter (3:33–62). The story is followed by verses on conflicting claims by the people of the book (3:63–77) and by the people who change the scripture (3:78). We read about scripture and prophethood (3:79–83) and a list of prophets (3:84). There are descriptions of disbelief, punishment, repentance, reward (3:85–92) and inventing lies about God and scripture (3:93–4). There is mention of the faith of Ibrāhīm and the Ka'ba (3:95–7), people of the book (3:98–9 and 3:113–15), addresses to those who believe (3:100–12 and 3:118–43), those who disbelieve (3:116–17) and verses that declare that prophets die (3:144–5). Again, the readers are told that night and day are signs of God (3:190), followed by a description and prayer of those who believe (3:191–4), as well as God's response to them (3:195). There are words about the reward for those who do good (3:198), which includes people of the book, who 'would never sell God's revelation for a small price' (3:199), and a final command to those who believe to be patient and to have resolve (3:200). Throughout the sura one can find the idea of revelation and how people receive revelation: through acceptance (belief), rejection (disbelief), interpretation, or manipulation, which are then met with reward or punishment.

In this chapter, my focus is on one dimension of the idea of revelation and its reception: the literary themes of knowledge, control and consonance, as a means to look at the relationship that the narrator develops between God, the audience and the text. These themes are prominent in this story and in the sura, and they are useful for exploring the relationships between the narrator, the readers and the text in the Qur'ān. The first section of this chapter will concentrate on God's withholding of knowledge, the second on God's withholding of control and, finally, the last on God's creating consonance. All of the parts of the story in *Sūrat Āl 'Imrān* work towards putting the readers and even the characters in their place, by emphasising God's knowledge and control, and the readers' and characters' deficiency in either. At the same time, the story comforts people by developing consonance between the reader and the characters, and even between the reader and God, while also providing echoes that signal to the audience that they can understand more of the story if they read more of it in other places in the Qur'ān.

Here, I borrow the concept of performativity from discourse theory in order to analyse Qur'ānic language. According to this concept, language sometimes operates in such a way that, once something is said, it is made true.[5] For example, in a marriage ceremony, when an officiate says, 'I now pronounce you husband and wife', the couple indeed becomes husband and wife. In this Qur'ānic story, there exists several examples of performative language; as we will see, this perfectly illustrates Qur'ānic beliefs about God. Chapter 2 will also present different layers of narration, as previously discussed in the Introduction. Seymour Chatman, Gerald Prince and Gerard Genette offer useful frameworks to discuss the three layers of narration in Qur'ānic stories. Drawing from Genette, we will begin with narrative discourse to indicate the presentation of the story (the actions that are being described).[6] Within the first layer of narrative discourse, God as narrator addresses the audience. In another layer, God the narrator addresses the Prophet Muḥammad. Finally, within that layer, God as a character interacts with other characters. This chapter will demonstrate how narrative discourse is carried by dialogue, so that a character's speech perfectly reflects the direction that the story will take. The theory of layered narration will help to trace the themes of knowledge, control and consonance within the story.

II. Withholding Knowledge

The theme of knowledge emerges in a number of ways. As discussed above, the themes of knowledge and revelation appear before the story begins, in the verse that mentions clear and ambiguous verses (3:7).[7] In the story itself, we see first the reader's deficient knowledge, then the characters' deficient knowledge and, finally, the narrator's supreme knowledge. Some of the examples of the withholding of knowledge derive from ambiguities. Angelika Neuwirth argues that the ambiguities of the story of *Sūrat Āl 'Imrān* come from Rabbinic influences on this Medinan sura.[8] However, ambiguity and the withholding of knowledge also occur in *Sūrat Maryam*, *Sūrat Yūsuf* and

Sūrat al-Qaṣaṣ, all Meccan suras. Indeed, the withholding of knowledge is a part of Qur'ānic narrative technique that is used to instil in the audience belief in God's omniscience.

After a brief introduction, the narrator sets up the story in such a way that the audience quickly realises their deficient knowledge. The entire pericope is:

> 3:33 God chose Adam, Noah, Abraham's family, and the family of Imran, over all other people,
> 34 in one line of descent – God hears and knows all.
> 35 Imran's wife said, 'Lord, I have dedicated what is growing in my womb entirely to You; so accept this from me. You are the One who hears and knows all',
> 36 but when she gave birth, she said, 'My Lord! I have given birth to a girl' – God knew best what she had given birth to: the male is not like the female – ' I name her Mary and I commend her and her offspring to Your protection from the rejected Satan'.
> 37 Her Lord graciously accepted her and made her grow in goodness, and entrusted her to the charge of Zachariah. Whenever Zachariah went in to see her in her sanctuary, he found her supplied with provisions. He said, 'Mary, how is it you have these provisions?' and she said, 'They are from God: God provides limitlessly for whoever He will'.
> 38 There and then Zachariah prayed to his Lord, saying, 'Lord, from Your grace grant me virtuous offspring: You hear every prayer'.
> 39 The angels called out to him, while he stood praying in the sanctuary, 'God gives you news of John, confirming a Word from God. He will be noble and chaste, a prophet, one of the righteous'.
> 40 He said, 'My Lord, how can I have a son when I am so old and my wife is barren?' [An angel] said, 'It will be so: God does whatever He will'.
> 41 He said, 'My Lord, give me a sign'. 'Your sign', [the angel] said, 'is that you will not communicate with anyone for three days, except by gestures. Remember your Lord often; celebrate His glory in the evening and at dawn'.
> 42 The angels said to Mary: 'Mary, God has chosen you and made you pure: He has truly chosen you above all women.
> 43 Mary, be devout to your Lord, prostrate yourself in worship, bow down with those who pray'.

44 This is an account of things beyond your knowledge that We reveal to you [Muhammad]: you were not present among them when they cast lots to see which of them should take charge of Mary, you were not present with them when they argued [about her].
45 The angels said, 'Mary, God gives you news of a Word from Him, whose name will be the Messiah, Jesus, son of Mary, who will be held in honour in this world and the next, who will be one of those brought near to God.
46 He will speak to people in his infancy and in his adulthood. He will be one of the righteous'.
47 She said, 'My Lord, how can I have a son when no man has touched me?' [The angel] said, 'This is how God creates what He will: when He has ordained something, He only says, "Be", and it is.
48 He will teach him the Scripture and wisdom, the Torah and the Gospel,
49 He will send him as a messenger to the Children of Israel: "I have come to you with a sign from your Lord: I will make the shape of a bird for you out of clay, then breathe into it and, with God's permission, it will become a real bird; I will heal the blind and the leper, and bring the dead back to life with God's permission; I will tell you what you may eat and what you may store up in your houses. There truly is a sign for you in this, if you are believers.
50 I have come to confirm the truth of the Torah which preceded me, and to make some things lawful to you which used to be forbidden. I have come to you with a sign from your Lord. Be mindful of God, obey me:
51 God is my Lord and your Lord, so serve Him – that is a straight path".'
52 When Jesus realized they [still] did not believe, he said, 'Who will help me in God's cause?' The disciples said, 'We will be God's helpers; we believe in God – witness our devotion to Him.
53 Lord, we believe in what You have revealed and we follow the messenger: record us among those who bear witness [to the Truth]'.
54 The [disbelievers] schemed but God also schemed; God is the Best of Schemers.
55 God said, 'Jesus, I will take you back and raise you up to Me: I will purify you of the disbelievers. To the Day of Resurrection I will make those who follow you superior to those who disbelieved. Then you will all return to Me and I will judge between you regarding your differences.

56 I will make the disbelievers suffer severely in this world and the next; no one will help them'.
57 As for those who believe and do good deeds God will pay them their reward in full but God does not love evildoers.
58 We relate to you [Muhammad] this revelation, a decisive statement.
59 In God's eyes Jesus is just like Adam: He created him from dust, said to him, 'Be', and he was.
60 This is the truth from your Lord, so do not be one of those who doubt.
61 If anyone disputes this with you now that you have been given this knowledge, say, 'Come, let us gather our sons and your sons, our women and your women, ourselves and yourselves, and let us pray earnestly and invoke God's rejection on those of us who are lying.
62 This is the truth of the matter: there is no god but God; God is the Exalted, the Decider'.

With only a short introduction and no explanation of time or place, 3:35 begins a dialogue: 'Imran's wife said, "Lord, I have dedicated what is growing in my womb entirely to You; so accept this from me. You are the One who hears and knows all".' The audience jumps into the story, overhearing a woman's prayer to God. The reader does not know who she is and learns that she is pregnant only through her prayer. Here, God narrates the story and simultaneously is present within the story. God is in two places and fulfilling two roles at the same time; God is omnipotent.[9]

This selection of verses also exemplifies the centrality of dialogue in the Qur'ān – rather than explaining that something is the case, the text presents it through dialogue – and, due to this device, the readers recognize their deficient knowledge. This may be called the 'primacy of dialogue', a term inspired by the scholarship of Robert Alter and Marilyn Robinson Waldman. Waldman argues that what Alter calls a 'preference for direct speech, particularly dialogue' very much applies to Qur'ānic stories.[10] The audience realises their lack of knowledge and that they know things only if and when the narrator chooses to relate them. Of course, the audience was not present when this dialogue took place; therefore, the only way to know it is through the Qur'ānic telling of it.

Just as the narrator withholds information from the reader by making it known through inference in dialogue, the narrator also leaves unclear the identity of the speaker; thus, the audience once again faces their deficient knowledge. Maryam's mother delivers the mentioned baby and finds out that the baby is a girl, not a boy. In verse 3:36 someone says, 'the male is not like the female', but it is unclear whether the words are spoken by the woman or by God (by the character, or the narrator, or both simultaneously). Two modern scholars, Abboud and Khalafallāh, claim these are the mother's words.[11] This verse is reminiscent of verse 3:7, where we are told of two categories of verses, but not which are which, and that God – and it is unclear whether enlightened people are included here – knows the true meanings of the Qur'ān. If the speaker is the woman, she seems to point out that, while she wanted her child to serve God, the child is a girl, and hence she is worried since girls are different from boys. In Qur'ānic commentary, there can be found explanations that she specifically wanted her child to serve God in the temple, and that this was a role for men.[12] If the words come from the narrator, they would constitute an ironic statement, since God knows that girls are different from boys; in this context, a girl is exactly what is needed to fulfil God's plan, since the girl is Maryam who will be the mother of 'Īsā. (The readers still are not presented with any of this information, again exemplifying the very controlled release of information to the reader.) Ironically, the reader does not know who has spoken which words: We are ignorant about the source of our ignorance. Regardless of who the speaker is, as the story progresses, it becomes clear that the mother's fears are unfounded, as her child does indeed grow up in a place of worship. Thus, the narrator points out the mother's deficient knowledge and, simultaneously, the reader's. There is the same delayed release of information, highlighting the reader's lack of knowledge, with the words: 'I name her Mary' (3:36). Only then does the mother make a point of mentioning the baby's name, and the audience learns who the child is.

In the next verse, the readers are told that Maryam was in the care of Zakariyyā, but not why or what happened to her mother (3:37). The readers thus face their ignorance in another aspect of the story.[13] Then, with an abrupt shift, '*kullamā*', 'whenever', we are told about a particular detail of Maryam's upbringing (3:37). Whenever Zakariyyā came to see Maryam in the temple, he would find her with provisions or food. Helen Blatherwick writes that this 'prefigures' the dates that Maryam is told to eat when she is in labour, in *Sūrat Maryam.*[14] This is an elegant connection between different Qur'ānic stories and different scenes in Maryam's life. Also, as will be seen below, Maryam is told that she will have a child in *Sūrat Āl 'Imrān* and *Sūrat Maryam*, but the readers are told about the labour and the dates only in *Sūrat Maryam.* Here, in *Sūrat Āl 'Imrān*, Zakariyyā asks from whence the food is coming and Maryam responds that it is from God (3:37).

This scene arouses readers' curiosity, as is evident in *tafsīr* discussions about the verse. While the Qur'ān itself does not seem to foreground plausible explanations for the incident, some commentators do. Abū al-Su'ūd explains that Maryam is so young that she does not quite understand the question and, therefore, is not surprised about the situation.[15] Al-Zamakhsharī says that she was as young as 'Īsā when he spoke as a baby.[16] *Tafsīr* texts on this verse discuss what kinds of provisions she receives – what season's fruits, and even what kinds of fruits.[17] The commentators' efforts to explain the details of this verse show that their curiosity was piqued, but not satisfied. Here, as elsewhere, the commentators are responding to the indeterminacy of the text, which they treat as a mystery to explore. For other stories, *tafsīr* works try to fill in details; their authors attempt to specify the age of people, specific locations and more. Clearly, the narrative inspires curiosity, and the narrator exploits this curiosity to instil beliefs about God. One such belief is to highlight the blessings of one who is close to God, by showing that what is impossible for some becomes possible for Maryam because of God's will.

Just as the story inspires the reader's curiosity in the description of Maryam's provisions, it also inspires curiosity later in the story, when Zakariyyā is surprised by news of the child for whom he had been praying (3:40). Here we may wonder why Zakariyyā is portrayed as praying for something that he later is surprised to see fulfilled. Much like this scene inspires our curiosity, it also inspires commentators' curiosity, as is evident from their explanations of the verses. Abū al-Su'ūd writes of an unsatisfactory explanation given for Zakariyyā's surprise: He had said the prayer sixty years before he received the news and then forgotten about it.[18] One may consider this an unsatisfactory explanation because the narrator is depicting a miracle, and a miracle would seem less remarkable if the person asking for it had forgotten about it. Yet, it may also be that Zakariyyā is surprised because so much time has passed; perhaps he had given up hope. Clearly, Abū al-Suʿūd is unable to come to terms with the scene, since he himself finds this explanation unsatisfactory. Sayyid Quṭb explains Zakariyyā's surprise as stemming from a tendency to think of laws and of God's actions as being restricted to those laws; thus, he is surprised when something defies those laws.[19] Elsewhere, Quṭb explains that it is natural that Zakariyyā is surprised about the child. People cannot defy reality, and so he desires to know how God does so.[20] This still does not explain why he would pray for something that defies the laws. The commentators' impulse to fill in the blanks here quite strikingly demonstrates that I am not the only reader whose curiosity is piqued by this scene.

In the context of the theme of knowledge within the story, Zakariyyā is perhaps shown as willing to pray for something, even if logically he does not understand how it could happen, in order to demonstrate that there are different levels to knowledge and understanding. Here we can recall the earlier discussion about knowledge revolving around verse 3:7, which mentions 'those firmly grounded in knowledge' (*al-rāsikhūn fi-l-ʿilm*) and 'those with real perception' (*ūlū-l-albāb*). We do not know who these people are, whether these are different categories or levels of knowledge, and we may wonder where Zakariyyā and his beliefs about his prayer would fit. Also, one may recall Bauer's work on different locations of knowledge and feeling in the Qur'ān for the heart and mind – *qalb*, *ṣadr*, *fu'ād* and *lubb*.[21] Zakariyyā might believe that God can do anything, but still not understand how it actually happens. Another perspective is that Zakariyyā does not know what he is willing to believe.

As this story piques the curiosity of the audience with the intent to point out their deficient knowledge, it also portrays characters giving unclear or cryptic answers to questions, to the same effect. One cryptic phrase occurs when Zakariyyā asks Maryam about her provisions and she responds that God 'provides limitlessly for whoever He will', *yarzuqu man yashā' bi-ghayri ḥisāb* (3:37). This may mean that the provisions are in an amount without account, meaning that they are plentiful, or it may mean that the giving is performed in a manner without account, implying that one does not know when or how they appear. The vagueness of the phrase exemplifies that yet again we are not to understand everything, and somehow this is satisfying to the characters here. When comparing the characters' reactions to those of the audience, there is variety in both: those who do not understand, those who think they do, those who wait and see, and those who are satisfied with not knowing.

Importantly, the phrasing in Maryam's words is almost exactly the same as an earlier verse in which a second-person addressee is told to say to God: 'You provide limitlessly for whoever You will', *tarzuqu man tashā' bi-ghayri ḥisāb* (3:27). Maryam's words echoing the earlier phrase show the strength of her faith, and that she says exactly what God tells people to say. Here, then, once again we see how much God has blessed her, which is what Maryam's mother had wanted. Maryam's words submit to God's words.

Another example of a cryptic answer to a clear question occurs after Zakariyyā is told that he will have a child. He asks how this could happen, and '[an angel] said, "It will be so: God does whatever He will" ' (3:40).[22] The translator, Abdel Haleem, inserts that '[an angel] said', although the Arabic merely says *qāla*, 'he said'. It is thus unclear whether the speaker is God talking about Himself in the third person, or one of the angels who spoke previously. We do not know who the speaker is, and the speaker tells the character, Zakariyyā and the reader simultaneously that God does what God wills. This brief phrase reminds the readers of God's place and of humankind's place – again, an explanation that is not an explanation. On one level, this provides a satisfactory answer (God can give whatever He wants to whomever He wants), but at the same time it is not (how exactly does God bestow these things?).

Through a variety of tactics, the audience is made aware of their ignorance; similarly, characters in the story are portrayed not knowing things. After Maryam's mother's speech about giving birth to a girl and the speech by an unknown speaker (3:36), the narrator explains: 'Her Lord graciously accepted her and made her grow in goodness' (3:37). As if to allay the mother's fears and to show the audience that Maryam's gender was part of God's plan, there is much positivity in this verse. It exudes goodness, with the root *ḥ-s-n* repeated twice: God not only accepts the child, but God does so in a good way (*ḥasanin*), and God 'made her grow in goodness' (*wa anbatahā nabātan ḥasanan*). God has blessed Maryam and her child, just as her mother had prayed. This shows that Maryam's mother's fears about having a girl were unfounded. Just as the audience is deliberately left ignorant of important facts, so too are the characters in the story mistaken in some of their assumptions and fears.

Later in the story, there exists even more evidence that Maryam's mother's fears were unfounded. The story describes a scene in which Maryam is praised: 'The angels said to Mary: "Mary, God has chosen you and made you pure: He has truly chosen you above all women"' (3:42). The word for chosen, '*iṣṭafāki*' is repeated twice and constitutes the same word used at the beginning of the story (3:33), when introducing Maryam's lineage. In 3:42, Maryam is described as being chosen over the women of the world; in verse 3:33, her family is chosen over the worlds. The echoes are loud and clear and serve to bring the stories together, while showing that Maryam's mother's fears were unfounded, and that God especially selected her child and her lineage. Maryam is then told to 'be devout' (*uqnutī*) to her Lord, to bow and to prostrate with those who prostrate (3:43). Once again, although her mother – possibly – was worried about being able to dedicate her to God since she is a girl, the story illustrates that gender is not a problem. We repeatedly see that Maryam's mother's expectations and fears were wrong; she was wrong about what she thought she knew.

While characters are shown not knowing things, and while the audience is also made aware that they do not know things, the narrator asserts what God knows throughout the story. Twice the narrator shows God's knowledge of characters that have not yet been born. Zakariyyā is told of the child whose birth he prayed for: 'The angels called out to him, while he stood praying in the sanctuary: "God gives you news of John, confirming a Word from God. He will be noble and chaste, a prophet, one of the righteous"' (3:39). He is not told that he will have a child and name him Yaḥyā; rather, he is told the name and characteristics of the child that is yet to be born. The unborn Yaḥyā is a fully fleshed character already: His identity is solid, and he already is what he is supposed to become. Sayyid Quṭb seems to be struck by this verse and comments that Yaḥyā's name and characteristics are known before he is born.[23] Through this verse, the narrator shows God's omniscience and omnipotence – God knows Yaḥyā's name and personality before he even exists. This presents an example of an issue presented above, in the Introduction: How does a being not bounded by sequence and causality tell a story to creatures who are limited by both?

In addition, this example uses a phrase that readers cannot quite understand. In the verse mentioned above, Yaḥyā is described as 'confirming a Word from God', *muṣaddiqan bi-kalimatin min allāh* (3:39). Some commentators write that this phrase means that Yaḥyā confirms 'Īsā, who is referred to as a word from God. Sayyid Quṭb writes that there is no proof for such an interpretation.[24] Other commentators not only take this as the meaning of the verse, but also add a story to explain it. Al-Ṭabarī writes that 'Īsā and Yaḥyā's mothers were pregnant at the same time, and one day Yaḥyā's mother told Maryam that she felt the child in her womb (Yaḥyā) move or even prostrate to that in Maryam's womb ('Īsā).[25] As we have seen repeatedly, commentators seem intrigued by this verse and include a number of details to explain it.

In Maryam's story in verses 3:45–8, there is another example of the narrator showing God's knowledge of characters that are not yet born, again using the term 'Word'. Maryam is told of 'news of a Word from Him', *bi-kalimatin minhu*, words that leave us pondering the meaning of 'Word' (3:45). Mustansir Mir explains: 'Jesus is only one of the many "words" of God and that, like many other events, the birth of Jesus was brought about by God's utterance of the simple command "Be!"'[26] Mir connects God's saying 'Be and it is' to the description of 'Isā as a word: 'Isā comes from God's word, 'be', *kun*. One may also add that in *Sūrat Maryam*, when Maryam comes to her people with her baby, they question her about him, and since she has vowed to abstain from talking, she points to him and he speaks. In effect, he becomes her word (19:27–33).

Maryam is told of the birth of 'Īsā: 'The angels said, "Mary, God gives you news of a Word from Him, whose name will be the Messiah, Jesus, son of Mary [*ismuhu 'Īsā ibnu Maryam*], who will be held in honour in this world and the next, who will be one of those brought near to God"' (3:45). With the phrase 'will be', Abdel Haleem's translation facilitates easier comprehension, by rendering the Arabic clearly in future tense. In fact, the Arabic uses nominal phrases (usually explained as 'is') without indication of tense. Abdel Haleem must have found it jarring to say that someone unborn (and maybe not even yet conceived) has a name; therefore, he translated the phrase in the future tense. The Arabic text does not seem to mind that the reader may find this jarring. A linear conception of time does not matter to the narrator. The verse continues to describe 'Īsā, as does the next.

A different layer of narration in the story occurs in a verse that is interpreted as addressing the Prophet Muḥammad: 'This is an account of things beyond your knowledge that We reveal to you [Muhammad]: you were not present among them when they cast lots to see which of them should take charge of Mary, you were not present with them when they argued [about her]' (3:44). Here the narrator shows what God knows, while simultaneously demonstrating to the audience and the Prophet Muḥammad their lack of knowledge. God the narrator is addressing a second-person singular addressee, mentioning that the story heard is from the *ghayb*, or unknown, and then adds more details about the story. Ironically, the verse renders the readers ignorant because it adds information which it previously did not disclose. Here, then, lies an example of performative language: God says this was unknown, and so it was unknown.[27] Moreover, these details were unknown because they were not part of the earlier narration. God is the narrator and the maker of everything; if God says something is unknown, then it is unknown; 'Be and it is'. Thus, God is the source of knowledge, which God bestows as He wills. This also opens the mind of the audience to the ideas of revelation, the message and messengers, all of which are topics discussed elsewhere in this sura.[28]

III. Withholding Control

Just as the story in *Sūrat Āl 'Imrān* makes it a point to show the audience's and the characters' limited knowledge while highlighting the narrator's supreme knowledge, it also indicates the reader's and characters' limited control while highlighting the narrator's complete control. In order to examine the audience's lack of control, one may look at the ways in which their expectations and understandings of reality are defied. While the audience obviously has no control over the telling of the story, they might expect it to cater to their understandings of reality. However, this does not happen here. The presentation of unborn children having names and personalities already served as one example of the reader's assumptions about the portrayal of time being crushed.

Something similar happens in the use of dialogue in the story. The narrator presents God as omniscient and asserts that the text holds no contradictions;[29] yet, in the different iterations of a story, God does not always convey the same dialogue with the same words. For instance, Zakariyyā responds, surprised about having a child: 'He said, "My Lord, how can I have a son when I am so old and my wife is barren?"' (3:40). Verse 19:8 is the only other verse in the Qur'ān that mentions this incident, and both verses begin with the same words, '*qāla rabbi ānnā yakūnu lī ghulāmun*', 'He said, "My Lord, how can I have a son"'. He then continues to say that he is old and his wife is barren (3:40), or the same in the opposite order (19:8). We must stop to wonder why an omniscient narrator portrays the dialogue of a historical occurrence in two different ways. What narrative purpose does it serve to have the transcript of a dialogue that supposedly took place one time in history in two different versions? Perhaps the answer once again lies in the idea of God's omnipotence. Limited human conception and understanding of dialogue and history do not matter; the narrator portrays things as He wills. Perhaps the difference in the order shows that to Zakariyyā there is no difference in priority, meaning that neither he nor his wife is to blame for their barrenness any more than the other. Or perhaps the narrator hints that one can say something and think something else simultaneously. Maybe the narrator is showing the limits of language in conveying thoughts. Or the narrator may be showing the audience that they cannot understand everything.[30]

While the narrator shows the audience their limited control in the portrayal and understanding of dialogue, the narrator also conveys their lack of control in the portrayal and understanding of time and place. Unexplained time leaps are frequent in Qur'ānic stories, and this stylistic device establishes the narrator's supremacy over the reader and the text – God does not portray time in a way that conforms to the reader's understanding of it. One leap of time and place occurs after Zakariyyā is told that he will have a child (3:39), and he asks for a sign and is told to fast for three days (3:41). In the next verse, angels tell Maryam that God has chosen her (3:42). The reader assumes and knows from another iteration (19:12) that Yaḥyā, the child promised to Zakariyyā, was born and that he had a good character, as promised. The reader also assumes that Zakariyyā has not spoken and thus fulfilled the sign. None of this is mentioned, so that the reader is at the mercy of the narrator; since God has said something will happen, the reader can assume that it did. The leap in time and space without explanation serves to demonstrate to the audience their lack of control – over the telling and understanding of this story, over time and place – while teaching them to rely on the narrator, even when not knowing what will come next or not fully understanding what has already come to pass.

Much like the audience is made to see their lack of control, so are the characters in the story. One dimension through which this becomes clear is that the characters' words sometimes submit to the movement of the story. Here, I will use the concept of narrative discourse to indicate the presentation of the story (the sequence of actions that are being described), as does Genette.[31] The phrase 'narrative discourse' helps distinguish between the story itself and the way in which it is portrayed. Early in the story, Maryam's mother prays for Maryam and her children, among whom will be 'Īsā: '"I name her Mary and I commend her and her offspring to Your protection from the rejected Satan"' (3:36). Her words reflect the narrative discourse of the story and give an idea of the direction that the story will take. Through her prayer, a connection is made to future generations, and the story moves along accordingly, eventually moving to Maryam's son, 'Isā (3:45–55). Thus, the dialogue in the story works to set the tone for the narrative discourse.

While Maryam's mother's words are depicted as advancing the narrative discourse, something similar also happens with Zakariyyā and Maryam's mother. In verse 3:34, God characterises Himself thus: 'God hears and knows all' (*samī'un 'alīm*). Then, Maryam's mother characterises God as 'the One who hears and knows all' (*al-samī' al-'alīm*, 3:35). And again, Zakariyyā concludes his supplication by praising God: 'You hear every prayer' (*samī' al-du'ā'*, 3:38). Thus, we see God the narrator first asserting that God is hearing and knowing; then, the characters in the story use the same epithets, rather than many others they could choose. The portrayal of their speeches thus submits to or is made to submit to God's characterisation of Himself. Of course, every story is ultimately written by its author, and the speeches of the characters are, too, but here the narrator seems to care little about maintaining a facade of individuality and autonomy for the characters' speech. Rather, God asserts Himself through the characters' speeches and simultaneously His control over them. I further explore this in Chapter 5 on *Sūrat Ṭaha*, where we see the narrator confirming God's words, as well as people's words.

Much like the present examples of a character's words submitting to the discourse of the story, an instance of a character's words and actions submitting to it can be found. After Maryam tells Zakariyyā that her provisions are from God (3:37), he is depicted as saying a prayer to God, asking to have a child (3:38). The timing of this verse and the use of the word '*hunālika*', 'there and then', makes it seem as if this is Zakariyyā's response to the miracle of Maryam's provisions, that if God can provide Maryam with food from nowhere, God can provide Zakariyyā with offspring. Al-Jalālayn and al-Ṭabarī explain that the fruits were out of season, and when Zakariyyā saw the possibility of something arriving out of season, he prayed to have a child, even though its time had passed.[32] While this may seem to be a plausible and tempting explanation, the connection between Maryam's response and Zakariyyā's prayer is not made clear, and the missing link (the fruits out of season) is not in the Qur'ān, but only in the *tafsīr*. The Qur'ān seems to be indifferent to the possibility of a connection; perhaps this is because it does not matter whether readers understand why Zakariyyā chose to say his prayer at that time and whether it really is a response to Maryam's words. It appears that Zakariyyā's logic or his motive are not important to the storyteller, but rather the action – that he performs this prayer. Zakariyyā's motive and the reader's understanding of it are unimportant. We are not to know people's intentions, a narrative technique that will be explored in the discussion on *Sūrat Yūsuf*. Here emerges strict Qur'ānic control over the story and its characters. The characters' speech and actions are controlled by the narrative discourse.

Similarly, Zakariyyā and Maryam use speech that perfectly submits to the idea of God having complete control. After first Zakariyyā (3:39) and then Maryam (3:45) are told by angels that they will have children, they both respond by addressing God. About Zakariyyā, it says twice, 'He said, "My Lord"' (3:40 and 3:41) and about Maryam it says, 'She said, "My Lord"' (3:47). Although angels address them, they respond to God, which al-Ṭabrisī mentions.[33] Maryam and Zakariyyā are shown knowing where all power and knowledge lies – with God – and thus address God directly.

Thus far we have explored the audience's and character's lack of control, as well as the various ways in which this is manifested in the story. The reverse to this lies in the narrator's supreme control. One area where this is found consists of the narrator's selective narration. Once again, the scene of Zakariyyā asking Maryam about her provisions can serve as example. The readers do not know that Maryam has been receiving any mysterious provisions, until Zakariyyā asks her about them. At that point, he seems to ask the question that the reader wants to have answered. However, Maryam does not answer it completely. She says, '"They are from God: God provides limitlessly for whoever He will"' (3:37). She presumably thinks that this is a satisfactory response, and Zakariyyā does not respond with a follow-up question (or is not portrayed as doing so); perhaps it is a satisfactory response. However, one must wonder why the narrator makes a character ask the reader's question, but then does not provide a comprehensible answer. What purpose does it serve to build up the reader's curiosity and then not satisfy it? All of this serves to show the reader how much control the narrator holds, and how little control the reader has; the reader is at the mercy of the narrator, just as the characters are at the mercy of the narrator (God). At the same time, the narrator seems to be teaching the audience what satisfactory questions and answers are, to begin with. Questions are acceptable, but not when they are excessive. Answers may not seem complete, but they are when they acknowledge God's role in the world. Ultimately, the audience cannot ask the narrator their questions and cannot hear an answer, and thus the narrator asserts His control, not only over the audience as an audience (completely unable to direct the story, even when they want to), but also over the audience as subjects of God (being taught what questions and answers are appropriate).

While the narrator shows God's control through the details in a particular iteration of the story, God also shows His control by making assertions and using them as proof – another instance of the performative. When Zakariyyā is informed that he will have a child, his response is to ask for a sign, and he is told that his sign is to abstain from speaking: 'He said, "My Lord, give me a sign". "Your sign," [the angel] said, "is that you will not communicate with anyone for three days, except by gestures. Remember your Lord often; celebrate His glory in the evening and at dawn"' (3:41). There is no indication of whether Zakariyyā is unable to talk for three days, or if he chooses not to talk. Whichever may be the case, we are not told why this is actually a sign. Why is this a sign and not, for example, a punishment?

If we turn to *tafsīr*, al-Zamakhsharī explains that Zakariyyā is unable to speak in order to devote his time to remembrance of God, instead of being occupied with human endeavours. He further explains that this is to express thankfulness, *shukr*.[34] Quṭb similarly writes that Zakariyyā is unable to talk with people so that he will connect with God instead.[35] Elsewhere, Quṭb emphasises the irony in this: That he is unable to talk to people, but can communicate with God.[36] These interpretations assume that Zakariyyā's being made unable to speak is a miracle, because he was previously healthy and able to speak. However, the Qur'ānic text does not make it clear whether he is unable to or chooses not to speak. If he chooses not to speak because God tells him so, why is this a sign? Although Zakariyyā has previously stood for the reader and asked Maryam our question about her provisions, he does not ask for clarification and instead seems satisfied with the sign that he is given. The character and audience face their ignorance juxtaposed with God's control. This is an example of performative language: Because God says this is a sign, it is a sign, and it seems to work for Zakariyyā as such.

Another occurrence of the performative in the story appears towards the end. In verse 3:61, it seems that the Prophet Muḥammad is addressed in the second person, and he is told:

> 3:61 If anyone disputes this with you now that you have been given this knowledge, say, 'Come, let us gather our sons and your sons, our women and your women, ourselves and yourselves, and let us pray earnestly and invoke God's rejection on those of us who are lying'.

This challenge to swear and ask for God's curse to be upon them reflects the performative: To say something is to make it so. There is no point to this challenge, unless this message actually is from God, for if there is no God and/or this message is not from God, then there is no danger in this challenge.[37] The confidence in the language of the challenge – the assumption that it actually is a challenge – gives it force and power. This verse is typical of the Qur'ānic narrative style that we have seen thus far: It makes assertions and shows these assertions through its style.

Another instance of God's control affirmed through the performative can be found in the narrative about 'Īsā. When Maryam is told that she will have a child and reacts with surprise, a speaker of unknown identity responds to Maryam: '"This is how God creates what He will: when He has ordained something, He only says, 'Be', and it is"' (3:47). The next verse (3:48) explains that 'Īsā teaches people the Torah and the Gospel. Verse 3:49

confirms this. Abdel Haleem translates the beginning of the verse as: 'He will send him as a messenger to the Children of Israel: "I have come to you . . ."' The Arabic text, '*wa rasūlan ilā banī isrā'īl annī qad ji'tukum*' flows subtly from narration about 'Īsā to 'Īsā's words. The short word, '*annī*' is the reader's signal that 'Īsā is talking. This is an abrupt shift from Maryam being told that she would have a child, to 'Īsā speaking as a messenger. Abdel Haleem aptly reflects this with a colon followed by a parenthesis and 'Īsā's speech. There is no other indication of a time leap in which the angels leave Maryam, Maryam is pregnant and delivers the baby, and 'Īsā is born. Instead, Maryam is told that she will have a child and then learns about his character and role as a prophet; from there, he is delivering his message. Maryam was told that, when God says 'Be', it is, and this is what the text shows the reader. God says that 'Īsā would be born and serve as messenger, and he is portrayed as such through performative language that seems almost as quick as 'be and it is'. God said it, and so it is. It should come as no surprise that there exist so many examples of the performative in this story; it is a perfect literary technique to show '"be" and it is' (3:47).

Throughout the story, God asserts His control over the characters and the audience; in the conclusion, God asserts His control over the story itself. Verses 3:58–62 seem to be the conclusion to the story, and one may consider 3:62 as the last verse in this story, because it comments on the stories, '*al-qaṣaṣ*'. Verse 3:58 also comments on the narration: 'We relate to you [Muhammad] this revelation [*al-āyāt*], a decisive statement'. The readers are thus reminded that this story is just one of the signs – *āyāt* is a concept that will be examined in the subsequent chapters. Through this, the story we have read is put in its place, as is the reader. The reader is made to understand that the story is just a part – a part of the entire story, and a part of the many stories and vast knowledge of God – and that the reader only knows this much because God chooses to reveal it. This is confirmed in the following verse, when the readers are reminded of God's power in regard to two stories: 'In God's eyes Jesus is just like Adam: He created him from dust, said to him, 'Be', and he was' (3:59). The next verse tells that God is the source of truth (3:60). God has all the power and knowledge over His subject and is thus the ultimate narrator.

IV. Creating Consonance

While the Qur'ān repeatedly works to put the characters, readers and God in their places by asserting the characters' and readers' lack of knowledge and control, as opposed to God's ultimate knowledge and control, it does not alienate the reader. Instead, the story brings consonance between the readers and the characters, the readers and God, and the readers and the story itself. I will first investigate how the story builds consonance between the reader and the characters. As discussed previously, early in the story the readers are told that Zakariyyā took care of Maryam and that, whenever he would come to see her in the temple, he would find her with provisions (3:37). A reader or listener would probably wonder where the provisions are coming from; fortunately, Zakariyyā asks exactly this very question. (The narrator here uses dialogue instead of narration to explain the event, an example of the above-mentioned primacy of dialogue in Qur'ānic stories.) The Qur'ān thus uses this question to create an identification between the audience and the character, insofar as both want to know the source of the provisions. Thus, Zakariyyā stands in for the audience, and the audience finds themselves in consonance with a character in the story.

Similarly, the audience can identify with a character at the end of the story, also in a state of puzzlement. After hearing about 'Īsā, we are told, 'When Jesus realized they [still] did not believe, he said, "Who will help me in God's cause?" The disciples said, "We will be God's helpers; we believe in God – witness our devotion to Him"' (3:52). The verse plunges readers into a state of unknowing, based on the use of the word '*minhum*', which refers to a group of people of an identity unknown to the readers (3:52). First occurs the pronoun, then the word for the disciples. Earlier, 'Īsā is talking to his people, and he addresses them with the second person plural, '*lakum*' (3:50). One might assume that the narrator in 3:52 is talking about the people to whom 'Īsā was speaking. Alternately, one may assume that he is speaking to the disciples, since they are mentioned somewhat later in 3:52; however, the text does not make this clear, and even if it did, we still do not know who they are. The next verse does not tell more about the disciples, but instead gives their speech (3:53). Then comes a verse that is puzzling and intriguing at the same time: '*wa makarū wa makara allāhu wa allāhu khayrū al-mākirīn*', 'The [disbelievers] schemed but God also schemed; God is the

Best of Schemers' (3:54). Abdel Haleem tries to make the Arabic text easier by inserting the words 'the [disbelievers]' in the translation, and this also conforms to al-Ṭabrisī's interpretation.[38] In the Arabic, there merely appears the verb in the third person plural, 'they'. Who are 'they'?

We receive no answer to this question, nor further explanation, and instead move to a new scene, a dialogue between God and 'Īsā. This verse quotes God as telling 'Īsā: '"Jesus, I will take you back and raise you up to Me: I will purify you of the disbelievers"' (3:55). It is not clear what is meant by raising and purifying him, and much discussion stems from this phrasing. Additionally, 'the disbelievers' is clearly stated, but their identity is not revealed. Just as consonance developed between Zakariyyā and the reader in their curiosity about Maryam's provisions, here consonance develops between 'Īsā and the audience in terms of wondering who the disbelievers are. God says, 'I will judge between you' (3:55), and this seems to be the point: Even though 'Īsā does not know who his supporters are or are not (3:52), and even though the audience clearly knows even less, God knows everything and will judge people and punish or reward them accordingly (3:55–7). This idea will re-emerge in Chapter 4 on *Sūrat Yūsuf.*

While one can discern consonance developing between the audience and the characters in the story, it also grows between the audience and God, through the prayers of Maryam's mother and Zakariyyā. About Zakariyyā, the Qur'ān says: 'There and then Zachariah prayed to his Lord, saying, "Lord, from Your grace grant me virtuous offspring: You hear every prayer"' (3:38). Given the previous discussion of the ways in which the story shows the audience their limited knowledge, it is striking that only through this prayer are readers told that Zakariyyā's childlessness was problematic. While Zakariyyā praises God for hearing supplications, the audience also overhears his supplication. In the same way, the audience overhears Maryam's mother's prayer to God earlier (3:35–6). Here, consonance is allowed to develop between God and the reader in that they both overhear the same (private) prayers, and between the reader and the characters. Of course, God the narrator chooses to form this union, and it adds complexity to the reader's image of the narrator. God the narrator is controlling, but God also chooses to share His knowledge at certain times and in limited ways, which, essentially, parallels God's revelation.

We can further advance our understanding when examining how the narrator develops consonance between the reader and the story itself. For example, after Maryam is told about 'Īsā, he discusses different miracles that he will perform 'with God's permission' (3:49). His speech is unusually long for Qur'ānic characters and continues for two more verses (through verse 3:51). Without any clear indication, the readers have left Maryam's story; al-Ṭabrisī notes this as well.[39] The reader only knows that Maryam is no longer present in the text. If the audience wants to know more about her story, they will have to read elsewhere in the Qur'ān; in fact there is a good deal of detail about her labour and delivery of 'Īsā in another sura (19:16–29). The Qur'ān signals this to the reader because, in fact, 'Īsā's words in verse 3:51 are identical with 19:36, except for a one-letter conjunction (the latter starts with a '*wāw*' that is not in the former). As the Qur'ān is a text that is often recited aloud, the verbal echo and the difference in it stand out. Thus, the conjunction can be considered a signal to the audience that there is more of this story in other places. Similarly, one finds echoing phrases in 'Īsā's words in verse 3:49 and God's description of 'Īsā in verse 5:110. It is worth noting that part of the echo comes from the repetition of *bi-idhni allāh* (3:49) and *bi-idhnī* (5:110). Thus, God emphasises that 'Īsā performs miracles by God's will, and 'Īsā emphasises this, too, with the same word.

While the audience may be curious to receive more information, they do not become irritated about the lack of it, or about the shift to a different focus in the story, because they know that they can read more elsewhere. In this way, one of the effects of concealment or withholding of information in Qur'ānic stories is to keep the audience interested and to encourage them to read more of the Qur'ān. The same can be said for other mysteries found in the sura, such as the passage about ambiguous and clear verses. A reader who is familiar with the Qur'ān or who analyses it carefully will be rewarded by this tactic; more casual readers may miss this. Such an approach is appropriate, since the Qur'ān explains that the revelation and even the stories are for those who 'reflect'.[40] Consequently, the audience feels satisfied that they know the story and the book, and that they can navigate it, too. They are rewarded and empowered by this awareness, and rather than feeling alienated from the story, they may feel familiar with it, or they may even feel that they know some of its secrets. Sarra Tlili, writing about the depiction of humans in the Qur'ān, concludes that 'it is only when they engage in a relationship with God, as His subjects who worship and are conscious of Him, that they start realizing their potential'.[41] When the Qur'ānic audience engages with the text carefully, they become connected with it and its secrets. They are elevated and humbled by the text; they find consonance with God and God's text, while they also face their limited knowledge and control. This seems a just reward, since elsewhere in the Qur'ān, and even in this story, it is mentioned : 'As for those who believe and do good deeds God will pay them their reward in full' (3:57).

V. Conclusion

In the last verse in the story, the narrator simultaneously asserts the truth of the story, the oneness of God and the omnipotence of God. The verse reads: 'This is the truth of the matter: there is no god but God; God is the Exalted, the Decider' (3:62). Throughout the story, the narration moves to show the reader exactly these aspects. The story overtly talks about God's power; when God says 'be', it is, and the narration shows this in the births of Yaḥyā and 'Īsā and through the use of performative language. Almost as instant as the phrase 'be, and it is' is the telling of their births and their realisation. Similarly, the narration repeatedly shows the audience that they and the characters in the story are at the mercy of the narrator, God, as God alone has complete knowledge and complete control. This becomes obvious through the use of layers of narration in the story. Cryptic explanations, such as Maryam's words about the provisions she receives, also lead the reader in the same direction and to the same beliefs. Leaps through time, with very little explanation attached, signal to the audience that their conception of time as linear is weak. Portrayals of dialogues that do not fit our conceptions of historical reality also hint at how limited these conceptions may be. In the end, the narrative techniques underpin what God the narrator asserts – that God is the source of all knowledge and that the little we know is what God chooses to tell us. And even when God chooses to tell us something, we may or may not understand it fully. This is God's will, because it serves to reinforce theological beliefs in God's supreme knowledge. This is emblematic of the ideas of God's message and how people receive, understand and interpret the message, which one can see in the non-narrative verses of the sura.

Notes

1. Similar to this is Mustansir Mir's description of *Sūrat Yūsuf.* See Mir, 'The Qur'anic Story of Joseph' 5–7.
2. I discuss this type of verse in more detail in Chapter 4 on *Sūrat Yūsuf.*
3. Bauer 14–15.
4. Ernst 171–5. Ernst argues that the roots *b-gh-y* and *f-t-n* are also both gendered; a comprehensive study of both words in the Qur'ān would be enlightening. See also Zahniser, 'The Word of God and the Apostleship of 'Isa' 84–7.
5. Austin 6.
6. Genette 36.
7. For more on this verse, see Nguyen 7–8.
8. Neuwirth, *Scripture, Poetry, and the Making of a Community* 42–3.
9. Ozgur Alhassen, 'You Were Not There' 85.
10. Waldman 52; Alter, *The Art of Biblical Narrative* 68; see also 69–70 and 87.
11. Abboud 154. Khalafallāh 246. Similarly, Reynolds writes: 'The Qur'ān here implies that 'Imrān's wife was not only surprised to discover that her child was a girl, she was also disappointed'. Reynolds 131.
12. See, for example, al-Ṭabrisī's commentary on 3:35. www.altafsir.com/Tafasir.asp?tMadhNo=4&tTafsirNo=3&tSoraNo=3&tAyahNo=36&tDisplay=yes&UserProfile=0&LanguageId=1
13. Ozgur Alhassen, 'You Were Not There' 85.
14. Blatherwick 35.
15. Al-'Amārī, vol. 2, 30.
16. Al-Zamakhsharī, vol. 1, 427.
17. Al-Maḥallī and al-Suyūṭī 71 and al-Ṭabarī, vol. 3, 1757–60 say that they are fruits of winter in the summer and fruits of summer in the winter. Al-Tha'ālibī, vol. 1, 249 says the same and also remarks that they are fruits of paradise (*janna*).
18. Al-'Amārī, vol. 2, 33.
19. Quṭb, vol. 1, 394.
20. Quṭb, vol. 4, 2303.
21. Bauer 14–15.
22. This verse is similar to 19:9: 'He said, "This is what your Lord has said: 'It is easy for Me: I created you, though you were nothing before'" '.
23. Quṭb, vol. 1, 394.
24. Quṭb, vol. 1, 394, note 1.
25. Al-Ṭabarī, vol. 3, 1766–7.

26. Mir, *Understanding the Islamic Scripture* 86.
27. Austin 6.
28. Ozgur Alhassen, 'You Were Not There' 85, 88–9.
29. See, for example, verse 4:82: 'Will they not think about this Qur'an? If it had been from anyone other than God, they would have found much inconsistency in it'.
30. The portrayal of the same dialogue in different ways occurs in other Qur'ānic stories, and I will revisit this concept.
31. Genette 36.
32. Al-Maḥallī and al-Suyūṭī 71 state that, when he saw the possibility of something happening when it is not its time, he made this supplication. Al-Ṭabarī, vol. 3, 1760–1 proposes the same. Similar is the commentary of al-Ṭabrisī, www.altafsir.com/Tafasir.asp?tMadhNo=4&tTafsirNo=3&tSoraNo=3&tAyahNo=38&tDisplay=yes&UserProfile=0&LanguageId=1
33. See: www.altafsir.com/Tafasir.asp?tMadhNo=4&tTafsirNo=3&tSoraNo=3&tAyahNo=40&tDisplay=yes&UserProfile=0&LanguageId=1
34. Al-Zamakhsharī, vol. 1, 429. Similar is Maybudī 148 and al-Ṭabrisī, www.altafsir.com/Tafasir.asp?tMadhNo=4&tTafsirNo=3&tSoraNo=3&tAyahNo=41&tDisplay=yes&UserProfile=0&LanguageId=1
35. Quṭb, vol. 4, 2303.
36. Quṭb, vol. 1, 395.
37. Ozgur Alhassen, 'You Were Not There' 89.
38. www.altafsir.com/Tafasir.asp?tMadhNo=4&tTafsirNo=3&tSoraNo=3&tAyahNo=52&tDisplay=yes&Page=2&Size=1&LanguageId=1
39. www.altafsir.com/Tafasir.asp?tMadhNo=4&tTafsirNo=3&tSoraNo=3&tAyahNo=48&tDisplay=yes&Page=2&Size=1&LanguageId=1
40. For example, 'In this way, God makes His messages clear to you, so that you may reflect' (2:219 and 2:266) and 'Tell them the story so that they may reflect' (7:176).
41. Tlili 244.

3

God, Families and Secrets in the Story of *Sūrat Maryam* 19:1–58[1]

I. Introduction

Several scholars have analysed *Sūrat Maryam* from a variety of perspectives. These include studies that focus on commentary on *Sūrat Maryam*,[2] modern Western scholarship 'centred largely on the virtue and piety of Mary' and on 'Īsā, studies in 'the interfaith community' and works that look at the 'similarities between the accounts of the births of John and of Jesus'.[3] In addition, Hosn Abboud uses extra-Qur'ānic sources and concentrates on the Qur'ānic concept of the feminine, arguing that in this very sura Maryam is 'a mother archetype celebrated for her power of fertility'.[4] Paying close attention to the literary characteristics of the story, Loren D. Lybarger focuses on the nature of prophecy in the Qur'ān.[5] Jane I. Smith and Yvonne Y. Haddad, and Brannon Wheeler examine the commentary on the events of Maryam's life as described in the Qur'ān,[6] while Neal Robinson investigates the commentary on 19:17–22.[7] Many of these studies revolve around commentary or extra-Qur'ānic biblical and historiographic sources.

What follows is a literary analysis concerning structure and theme within *Sūrat Maryam* 19:1–58 itself. I emphasise these specific verses because they include a story, and this chapter will also examine connections between the story and the non-narrative verses of the sura, discussing the structure of the story and the dramatic tension and irony in the subtextual juxtaposition of the signs for secrets concealed and secrets revealed. Here, the story of Zakariyyā, Maryam and 'Īsā flows into a number of stories of other characters. This is the only such instance with this structural feature which I will examine; hence, it is only in the context of this chapter that the structure of the story will receive analysis. One may wonder why these various stories are grouped together and how they relate to and interact with each other. A focus on structure will yield an answer to these questions.

The first part of this chapter sheds light on the formation of connections through the structure of the story. In its second part, the chapter turns to the making of connections between the story and the non-narrative verses of the sura (19:59–98). Finally, we move on to the withholding of knowledge, a technique discussed in the previous chapter, but re-examined here in terms of signs and secrets. The story in *Sūrat Maryam* 19:1–58 begins with the themes of God and family, but this becomes less prominent and is eventually replaced by the theme of God and faith. Thus, God the narrator initially makes Himself central to the family, and eventually replaces the family. At the same time, the story features signs that signify secrets and secrecy in various forms – people's secrets and God's secrets. People have secrets or seclude themselves, sometimes because it is a command of God, sometimes without a reason given, and it is these human secrets that are revealed in the story. However, God also holds secrets, and these remain as such. I will explore these secrets and signs and how they relate to the structure and the way in which God portrays Himself in this Qur'ānic story. We are to understand that the relationship with God is more important than a familial relationship, and then we are told more about this relationship: God alone knows everything, and nothing is secret from God.

II. Structural Connections in the Story

This chapter shows how, in *Sūrat Maryam* 19:1–58, the Qur'ān establishes structure by means of echoing letters, words, phrases and sections. Once the structure is established, it changes as the sura progresses. This constitutes part of the Qur'ānic narrative technique, which sometimes sets patterns and then breaks them, and it does so for a reason. This is similar to what Robert Alter discusses in the context of the Bible, analysing both repetition and 'divergence' or 'suppression' from repetition.[8] In *Sūrat Maryam*, the story begins by foregrounding family, but by the end God has moved to the fore and replaced the family. At the same time, the various sections in the story become progressively shorter. This decreasing length causes readers to identify less with the characters, while the narrator's voice becomes more pronounced, the commentary increases, and God's role becomes more dominant.

The entire pericope is:

19:1 *Kaf Ha Ya 'Ayn Sad*
2 This is an account of your Lord's grace towards His servant, Zachariah,
3 when he called to his Lord secretly, saying,
4 'Lord, my bones have weakened and my hair is ashen grey, but never, Lord, have I ever prayed to You in vain:
5 I fear [what] my kinsmen [will do] when I am gone, for my wife is barren, so grant me a successor – a gift from You –
6 to be my heir and the heir of the family of Jacob. Lord, make him well pleasing [to You]'.
7 'Zachariah, We bring you good news of a son whose name will be John – We have chosen this name for no one before him'.
8 He said, 'Lord, how can I have a son when my wife is barren, and I am old and frail?'
9 He said, 'This is what your Lord has said: "It is easy for Me: I created you, though you were nothing before"'.
10 He said, 'Give me a sign, Lord'. He said, 'Your sign is that you will not speak to anyone for three full [days and] nights'.
11 He went out of the sanctuary to his people and signalled to them to praise God morning and evening.
12 [We said], 'John, hold on to the Scripture firmly'. While he was still a boy, We granted him wisdom,
13 tenderness from Us, and purity. He was devout,
14 kind to his parents, not domineering or rebellious.
15 Peace on him the day he was born, on the day of his death, and on him the day he is raised to life again.
16 Mention in the Scripture the story of Mary. She withdrew from her family to a place east
17 and secluded herself away; We sent Our Spirit to appear before her in the form of a normal human.
18 She said, 'I seek the Lord of Mercy's protection against you: if you have any fear of Him [do not approach]!'
19 but he said, 'I am but a Messenger from your Lord, [come] to announce to you the gift of a pure son'.

20 She said, 'How can I have a son when no man has touched me? I have not been unchaste',
21 and he said, 'This is what your Lord said: "It is easy for Me – We shall make him a sign to all people, a blessing from Us" '.
22 And so it was ordained: she conceived him. She withdrew to a distant place
23 and, when the pains of childbirth drove her to [cling to] the trunk of a palm tree, she exclaimed, 'I wish I had been dead and forgotten long before all this!'
24 but a voice cried to her from below, 'Do not worry: your Lord has provided a stream at your feet
25 and, if you shake the trunk of the palm tree towards you, it will deliver fresh ripe dates for you,
26 so eat, drink, be glad, and say to anyone you may see: "I have vowed to the Lord of Mercy to abstain from conversation, and I will not talk to anyone today" '.
27 She went back to her people carrying the child, and they said, 'Mary! You have done something terrible!
28 Sister of Aaron! Your father was not a bad man; your mother was not unchaste!'
29 She pointed at him. They said, 'How can we converse with an infant?'
30 [But] he said: 'I am a servant of God. He has granted me the Scripture; made me a prophet;
31 made me blessed wherever I may be. He commanded me to pray, to give alms as long as I live,
32 to cherish my mother. He did not make me domineering or graceless.
33 Peace was on me the day I was born, and will be on me the day I die and the day I am raised to life again'.
34 Such was Jesus, son of Mary. [This is] a statement of the Truth about which they are in doubt:
35 it would not befit God to have a child. He is far above that: when He decrees something, He says only, 'Be', and it is.
36 'God is my Lord and your Lord, so serve Him: that is a straight path'.

37 But factions have differed among themselves. What suffering will come
to those who obscure the truth when a dreadful Day arrives!
38 How sharp of hearing, how sharp of sight they will be when they come
to Us, although now they are clearly off course!
39 Warn them [Muhammad] of the Day of Remorse when the matter will
be decided, for they are heedless and do not believe.
40 It is We who will inherit the earth and all who are on it: they will all be
returned to Us.
41 Mention too, in the Scripture, the story of Abraham. He was a man of
truth, a prophet.
42 He said to his father, 'Father, why do you worship something that can
neither hear nor see nor benefit you in any way?
43 Father, knowledge that has not reached you has come to me, so follow
me: I will guide you to an even path.
44 Father, do not worship Satan – Satan has rebelled against the Lord of
Mercy.
45 Father, I fear that a punishment from the Lord of Mercy may afflict you
and that you may become Satan's companion [in Hell]'.
46 His father answered, 'Abraham, do you reject my gods? I will stone you
if you do not stop this. Keep away from me for a long time!'
47 Abraham said, 'Peace be with you: I will beg my Lord to forgive you
– He is always gracious to me –
48 but for now I will leave you, and the idols you all pray to, and I will pray
to my Lord and trust that my prayer will not be in vain'.
49 When he left his people and those they served beside God, We granted
him Isaac and Jacob and made them both prophets:
50 We granted Our grace to all of them, and gave them a noble
reputation.
51 Mention too, in the Scripture, the story of Moses. He was specially
chosen, a messenger and a prophet:
52 We called to him from the right-hand side of the mountain and brought
him close to Us in secret communion;
53 out of Our grace We granted him his brother Aaron as a prophet.
54 Mention too, in the Scripture, the story of Ishmael. He was true to his
promise, a messenger and a prophet.

55 He commanded his household to pray and give alms, and his Lord was well pleased with him.
56 Mention too, in the Scripture, the story of Idris. He was a man of truth, a prophet.
57 We raised him to a high position.
58 These were the prophets God blessed – from the seed of Adam, of those We carried in the Ark with Noah, from the seed of Abraham and Israel – and those We guided and chose. When the revelations of the Lord of Mercy were recited to them, they fell to their knees and wept,

A number of scholars have discussed the structure of *Sūrat Maryam*. Shawkat Toorawa writes at some length about this issue and offers various perspectives. The models he summarises examine the whole sura, whereas here I focus only on the structure of 19:1–58. For these verses, the structure I investigate is almost identical to that of Bilal Gökkir. The difference lies in the fact that I include 19:1, while he does not. As will be seen, 19:1 is exceptional in some ways and does not exactly fit into the structure I propose, yet it matches thematically. Thus, it is worth including it in the present discussion. Table 3.1 illustrates various structural models for 19:1–58 (some based on Toorawa 28–30):

Toorawa writes about the models by Gökkir, Neuwirth and Robinson: 'Although repetition is implicit in all three of these breakdowns of Q. 19, none of them make lexical echoes and repetition in the sura explicit'.[9] My own analysis of the structure adds to their work because it shows not only how the structure of 19:1–58 is developed through 'lexical echoes and repetition', but also that the structure serves a narrative, rhetorical and thematic purpose.

One way in which structure is established in this story occurs through echoing or repeated letters. A look at the letters ending all of the verses in the sura will give an idea of the overall structure. Toorawa argues that 'rhyme is without doubt a crucial aspect of the structure of suras generally, a fact that, regrettably, has not sufficiently informed scholarship on the Qur'ān'.[10] As Toorawa asserts, rhyme helps establish the structure in this sura. This can be seen in the chart below: Most of the verses end with the same letter, *alif*. The remaining verses end in *nūn* (19:34–5, 38–40) and *mīm* (19:36–7). These

Table 3.1 Various models of the structure of 19:1–58

Gökkir	Robinson	Neuwirth[a]	Abboud[b]
19:2–15 (I would make this 19:1–15)	19:1–2 19:3–15	A) Zachariah: 19:1–15, subdivided as follows: 19:1, 2, 3–6, 7–11, 12–15	19:1–2 19:3–6 19:7–11 19:12–15
19:16–40	19:16–33 19:34–40	B) Mary: 19:16–40, subdivided as follows: 19:16–21, 22–6, 27–9, 30–3, 34–6, 37–40	19:16–21 19:22–6 19:27–9 19:30–3 19:34–6 19:37–40
19:41–50 19:51–3 19:54–5 19:56–7 19:58...	19:41–50 19:51–3 19:54–5 19:56–7 19:58...	C) Abraham and other envoys: 19:41–65, subdivided as follows: 19:41–6, 47–50, 51–3, 54–5, 56–7, 58–9, 60–3, 64–5...	19:41–50 19:51–3 19:54–5 19:56–7 19:58–63

[a] Also explained in Ernst 218–19.
[b] Abboud 40–4. She describes this structure as stemming from colometric analysis, 38.

letters are similar in pronunciation; they are both nasals, and in the recitation of the Qur'ān one sometimes replaces the other. When considering them as reasonably similar letters, verses 19:34–40 form a category different from the rest of the verses, in addition to 19:1.

Of the remaining verses, one ends in the letter *ṣād*, and this is the first verse, 19:1. This verse is exceptional within the sura, as it is composed of disconnected letters;[11] in general, verses with these letters are extraordinary in the Qur'ān. It is also exceptional when compared to other such disconnected letters in the Qur'ān – while some disconnected letters occur more than once in the Qur'ān, the combination, *kāf–hā'–yā'–'ayn–ṣād* (19:1) appears only once. In terms of how these letters function in this sura, Toorawa writes that it is the 'lone non-rhyming "word" in the sura' and thus 'does not rhyme with what follows'. This, he claims, is unlike the other disconnected letters in the Qur'ān.[12] Thus, this verse is unusual in the way in which it functions in this sura, as opposed to other suras.

Table 3.2 illustrates a circular structure in the verse endings of 19:2–98:

Table 3.2 Verse endings in *Sūrat Maryam*

Verse Number	Letters Ending the Verse
19:1	*ṣād*
19:2–33	*alif*
19:34–40	*nūn/mīm*
19:41–98	*alif*

two lengthy sections ending in *alif* (19:2–33 and 19:41–98) surround a section with a *nūn/mīm* rhyme (19:34–40). I will discuss this section in more detail below, drawing on the insights of Michel Cuypers concerning Semitic rhetoric and symmetry.

Much like the Qur'ān establishes structure here through end-rhyme, it also does so in the story through words, phrases, number of verses and sub-sections; this structure serves to advance an overall message. Here, I will analyse in greater detail how structure is created and how it changes, connecting structure to the theme that is being developed and at the same time connecting it to other dominant themes in the sura and the Qur'ān. Table 3.3 summarises the structure established through sections and sub-sections, phrases, words and letters in these verses. Most of the sections begin with a person and connect him or her to a relative in a sub-section. Toorawa implies that kinship is a theme of the sura; I will demonstrate that this is indeed the case.[13]

The story in verses 19:1–58 comprises seven sections, each of which starts with a word from the three-letter root, *dhāl kāf rā'*. This root alludes to mentioning, reminding, being mindful and remembering. Most of the time, this root is paired with the word *kitāb*, book, in the phrase, 'mention in the book'. In addition, most of the sections include the root *rā' ḥā' mīm*. This three-letter root plays a role in establishing not only structure, but also a theme within the story. Alluding to mercy, this root goes hand-in-hand with the theme of family. Four times it is used for God's mercy (19:2, 19:21, 19:50 and 19:53), while in the remaining instances it refers to God as *al-raḥmān*. Muḥammad Al-Ghazālī also mentions the use of the word '*raḥmān*' and '*raḥma*' in the sura.[14] From this root can be derived a word that indicates 'womb', 'relationship' and 'kinship' (*raḥim*). Thus, *rā' ḥā' mīm* simultaneously conveys the concepts of mercy and family, and it adds depth to our understanding of and focus on family within the story. The root occurs a total of twenty times in the

Table 3.3 Structure in *Sūrat Maryam* 19:1–58

Section	Verses	Number of Verses	Main Character	Subsection	*Dhāl kāf rā'*[a]	*Kāf tā' bā'*	*Rā' ḥā' mīm*	Letter Ending the Verse
N/A	19:1	1	N/A	N/A	N/A	N/A	N/A	*ṣād*
1	19:2–15	14	Zakariyyā	19:12–15, son (Yaḥyā)	19:2 *dhikr*	19:12 *kitāb*	19:2	*alif*
2	19:16–40	25	Maryam	19:30–40, son ('Īsā)	19:16 *wa-dhkur*	19:16, 19:30 *kitāb*	19:18, 19:21, 19:26	*alif* *nūn/mīm* (19:34–40)
3	19:41–50	10	Ibrāhīm	19:49-50, son (Isḥāq) and grandson (Ya'qūb)	19:41 *wa-dhkur*	19:41 *kitāb*	19:44, 19:45, 19:50	*alif*
4	19:51–3	3	Mūsā	19:53, brother (Hārūn)	19:51 *wa-dhkur*	19:51 *kitāb*	19:53	*alif*
5	19:54–5	2	Ismā'īl	19:55, *ahl* (people)	19:54 *wa-dhkur*	19:54 *kitāb*	none	*alif*
6	19:56–7	2	Idrīs	none	19:56 *wa-dhkur*	19:56 *kitāb*	none	*alif*
7	19:58	1	none (conclusion)	none	none	none	19:58	*alif*

[a] The root also occurs in the sura outside of verses Q. 19:1–58, in Q. 19:67. Toorawa 37

sura (in 19:2, 19:18, 19:21, 19:26, 19:44, 19:45, 19:50, 19:53, 19:58, 19:61, 19:69, 19:75, 19:78, 19:85, 19:87, 19:88, 19:91, 19:92, 19:93 and 19:96).

When scrutinising each section in greater detail, one gains an understanding of the development of and change in the structure that takes place in this story. The first section of the story comprises 19:2–11, in which Zakariyyā asks for a child. Verse 19:2 begins the section with the word *dhikr* (translated by Abdel Haleem as 'an account'), which presents a beginning different from the rest of the sections. Thus, we do not find the word *kitāb* in the opening phrase, although it figures in this section in verse 19:12. Our story begins with Zakariyyā making a supplication to God, asking to be granted a child. Thus, with Zakariyyā's asking for a child, the family takes a central place in this section. In addition, the parent plays an active role: the soon-to-be father is asking to be made a father. At the same time, Zakariyyā is appealing to God (19:3–6, in 19:10 he asks God for a sign), and there also appears a mysterious speaker presumably sent by God in a sub-section (19:7–10). Hence, even in a story about a parent-child relationship, God has a role. As will be seen later, this contrasts with a disbeliever who does not ask God for children but assumes that he will be given children nonetheless (19:77). The root *rā' ḥā' mīm* occurs in verse 19:2, translated by Abdel Haleem as 'grace': 'This is an account of your Lord's grace towards His servant, Zachariah' (19:2). The section includes a sub-section in which God addresses Yaḥyā directly, praises him and wishes peace upon him (19:12–15). The child, therefore, holds an important and positive place in this section.

Section two (19:16–40) begins with the root *dhāl kāf rā'* in the phrase *wa-dhkur fi-l-kitāb*, which we will see as a signal for the beginning of this and the next four sections: 'Mention in the Scripture' (19:16). This section presents Maryam, who does not ask for a child; yet, a messenger comes to tell her that she will have one: 'but he said, "I am but a Messenger from your Lord, [come] to announce to you the gift of a pure son"' (19:19). Maryam and her future motherhood constitute the focus of the section. Thus, as with the first section, the parent can be found in a fundamental role. Also like in the first section, a mysterious speaker tells her that she is to have a child (19:17–21) and that he is sent by God. There is another or possibly the same speaker who mentions God and comforts Maryam in childbirth (19:24–6). In addition, Maryam actively appeals to God (19:18). In this way, even when the parent-child relationship takes on the greatest significance, God still plays a critical role in the story. The root *rā' ḥā' mīm* occurs three times in this section: once, Maryam calls God '*al-raḥman*' or 'Lord of Mercy' (19:18); once she is told to abstain from speaking and to say that she has made a vow to '*al-raḥman*' not to speak (19:26); and the third time, when the messenger tells Maryam about her future child, she is told that he will be a *raḥma* or 'a blessing' from God (19:21).

In the sub-section, 'Īsā speaks at length (19:30–3). When 'Īsā speaks for his mother and defends her from people's accusations, there begins a divergence from the established pattern: The child is now in a dominant role in comparison to the parent, and he constitutes the focal point of this section. Neuwirth describes 'Īsā's speech (19:30) as a 'very undramatic self-introduction'.[15] However, when read in its textual context, one may consider it rather dramatic, based on the sharp contrast between the situation and 'Īsā's straightforward but weighty words. Maryam has been commanded not to speak, and when her people ask her how she could possibly have given birth to a child, all she does is point to her new-born. Not surprisingly, the people respond by asking how they could speak to a baby, but then the baby speaks for her and introduces himself. As discussed in the previous chapter, 'Īsā is God's word and then becomes Maryam's word (3:45).

Then follows the exceptional section in which God the narrator discusses 'Īsā and the existing debates about him (19:34–40). Although the style here seems different from the rest, the content focuses on 'Īsā. The child ('Īsā) plays a prominent role in this section, just as Yaḥyā has done in the previous one. Neuwirth argues that 19:34–40 is a 'later Meccan addition' which came as a result of historical circumstances. Part of her reasoning rests on the stylistic difference between 19:34–40 and the surrounding verses.[16]

The present study does not concern itself with gleaning historical information about the Qur'ān's audience from the Qur'ānic text; however, two Qur'ānic narrative techniques complicate Neuwirth's argument. First, the narrative style in 19:34–40, in its merging of narrative and non-narrative, by way of merging a character's and God's speech, is not completely unique in the Qur'ānic stories. Here occurs a switch from 'Īsā speaking in the first person, to the narrator speaking about the issue, then a return to the story; the same technique can be observed in Mūsā's story in *Sūrat Ṭaha* (20:51–7). Chapter

5 on *Sūrat Ṭaha* will describe this narrative technique as a merging of Mūsā's and God's speech, with the text then returning to the dialogue between Mūsā and Fir'awn. Thus, Neuwirth's argument would need to explain this narrative technique in 20:51–7 and any other places where it occurs.

Furthermore, the structural centre functioning as a place of change presents another narrative feature of the text, and here the centre harmonises perfectly with the rest of the story. Neuwirth would have to explain how a historically later addition fits so well into the text. Cuypers argues that 'the center is always the turning point', and 'at the center there is often a change in the trend of thought, and an antithetical idea is introduced. After this the original trend is resumed and continued until the system is concluded'.[17] Structurally, 19:34–40 is the centre of the story with its exceptional *nūn/mīm* rhyme. This section serves as a turning point between an earlier story about two morally righteous family relationships, and the next story about the relationship between Ibrāhīm and his father, which includes reversals from the previous one. Hence, the stylistic difference in these verses signals divergence and contributes to their functioning as a thematic turning point to show changes from the pattern. Furthermore, Cuypers writes that 'rhetorical analysis shows that universal announcements are always found in a privileged place, rhetorically speaking – at the center of concentric constructions'.[18] Indeed, the centre in the story under discussion is 19:34–40: It ends differently from the former or the latter sections, does not constitute a narrative section and asserts God's existence as opposed to people's claims about God. Verse 19:34 may be considered a story, but verses 19:35–40 may not. Verse 19:34 also diverges from the previous ones, with a change in focalisation.[19] The use of a different letter to end these verses thus corresponds to the fact that they are non-narrative verses. Then, in verse 19:41 the readers are moved back to the narrative. The content and the end-rhyme of all of the sections match, and the auditory and logical structures mesh in these verses.

The third section comes after the turning point and diverges further from previous trends (19:41–50). The section starts in the same manner as earlier, with '*wa-dhkur fi-l-kitāb*', 'Mention too, in the Scripture' (19:41). Here, most strikingly, there occurs a reversal in which the child (Ibrāhīm) is given something (knowledge) and wants to share it with his father:

19:42 He said to his father, 'Father, why do you worship something that can neither hear nor see nor benefit you in any way?
43 Father, knowledge that has not reached you has come to me, so follow me: I will guide you to an even path.
44 Father, do not worship Satan – Satan has rebelled against the Lord of Mercy.
45 Father, I fear that a punishment from the Lord of Mercy may afflict you and that you may become Satan's companion [in Hell]'.

This section contrasts with the previous one in several ways. First, the child, and not the parent, is now a dominant focal point. Second, the child, and not the parent, is given something (knowledge, instead of a child). Third, whereas Zakariyyā was worried about inheritance (19:5–6), here the issue is reversed, and the son wants his father to inherit from his knowledge. Toorawa mentions this reversal in his study, calling this echoing a 'thematic inversion'.[20] This section and the previous sub-section in which 'Īsā speaks at length (19:30–3) show a reversal in the parent-child relationship, although in the case of Ibrāhīm the reversal is more drastic and features more manifestations. As mentioned above, contrasts and divergences from the pattern are part of Qur'ānic narrative technique, and they work to advance belief.

In the section on Ibrāhīm, the root *rā' ḥā' mīm* appears three times: twice Ibrāhīm calls God the 'Lord of Mercy' (19:44 and 19:45), and the third time, God mentions the 'grace' He has bestowed on Ibrāhīm, Isḥāq and Ya'qūb (19:50). Ibrāhīm speaks gently with his father, and the gentleness with which he speaks contrasts sharply with his father's response. Ibrāhīm uses an intimate manner to address his father, '*yā abati*', in verses 19:44 and 19:45, and, as mentioned, twice refers to God as the Lord of Mercy. Thus far, we have seen three examples of children being good to their parents: 'Īsā, Yaḥyā and Ibrāhīm.

Ibrāhīm's father responds by threatening him and telling him to go away: 'His father answered, "Abraham, do you reject my gods? I will stone you if you do not stop this. Keep away from me for a long time!"' (19:46). Here for the first time occurs a negative example of a family member. One may wonder whether Ibrāhīm's father serves as an anti-family figure in the story, further displacing the family and causing an end to the relationship. This idea fits well with Cuypers's claim that the centre constitutes the turning point. One should keep in mind, however, that the family is also presented as a blessing throughout the story (see for example 19:7, 19:14–15, 19:19, 19:31–3 and 19:49) and that God replaces the family, whether it is a negative or positive example.[21]

While Ibrāhīm does not seem to want to do so initially, he leaves his father (19:48). However, he is rewarded with not just one, but two family members: a child, Isḥāq and a grandchild, Ya'qūb (19:49–50). His one lost family member is replaced by two new members and, in the end, he has gained doubly. His gain moves generations into the future, in contrast to his father, who represents the past generation. This is clear to at least one commentator, and Abū al-Su'ūd mentions that Isḥāq and Ya'qūb replace Ibrāhīm's disbelieving relatives.[22]

In the fourth section (19:51–3), which also begins with '*wa-dhkur fī-l-kitāb*' (19:51), Mūsā is mentioned; this specific sub-section mentions his brother (19:53):

> 19:51 Mention too, in the Scripture, the story of Moses. He was specially chosen, a messenger and a prophet:
> 52 We called to him from the right-hand side of the mountain and brought him close to Us in secret communion;
> 53 out of Our grace We granted him his brother Aaron as a prophet.

Based on Qur'ānic rules of inheritance, one might propose that a brother is a relative more distant than a child,[23] and that the family is gradually becoming less prominent in the story. Moreover, Hārūn is an assistant to help fulfil God's will; he is an answer to a prayer that Mūsā makes elsewhere (20:29–36). Thus, although he is a family member, his role hinges on serving God as a prophet and being part of God's will. Before the mention of the brother, God the narrator mentions calling Mūsā in communion: God brings Mūsā close to Himself, giving God a more prominent role in the story (19:52). In this way, as the family is de-emphasised in this section, God is emphasised.

The root *rā' ḥā' mīm* is also present, as an explanation for God's making Hārūn a helper for Mūsā: 'out of Our grace [*min raḥmatinā*] We granted him his brother Aaron as a prophet' (19:53). Here, then, the root for mercy and womb (*r-ḥ-m*) does not hinge on family but, instead, on God. This section is shorter than the others, with only three verses, as opposed to the fourteen, twenty-five and ten verses in the previous sections. And the sections will continue to become even shorter.

Now one may review the parent-child theme as it has developed and diverged thus far. First there appears a person asking God to grant him a child. Second appears someone being told she will have a child. Then arrives a turning point, and in the third section, a child wants to give the parent something. In the fourth section, someone is described as a prophet; moreover, he is granted a brother, also a prophet, to assist him. Hence, the focus moves from someone praying to God to have a child, to siblings serving God together. One can observe a shift from God being periphery and family central, to God being central and family periphery.

The fifth section (19:54–5) begins with '*wa-dhkur fi-l-kitāb*' (19:54) and mentions Ismāʿīl: 'Mention too, in the Scripture, the story of Ishmael. He was true to his promise, a messenger and a prophet. He commanded his household to pray and give alms, and his Lord was well pleased with him' (19:54–5). Ismāʿīl is identified in the Qur'ān as Ibrāhīm's son (14:39), but while he is not mentioned in Ibrāhīm's sub-section, he receives mention here. This is a very subtle vestige of the mention of family in the story. In addition, Ismāʿīl's sub-section mentions his *ahl*, which can be translated as household, people, or community (19:55).[24] This relationship is even more distant and less defined than that to a child or a brother. In examining context and structure, this analysis and that of verses 19:49–50 help to address some scholarly confusion about why Isḥāq and Yaʿqūb are listed together, and why Ismāʿīl is listed separately here.[25] Isḥāq and Yaʿqūb are mentioned in Ibrāhīm's sub-section, as extensions of him, reaching into the future, when he is cut off from the past (his father). Here, Ismāʿīl himself represents the connection to his father; yet, he is separated from his father in terms of textual location, because the focus is instead on Ismāʿīl's role as a prophet and his connection to God. In this section the root *rā' ḥā' mīm* does not appear, an absence I will explain below. Again, as seen before, there exists a building up of divergences from the patterns that were first established. This serves to show that the family is less pivotal and, instead, one's connection to God takes on central importance.

Section six (19:56–7) also begins with '*wa-dhkur fi-l-kitāb*' (19:56) and then mentions Idrīs, although neither family nor the root *rā' ḥā' mīm* appear: 'Mention too, in the Scripture, the story of Idris. He was a man of truth, a prophet. We raised him to a high position' (19:56–7). Since there is no mention of family, there is also no sub-section. Here, rather than about family, we are told about God giving Idrīs 'a high position' (19:57). The focus has completely shifted to God and God's relationship with Idrīs.

Finally, section seven (19:58) serves as conclusion and climax to the story. Neuwirth suggests that this verse is a later insertion because of its unusual 'form';[26] however, the previous verses have been gradually building up to this one, both thematically and stylistically. The differences in this verse, the variations from the pattern, are part of Qur'ānic narrative technique – the contrast draws attention. Verse 19:58 does not begin with '*wa-dhkur fi-l-kitāb*' or any other form of the root *dhāl kāf rā'*. God mentions the prophets He blessed and their faith in God:

> 19:58 These were the prophets God blessed – from the seed of Adam, of those We carried in the Ark with Noah, from the seed of Abraham and Israel – and those We guided and chose. When the revelations of the Lord of Mercy were recited to them, they fell to their knees and wept.

No family is mentioned, although the concept of lineage (blessed by God) is present. In addition, the root *rā' ḥā' mīm* does appear in reference to God, showing that mercy is still important, even though the family is no longer present. Mercy does not hinge on the family, but on God. In the first part of the verse, God is the subject of the sentence (showing God's dominance), and even when the prophets act, they bow in prostration to God (19:58). This section is only one verse in length – the sections have progressively become shorter and shorter, until this verse, which seems to arrive at the theological essentials: God and God's prophets.

While the other sections contain narrative and dialogue, this section is commentary alone. Without the narrator's commentary, there would be nothing left here. Thus, God the narrator is essential in the content. Similarly, we no longer have one or two main characters upon whom to focus or with whom to identify; rather, there figure God and the names of various prophets. There is no scene on which to focus, but the concepts of guidance and submission and submission's manifestation in prostration. Throughout the story, through the establishment of and change in structure, prophetic narratives have been replaced by the concept of faith, and the family has been replaced by God. Narrative has been replaced by meta-narrative.

III. Connections with the Non-narrative Verses of the Sura

One way of discovering the connections between the story and the non-narrative verses of the sura is to look for echoing words, this time for semantic connections between the story and the end of the sura. As Toorawa discusses and lists,[27] there exists a number of words in the story that are echoed in the later verses. After the story (19:1–58), the sura moves to non-narrative verses about the afterlife (19:59–72), the acceptance or rejection of guidance (19:73–84), once again the afterlife (19:85–7), the grave mistake of saying that God has a son (19:88–92) and the afterlife again (19:93–8). There is no further mention of Zakariyyā, Maryam or ʿIsā by name, but an obvious thematic connection between the story of the birth of ʿĪsā and the Qur'ān's declarations that God does not have a son (19:88–92). Importantly, we do not see the names of any being other than God in both parts of the sura; Allāh is mentioned throughout, but the characters are only mentioned by name in the story.[28] This in itself continues the narrative trend of replacing family with God. It is also worth mentioning that the root *r-b-b*, always as the word *rabb*, 'Lord', occurs in four of the seven sections of the story above, as well as in five verses in the non-narrative section.[29]

Given the prominence of the theme of family in the story, one may wonder if and how it appears in the rest of the sura. One can answer this question by scrutinising the roots related to this concept throughout the sura. For example, the root *w-r-th* signals the idea of inheritance, in the story and in other verses in the sura. In the story, Zakariyyā is concerned about not having someone to inherit from him, and he asks God to bless him with a child: '"I fear [what] my kinsmen [will do] when I am gone, for my wife is barren, so grant me a successor – a gift from You – to be my heir [*yarithunī*] and the heir [*yarithu*] of the family of Jacob. Lord, make him well pleasing [to You]"' (19:5–6). The same root letters, *w-r-th*, occur when God says that God inherits everything: 'It is We who will inherit [*narithu*] the earth and all who are on it: they will all be returned to Us' (19:40). Here emerges a contrast between Zakariyyā's concerns and the reality that God tells the readers – that is, that God inherits everything. This offers a parallel to Maryam's mother's unfounded concerns discussed in Chapter 2 on *Sūrat Āl 'Imrān*: Maryam's mother worries about how she will dedicate a girl to God, but a girl is exactly what God wanted to fulfil His will; Zakariyyā worries about who will inherit from him, but God is the one who ultimately inherits everything. Then the concept of inheritance becomes further complicated: 'That is the Garden We shall give as their own [*nuwrithu*] to those of Our servants who were devout' (19:63). Thus, God lets believers inherit the Garden, *al-janna*. Finally, the reader is presented with a verse about one who disbelieves: 'We shall inherit from him [*narithuhu*] all that he speaks of and he will come to Us all alone' (19:80). The idea of inheritance that Zakariyyā initially brings to the fore is repeatedly complicated by God in the rest of the sura.

Concerning inheritance, throughout the sura one can find the ideas of a parent giving his inheritance to his child and of God inheriting the earth and everything on it; this can be understood as emphasising God's immortality in contrast to human mortality. It contrasts with the notion that God lets believers inherit the Garden, and this, in turn, contrasts with the idea that God inherits – or knows – everything that people say and do. Inheritance moves from being a family-focused issue to revolving around God: God inherits everything because God is eternal, and God inherits everything that a person says or does. This reflects different verses in the Qur'ān, such as: 'Everyone on earth perishes; all that remains is the Face of your Lord, full of majesty, bestowing honour' (55:26–7; see also 28:88). Much like throughout the story as a whole, one can see a shift from the family as central to God as central, only here it happens in terms of inheritance: Inheritance moves from being family-centred to God-centred. As with the earlier section of the story, the presentation and development of a theme is strengthened by echoing words.

The root *w-l-d* is instrumental in tracing the idea of family in the sura. Neuwirth discusses the use of the root *w-l-d* in this sura, but does not mention that it is present in the story sequence (19:1–58), as well as in two sections that she argues do 'not fit' into *Sūrat Maryam* (19:34–40 and 19:66–98).[30] In the first few verses, the root appears as 'parents', *bi-wālidayhi* (19:14), 'he was born', *wulida* (19:15), 'mother', *bi-wālidatī* (19:32) and 'I was born', *wulidtu* (19:33). We then move to a verse that states that God does not have a child, *walad* (19:35). Further there is a verse about the disbeliever who assumes he will be blessed with wealth and children, *waladan* (19:77). This contrasts thematically with Zakariyyā praying to be blessed with a child – the disbeliever assumes, whereas Zakariyyā knows to ask God. Two verses tell about people who say that God has a son, *waladan* (19:88 and 19:91) and about God's rejection of the claim that God has a son, *waladan* (19:92). Interestingly, Zakariyyā uses the word *waliyy*, 'successor', in his prayer for a child (19:5) – connecting the child to the idea of inheritance. Maryam and the angel refer to her child as *ghulām*, 'son' (19:19 and 19:20). The root *w-l-d* connects directly to the idea of birth, mothers, fathers and parents. In the sura, birth, parents and the child that people claim God has are all expressed with the root *w-l-d*, making clear the absurdity of claiming that God has a child. In contrast, the children of Maryam and Zakariyyā are not referred to by the same root.

There exists an important confirmation of the patterns in the story with the root *j-y-'*, which occurs in the story and afterwards.[31] First are the contractions that come to Maryam (*ajā'hā*, 19:23). Then, because of the contractions, Maryam goes to her people, carrying her infant, and they tell her that she has come with a terrible thing (*ji'ti*, 19:27). Ibrāhīm tells his father about the knowledge that came to him (*jā'anī*, 19:43). As discussed earlier, knowledge replaces the child – here clearly reflected with the same root word. We may even suggest that knowledge displaces Ibrāhīm's son, Ismā'īl; thus, Ismā'īl is not present in Ibrāhīm's sub-section. Finally, the story is followed by two verses that say that those who claim God has a son come forward with something terrible (19:88–9). One can discern a definite echoing and contrast between the people's accusation of Maryam, *laqad ji'ti shay'an fariyyan* (19:27), and God's accusation of people claiming that God has a son, *laqad ji'tum shay'an iddan* (19:89). In addition to the same verb, both phrases have the same number of words, both include the words *laqad* and *shay'an*, and both accuse people of doing something terrible. Clearly, in one case, people are advancing the criticism while, in the other case, God is. The latter verse obviously comments on the earlier one, highlighting that Maryam was criticised by her people, but those who deserve criticism actually are the ones who claim that her son was God's son.

The root *kh-r-r* occurs twice in the sura. In the first instance, prophets hear God's recitation and fall in prostration: 'When the revelations of the Lord of Mercy were recited to them, they fell to their knees [*kharrū*] and wept' (19:58). The root re-occurs in the non-narrative section that rejects the claim that God has a child (19:88), in the comment, 'How terrible is this thing you assert: it almost causes the heavens to be torn apart, the earth to split asunder, the mountains to crumble [*wa-takhirru*] to pieces' (19:89–90). Through this shared root, a connection is forged between the faith of people and mountains – everything praises God (59:24), as opposed to those who believe that God has a child. We see the atrociousness of the claim that God has a child – mountains crumble in response to it, and this connects the story and the non-narrative verses in the sura.

The root, *q-ḍ-y* first occurs when a messenger tells Maryam about her having a child: 'and he said, "This is what your Lord said: 'It is easy for Me – We shall make him a sign to all people, a blessing from Us'." And so it was ordained: [*maqḍiyyan*]' (19:21).[32] About 'Īsā, we read: 'it would not befit God to have a child. He is far above that: when He decrees [*qaḍā*] something, He says only, "Be," and it is' (19:35). Thus, it is God's decree that Maryam would have a child, and this decree is how he came to be. The other two uses of the root have to do with Judgment Day, and God's decree: 'Warn them [Muhammad] of the Day of Remorse when the matter will be decided [*quḍiya*], for they are heedless and do not believe' (19:39), and 'but every single one of you will approach it, a decree from your Lord which must be fulfilled [*maqḍiyyan*]' (19:71). Here connections are being made between the certainty of God's will concerning Maryam having a child, creation more generally, and the Day of Judgment. Again, the narrative moves from family to God – in this case, God's creating people and holding them accountable.

As seen in Table 3.2, the root *k-t-b* appears in all the sections of the story, other than the conclusion, and it usually tells the second-person addressee to recall within the book the story of various characters. One also finds the root *k-t-b* in a non-narrative verse, that God will write down or record the words (19:79) of the one who rejects God's signs (*āyāt*) and says that he will be blessed with wealth and children (19:77). With the root *k-t-b*, we can observe a pivoting from the book of signs (*āyāt*) that tells stories of prophets and their children, to people's rejection of God's signs (*āyāt*) and claim that they will be blessed with wealth and children. This contrasts those who ask God to be blessed with children with those who do not ask God but assume that they will be granted children; both will be written about by God. Hence, while the story teaches the audience to centre God and decentre family, the disbeliever removes God, keeps the family and adds wealth (*mālan*).

As discussed above, all of the main sections of the story begin with the idea of remembrance, expressed with the root *dh-k-r*, which forms one of the building blocks of the story's structure. We also find this root in the non-narrative section: 'but does man not remember [*a-wa-lā yadhkuru al-insānu*] that We created him [*khalaqnāhu*] when he was nothing before?' (19:67). So people are told of the remembrance (19:2), then told to remember (19:16, 19:41, 19:51, 19:54 and 19:56) and, finally, rhetorically asked if they remember that God created them (19:67). In 19:67, the root *kh-l-q* re-emerges. The earlier appearance of this root occurs when the angel explains to Zakariyyā that God can create a child just as God created Zakariyyā [*khalaqtuka*] (19:9). The roots *dh-k-r* and *kh-l-q* offer reminders that relate to God's mercy and the stories in God's revelation, some of which discuss creation – both surprising and miraculous – and then one's own creation. The particular stories give way to creation and the creation of people in general.

The root *l-s-n* occurs twice, once in the narrative and once in the non-narrative section. About Isḥāq, Ya'qūb and maybe Ibrāhīm, it says: 'We granted Our grace to all of them, and gave them a noble reputation [*lisāna sidqin*]' (19:50). The non-narrative section contains a verse addressing the second-person singular, usually interpreted to be Prophet Muḥammad, about the revelation, 'We have made it easy, in your own language [*bi-lisānika*] [Prophet], so that you may bring glad news to the righteous and warnings to a stubborn people' (19:97). Hence, there is a connection being forged between the prophets in the story and the Prophet Muḥammad. This root connects the stories in the sura to the Qur'ān, its revelation and its story.

As for the root *d-'-w*, we find both Zakariyyā and Ibrāhīm mentioning their prayers to God. Zakariyyā asks for a child and adds, 'but never, Lord, have I ever prayed to You in vain [*wa-lam akun bi-du'ā'ika rabbi shaqiyyan*]' (19:4). Ibrāhīm uses the root three times when talking to his father: ' "but for now I will leave you, and the idols you all pray to [*tad'ūna*], and I will pray to [*ad'ū*] my Lord and trust that my prayer will not be in vain [*an-lā akūna bi-du'ā'i rabbī shaqiyyan*]" ' (19:48). The last phrase is almost the same as Zakariyyā's. Ibrāhīm also mentions the idols to which his people pray, and this usage of the root appears later in the sura as well: 'that they attribute [*da'aw*] offspring to the Lord of Mercy' (19:91). Therefore, Ibrāhīm's uses of the root *d-'-w* connect us to Zakariyyā and to the non-narrative verses of the sura. Through these verses, we encounter a contrast between praying to and believing in God, and belief in idols or offspring of God.

In these examples, words and ideas from the story are developed, refined and complicated in the rest of the sura. Echoing words serve a narrative and structural importance in the Qur'ān: They form structure within a story and connect it to other sections of the sura. They constitute a narrative technique that the Qur'ān uses to develop, complicate and comment on ideas and its stories.

IV. Withholding Knowledge through Signs and Secrets

Following the discussion of the structure of the story in *Sūrat Maryam* and its connections to the rest of the sura, I will now move on to the signs signifying secrecy and seclusion in the story. Here I am using 'sign' in the sense of Ferdinand de Saussure and Roland Barthes – a sign is made up of a signifier and signified.[33] Ian Netton uses the word 'theologeme' similarly.[34] In verses 19:1–58, one encounters a system of signs for secrecy and seclusion; these signs are overwhelmingly apparent throughout the story. These different kinds of secrets are manifest in the text in a number of ways: what is hidden and what is revealed, what can be said, what can be communicated by other means and what remains a secret. There is secrecy, the hiding of things, being in a state of isolation or solitude, being silent or unable to speak and things that are omitted or revealed. These all constitute signs for secrets.

The Qur'ān does not label these as secrets or signs; rather, I am. The word for 'secretly', '*khafiyyan*', does appear in the story (19:3). The word for sign, *āya*, also occurs in the story, as it does frequently in the Qur'ān. Zakariyyā asks for a sign, *āya*, that he will have a child and is offered one: abstaining from speech (19:10). Maryam does not ask for a sign or a child but is told that her child will be a sign, *āya*, for people, as well as a mercy (19:21). And in the last verse of the story, prophets bow down in prostration when they hear God's signs, *āyāt* (19:58). In general, as in this verse, people interpret *āyāt* both as signs of God and as the verses of the Qur'ān, which are signs of God.[35] In the non-narrative verses of *Sūrat Maryam*, those who reject God's signs when they hear them use the same phrasing as in 19:58 (*wa-idhā tutlā ʿalayhim āyātunā,* 'When Our revelations are recited to them', 19:73), as does the one who disbelieves in God's signs (*a-fa-raʾayta al-ladhī kafara bi-āyātinā,* 'Have you considered the man who rejects Our revelation', 19:77). We can thus see the notions of proof, secrecy and revelation expressed in the word 'sign', *āya.* Revelation here may mean that something is being made known, while it can also refer to the Qur'ān. God is the master of revelation in the sense of knowing and uncovering secrets, revealing the Qur'ān and narrating the stories in the Qur'ān.

There exist several signs through which secrets are revealed and seclusion is broken within the story. These instances raise a number of questions: If the seclusion is going to be broken eventually, why is the appearance maintained at the beginning, or to some extent? What is the narrator trying to accomplish with these broken secrets? These questions will determine the present analysis. We will see that the secrets that are maintained originate with God the narrator and relate to narrative choices – the narrator not revealing the meaning of certain letters or details, or the identity of some of the speakers in the story. One can also discover ways in which the Qur'ān makes the readers work, pushing them to read further, to ask questions, to analyse and to propose answers.

The sura begins with the disconnected letters, which I approach as an integral part of the text. Their meaning is a secret that the narrator keeps from the readers (19:1). There has been much research on and discussion of the disconnected letters, as will be further mentioned in the next chapter. For now, we may consider the disconnected letters as a sign signifying one of God's secrets that is maintained.

Unlike God's secret that is maintained, early on in the story emerges a human secret that is broken: Zakariyyā's quiet prayer to God and the fulfilment of his prayer. Zakariyyā's prayer is described as '*khafiyyan*', 'secretly' or quietly: 'when he called to his Lord secretly' (19:3). Then we learn about the content of Zakariyyā's prayer to God (19:4–6). He mentions his old age, his weakness and his fear for the future: '"Lord, my bones have weakened and my hair is ashen grey, but never, Lord, have I ever prayed to You in vain: I fear [what] my kinsmen [will do] when I am gone, for my wife is barren, so grant me a successor – a gift from You"' (19:4–5). This prayer is clearly intimate in nature, reflecting privileged information. Ironically, all readers and listeners of the Qur'ān are privy to it. What does the narrator seek to achieve by revealing secrets between Him and others?

In contrast to this secret that is revealed, Zakariyyā's story presents readers with a mystery that remains a mystery. A speaker tells Zakariyyā that he will have a child; however the speaker's identity remains secret from both Zakariyyā and the readers. The speaker uses the first person plural, '*innā nubashshiruka*', '"We bring you good news"' (19:7). Zakariyyā responds by asking God how this could be, '*rabbī annā yakūnu lī ghulāmun*' (19:8), which makes one wonder if the speaker with the good news may be God. The next verse, however, may be the speaker quoting God, which would imply that the speaker is not God, unless God is quoting Himself: 'He said, "This is what your Lord has said: 'It is easy for Me: I created you, though you were nothing before'"' (19:9). Then Zakariyyā again addresses God, asking for a sign (19:10). Thus, we could either have a number of speakers, or God speaking using the plural, or possibly one speaker quoting God speaking about Himself in the plural. Note that Abdel Haleem uses an upper case, 'We', in translating 19:7, implying that the speaker is God. Abū al-Suʿūd claims that the speaker is an angel, but he does not explain how he came to this conclusion.[36] In the end, one may argue that the speaker is or is not God, as seen in the interpretations of Abdel Haleem and Abū al-Suʿūd. The speaker's identity is a secret. Here, I am interested in the existence of this mystery as a result of narrative choices and as a sign for one of God's secrets remaining a secret.

While the readers are presented with God's secret messenger, they may also see a sign for a human secret that is revealed when Zakariyyā leaves the 'sanctuary' or *miḥrāb* (19:11) to encourage his people to praise God. With Zakariyyā exiting the *miḥrāb*, he is moving from a private to a public place. Again, the readers are told about this scene and, thus, what may have been secret no longer remains so. Zakariyyā's move from the *miḥrāb* is a signifier for a human secret that is revealed. What was secret becomes known through the Qur'ān.

Similarly, when Zakariyyā is told that he will have a child, he is also told the name of the child, '*innā nubashshiruka bi-ghulāmin ismuhu yaḥyā*' (19:7). Zakariyyā, and the readers, are revealed the name of a child who is *in utero* (a very secret, private place to be) or possibly has not even been conceived yet.

Zakariyyā asks for a sign, and with his sign another secret is revealed: 'He said, "Give me a sign, Lord." He said, "Your sign is that you will not speak to anyone for three full [days and] nights"' (19:10). Thus, he is to seclude or isolate himself. Ironically, although he is not to talk to people, he still signals to them to praise God day and night, or during public and private times. Commentators discuss the ways by which Zakariyyā 'signalled to them', '*fa-awḥā ilayhim*' (19:11), given that he was to abstain from speaking. For example, al-Thaʿālibī, al-Ṭabarī and al-Ṭabrisī explain that he signals by means of signs or by writing in the dirt; this interpretation contrasts the ideas of communicating and remaining silent.[37] Here, then, being told not to speak, but still communicating signifies a human attempt at breaking isolation.

Moreover, Zakariyyā is told that he will not speak for three nights (19:10), but that he is to praise God day and night (19:11). As discussed in the previous chapter, the detail of Zakariyyā's abstinence from speech and his simultaneous communicating day and night also receives mention in another verse (3:41). Due to the variation in the references to day and night, the contrast between public and private times becomes clear. In both iterations, Zakariyyā breaks his silence and communicates with people: the secret is not.

Just as Zakariyyā's secrets are revealed, so are some of Maryam's. Maryam's story begins with her withdrawing from her people to an eastern place: 'Mention in the Scripture the story of Mary. She withdrew from her family to a place east' (19:16). The reader cannot be sure why she isolates herself at this point, or where she goes – this is secret from the reader. Some commentators mention that she withdrew to purify herself after menstruation or to worship God and that the location was somewhere east of where her people lived, or east of the *miḥrāb*.[38] Other commentators explain that Maryam was usually in the *masjid*, and when she was menstruating she would go to her aunt's house until she was done and would purify herself before returning to the *masjid*.[39] Here, the narrative portrays isolation and secrecy, and based on the *tafsīr*, readers notice and respond to these issues.

But Maryam's seeming isolation is disturbed by a visitor: she '... secluded herself away; We sent Our Spirit to appear before her in the form of a normal human' (19:17). Abū al-Suʿūd and al-Zamakhsharī explain that an angel came and told her that she would have a child while she was purifying herself.[40] This makes Maryam's seclusion even more intimate, and it renders the intrusion upon her seclusion even more surprising. Al-Ṭabarī and al-Zamakhsharī mention that she was alone, away from her people.[41] Ironically, her 'chaste seclusion becomes far more akin to vulnerable isolation'.[42] Her seeming isolation is intruded upon; hence, her seclusion is not complete.[43] Maryam's pregnancy itself can be seen as an example of her body being invaded: her individual body is not private, as she is made to share it with her foetus. Here, then, is Maryam isolating herself in vain, as a signifier for a human attempt at isolation being futile. While this reading might initially seem controversial from a theological perspective, it does fit with the notions that God chooses and blesses Maryam (3:37), that God tests people (for example 2:155, 3:142, 29:1–3 and 67:2), that something may look negative but can in fact be good for someone (2:216 and 24:11) and that God is the best of planners (for example 3:54, 8:30, 13:42, 14:46 and 27:50–1).

Although Maryam's attempt at isolation is futile, her visitor's identity is a secret, from Maryam and the readers. He says that he is a messenger: 'but he said, "I am but a Messenger from your Lord, [come] to announce to you the gift of a pure son"' (*innamā anā rasūlu rabbiki* 19:19). Here the speaker's identity as a messenger is certain, but one may wonder if he is the same as the one who spoke to Zakariyyā. A compelling reason to think that it is the same character lies in the fact that he gives the same response to both of them after they ask how they could have a child: 'and he said, "This is what your Lord said: 'It is easy for Me – We shall make him a sign to all people, a blessing from Us'"' (19:21). The beginning of this response is the same as the response given to Zakariyyā (19:9). If the mysterious speaker is the same for both Maryam and Zakariyyā, it says clearly that Maryam's is a messenger (19:17–19), and he is described as 'Our Spirit' (19:17). What exactly this means remains unclear. In the end, we do not know who the speaker is, although al-Thaʿālibī, Abū al-Suʿūd, al-Ṭabarī and Sayyid Quṭb write that he is Jibrīl.[44] This mysterious visitor constitutes a sign through which the narrator signifies the withholding of information.

Maryam later similarly withdraws herself when she is pregnant: 'And so it was ordained: she conceived him. She withdrew to a distant place [*qaṣiyyan*]' (19:22). One commentator says that she went far away from her people.[45] The readers are not told why or where she goes – another secret from the readers – but this time one may assume that she chooses to isolate herself because she is pregnant and prefers to give birth in private, since she may be criticised for her pregnancy (19:27–8). Yet, her seclusion is incomplete once again. Maryam is in labour and in pain: 'and, when the pains of childbirth drove her to [cling to] the trunk of a palm tree, she exclaimed, "I wish I had been dead and forgotten long before all this!"' (19:23). The reader has just been told that she had withdrawn 'to a distant place' (19:22); hence, one can assume that she speaks her despair in private. However, the narrator is revealing the scene to the reader. This is rather ironic since the Qur'ān provides readers with a lasting record of her wish to be forgotten.

In the events of the story itself, the seclusion is not complete, because someone responds to Maryam's cry of despair:

> 19:24 but a voice cried to her from below, 'Do not worry: your Lord has provided a stream at your feet
> 25 and, if you shake the trunk of the palm tree towards you, it will deliver fresh ripe dates for you,
> 26 so eat, drink, be glad . . .'

The speaker comforts her. She is not alone, and her secret is not a secret, even though she has withdrawn from people. Since Maryam is pregnant, she could never be alone anyway – her foetus constantly accompanies her – until she gives birth. Karen Bauer aptly explains that Maryam is rewarded for her loneliness and anguish with company and relief.[46] This attempt at isolation being rewarded with comfort contrasts with her previous attempt at isolation being met with a surprising messenger and the message that she will give birth to a messenger. Perhaps this also helps to address any theological discomfort among the audience about Maryam's pregnancy – she is rewarded for some of the difficulties she endures. In the context of Maryam's labour, there appear a few signs signifying human attempts at isolation and secrets being revealed: She isolates herself and wishes to be forgotten, but we are told of this, and someone speaks to comfort her, even though she is in an isolated place.

But who is it that comforts Maryam? It is possible that it is a messenger from God, but there is no indication of his identity, or if he is the same messenger that came to her earlier. The surveyed commentators write that the speaker could be the newly born 'Īsā or Jibrīl, sometimes leaning one way or another.[47] Abū al-Su'ūd explains that the speaker is Jibrīl, who received the child as midwife, and hence, the voice comes from below her. He also mentions that 'Īsā could be the speaker.[48] Sayyid Quṭb assumes the speaker is 'Īsā comforting his mother.[49] Even if the speaker is 'Īsā, one may wonder if he is speaking from the womb or after his birth. As the range in opinions indicates, none of these commentators has compelling proof with which to determine the identity of the speaker, because the narrator gives the reader few clues.

This speaker tells Maryam not to talk to people, and she is thus isolated from them in speech, as was Zakariyyā (19:26). Ironically, however, while Maryam is told not to speak, she is at the same time ordered what to tell people: '. . . say to anyone you may see: "I have vowed to the Lord of Mercy to abstain from conversation, and I will not talk to anyone today"' (19:26). As with Zakariyyā's scene, given this seeming contradiction, some commentators discuss the nature of her abstinence from words. Muhammad Asad acknowledges the challenge in interpreting the verse when he explains that it literally tells her to 'say'; he translates this as to 'convey, since speech would contradict what follows'.[50] Al-Tha'ālibī claims that she could have used signs.[51] Although Maryam is told not to speak, she is told to say that she is not to speak. Thus, her silence is broken from the beginning. At the same time, Maryam's child is able to speak for her, even though he is a baby and, therefore, her isolation from people is incomplete (19:30–3). Even if she had wanted to maintain her silence, she would have been unable to, as 'Īsā speaks for her. Thus, Maryam's communicating and her child communicating in her place when she is told not to speak are signs signifying the incomplete nature of human isolation.

In contrast, there exists a secret in the narrative style when Maryam returns to her people and they greet her thus: 'they said, "Mary! You have done something terrible! Sister of Aaron! Your father was not a bad man; your mother was not unchaste!"' (19:27–8). Commentators are puzzled over why they call her the sister of Hārūn. The most straightforward reason they provide is that she has a brother named Hārūn.[52] Al-Zamakhsharī offers this explanation and adds that this could also be a reference to the brother of Mūsā,[53] given the fact that Mūsā's brother Hārūn is mentioned later in the story (19:53). Verses 19:28 and 19:53 are the only two verses in the sura with the root *'-kh-w*, and both mention Hārūn: '"Sister of Aaron,"' *ukhta hārūn* (19:28) and 'his brother Aaron', *akhāhu hārūn* (19:53). Clearly, this forms a semantic connection; however, one may ponder other connections between the stories, as the connection between Hārūn, the brother of Mūsā, and Maryam is obscure. Some explanations posit that Maryam's people were descendants of Hārūn, that Hārūn was the name of an upright person at that time, or, the opposite, that it was the name of an immoral person.[54] Another theory mentioned by Hosn Abboud draws similarities between the Maryam of this story and Miriam, the sister of Aaron and Moses in the Torah.[55] (The sister of Hārun and Mūsā is mentioned in the Qur'ān, but she is not named.) This range of explanations demonstrates that the meaning is unclear to readers; here is another mystery that the narrator presents to readers and listeners.

Muḥammad Aḥmad Khalafallāh discusses this issue and includes quotations from commentators who interpret Maryam as actually being the sister of Hārūn, an idea he calls a 'historical mistake'. He uses this example to advance a point he makes throughout his book – that is, that Muslims use Qur'ānic stories as a source of historical truth, when instead they should see them as literary art or rhetorical expression.[56] It seems that Khalafallāh underestimates and misunderstands the problem; the ambiguities do not merely concern historical matters, but are a very deliberate part of the Qur'ānic narrative and rhetorical style, as we have seen.

Just as the reference to Hārūn is unclear, there exists another secret that remains so in the story. As discussed above, verses 19:34–40 end with a letter different from the rest of the sura. These verses are distinct from the rest of the story, even though they flow immediately from 'Īsā's speech:

> 19:34 Such was Jesus, son of Mary. [This is] a statement of the Truth about which they are in doubt:
> 35 it would not befit God to have a child. He is far above that: when He decrees something, He says only, 'Be', and it is.
> 36 'God is my Lord and your Lord, so serve Him: that is a straight path'.
> 37 But factions have differed among themselves. What suffering will come to those who obscure the truth when a dreadful Day arrives!
> 38 How sharp of hearing, how sharp of sight they will be when they come to Us, although now they are clearly off course!
> 39 Warn them [Muhammad] of the Day of Remorse when the matter will be decided, for they are heedless and do not believe.

40 It is We who will inherit the earth and all who are on it: they will all be returned to Us.

Commentators offer several options for the identity of the speaker in these verses. One claims that verses 19:34–6 contain the words of the Prophet Muḥammad, while others write that verse 19:39 does.[57] Neal Robinson argues that 19:36 is 'Īsā's speech.[58] The commentators also say that verse 19:37 represents God's words.[59] The fact that the commentaries do not offer any consensus about the identity of the speaker shows the ambiguity of the verses; this then can be interpreted as a sign for God's secrets which remain secret.

Each mystery or secret functions to establish Qur'ānic theological beliefs. All these signs can be considered signifiers that work to constitute a new sign. This Qur'ānic story is highly symbolic in nature. For example, 'Īsā and Maryam being told not to communicate but communicating signifies the concept of the human secret that is revealed. The human secret that is revealed is at the same time a signifier, and the signified is God's supreme knowledge: Human secrets are revealed because God knows everything. Thus, when Zakariyyā performs a secret prayer, of which the Qur'ānic audience is made aware, we encounter the concept of the human secret that is revealed, which in turn signifies God's omniscience. This becomes especially clear when we contrast these signs with the mysteries and ambiguities in the text – God's secrets that are actually maintained as secrets.

All the characters' secrets and attempts at seclusion and isolation are defied in one way or another throughout the story. People's secrets are not

Table 3.4 Signs become more signs

Sign	
Signifier Example: Zakariyyā makes a secret prayer, which is revealed to the Qur'anic audience	Signified Example: The concept of the human secret that is revealed
Sign	
Signifier Example: The concept of the human secret that is revealed	Signified Example: God's supreme knowledge

truly secret because God knows them all. The process of the reader being told secrets by the narrator establishes the authority of the narrator, showing that God knows these private things. At the same time, this process brings the reader closer to the narrator and the characters. The audience feels that the narrator is sharing secrets with them, and they feel that they have intimate knowledge of the characters. From this, readers may infer that, since the narrator knows the past, God also knows the future, and when God warns about the Day of Judgment (19:37–40), the warning is not in vain.

The only secrets in the story that really are secret relate to the ways in which God the narrator narrates the story. Why does the narrator include disconnected letters in a verse, without explaining what the letters mean? Why does the narrator mention that someone spoke, but not reveal who the speaker is? From the variety of interpretations from commentators, one can understand that there exist many ambiguities in the text. Ironically, the reader would not even know of these secrets, had the narrator not included them to begin with. There is a 'deliberate confusion of the reader', as Booth describes it:[60] The narrator is mentioning things and doing so in ways that we cannot fully understand. Since God is infinite and the audience is finite, confusion may constitute an appropriate response to the address by an omniscient deity. The narrative empowers the readers, while challenging them and emphasising to them that their knowledge and understanding are limited, even though they have the potential to achieve more. It is useful here to recall the Qur'ānic usage of the word *āyāt* for God's creation, including people, their languages and colours and the verses of the Qur'ān (2:99, 2:129, 2:151, 3:7, 30:20–2, 45:4, etc.). They are all signs of God – they are all created by God, empowered and fundamentally limited at the same time. The Qur'ān presents itself as God's word and, thus, shows us that it is greater than us and that we cannot understand everything in it. Consequently, the audience realises that they would not know anything, if God the narrator did not relate it to them, reinforcing the belief that they would not exist if God had not willed it.

V. Conclusion

This chapter began with an analysis of the structure of the story in *Sūrat Maryam*, as it is established by means of themes, echoing words and phrases, the number of verses, the gradual progression in the moral argument being made, and the consistent patterns in sections and sub-sections. Because the story mentions multiple characters, I have analysed how those sections relate to each other. Through the structural development, the importance of the relationship between a person and their family is progressively decreased, and the relationship between a person and God increases in significance. The chapter then moved on to examine the relationship of an individual to God: God knows everything, and He tells what He wants and keeps secret what He wants. God reveals through *āyāt*, signs and verses of the revelation. In 19:1–58, various narrative choices work to instil beliefs about God. This analysis highlights the themes of relationships with family and with God, and various kinds of secrets, all of which may not have been very apparent without the analysis of the story's structure. In this way, we have been able to discern underlying structures within the text, structures not apparent on the surface.[61] As Toorawa indicates, lexical echoes and rhymes are critical for establishing structure in the story, and structure has ramifications for the message of the story.

Throughout the story of *Sūrat Maryam* 19:1–58, the relationship between God and people is reinforced. Fundamentally, God is central. Based on the structure of the story, one can see that the most important and lasting relationship is the relationship between God and people. Even the family, which is portrayed as a blessing, becomes less prominent in the story, while God becomes more prominent, until finally the story ends with a focus on the relationship between God and God's messengers (19:58).

Through the analysis of various echoing roots in the story and thereafter, the Qur'ān sets patterns and then diverges from them to make points, to complicate and develop them. Connections made through echoing words illustrate how Qur'ānic stories and non-narrative work together. The non-narrative verses in many ways act as commentary on and contrast to the earlier story.

At the same time, through the contrasting signs of human secrets that are revealed and God's secrets that are maintained, through the giving of information just sufficient to show that there is information being withheld (but not enough to actually reveal the secret), the Qur'ān further develops the relationship between God and people. God is the creator who knows everything; hence, there are no secrets from God. The narrative style thus reflects Qur'ānic verses such as this one in which 'Īsā tells God: '. . . You know all that is within me, though I do not know what is within You, You alone have full knowledge of things unseen' (5:116).

Notes

1. Earlier versions of parts of this chapter were previously published in the *Journal of Qur'anic Studies*. See Ozgur Alhassen, 'A Structural Analysis of *Sūrat Maryam* Q. 19:1–58'.
2. Lybarger 240, note 2.
3. Toorawa 25.
4. Abboud iii.
5. Lybarger.
6. Smith and Haddad, and Wheeler, *Prophets in the Quran* 299–301.
7. Robinson, *Christ in Christianity and Islam.*
8. Alter, *The Art of Biblical Narrative* 56, 60, 61.
9. Toorawa 27–31.
10. Toorawa 51.
11. These letters are also referred to as 'the mysterious letters' or '*al-fawātiḥ*', 'the introductory letters'.
12. Toorawa 52 and 55–6, respectively. There is much discussion about the meaning, origin and purpose of the *fawātiḥ* in general.
13. Toorawa 77, note 62.
14. al-Ghazālī 323–4.
15. Neuwirth, *Scripture, Poetry, and the Making of a Community* 351.
16. Neuwirth, *Scripture, Poetry, and the Making of a Community* 342–53.
17. Cuypers, *The Banquet* 35–6, based on Nils W. Lund. Also, Carl Ernst writes in some detail about Cuypers's work: Ernst 162–71.
18. Cuypers, *The Banquet* 304.
19. Sakaedani 64.
20. Toorawa 58.
21. For more on this story of Ibrāhīm in its larger Qur'ānic context, see: Ozgur Alhassen, 'A Narratological Analysis of the Story of Ibrāhīm in the Qur'ān'.
22. Al-'Amārī, vol. 5, 269.
23. See, for example, 4:11.
24. Al-Jalālayn 401 explains that *ahl* means his people, and al-Tha'ālibī, vol. 2, 331

gives the meaning of his people or his community.

25. Firestone writes: 'It is worth noting that the inconsistent qur'ānic references to Abraham's descendants have been an issue of some interest to Western scholars [. . .] A number of verses list Isaac and Isaac's son Jacob (q.v.) together as if they were both sons of Abraham (q 6:84; 11:71; 19:49; 21:72; 29:27). In a series of quite different passages, Ishmael is listed as if he had no familial connection to Abraham (q 6:86; 19:54–5; 21:85; 38:48) [. . .] Already in the nineteenth century C. S. Hurgronje (Het Mekkaansche Feest) theorized that this material reflects some confusion over the exact relationship between Abraham and his descendants, claiming that these verses date from the Meccan period of revelations, i.e. before Muḥammad came into regular contact with Jews or Christians. The verses that reproduce the biblical genealogy were held to date from Muḥammad's days in Medina, when he apparently had ongoing contact with the local Jewish community'. According to Hurgronje, then, the Bible writes the Qur'ān's history.
26. Neuwirth, *Scripture, Poetry, and the Making of a Community* 331–2.
27. Toorawa 33–50 and 60–61.
28. Toorawa 50.
29. Toorawa 38.
30. Neuwirth, *Scripture, Poetry, and the Making of a Community* 345.
31. Toorawa 36.
32. In Abdel Haleem's translation, 'And so it was ordained' is marked as verse 19:22, but it is actually part of 19:21.
33. See, for example, Saussure; Barthes, 'Mythologies'. For another example of analysis focused on signifiers and signifying, see Netton 68.
34. Netton 71–80.
35. For more on signs in the Qur'ān, see Ward Gwynne 27.
36. Al-'Amārī, vol. 5, 255.
37. Al-Tha'ālibī, vol. 2, 321, al-Ṭabarī, vol. 7, 5460–1 and www.altafsir.com/Tafasir.asp?tMadhNo=4&tTafsirNo=3&tSoraNo=19&tAyahNo=8&tDisplay=yes&Page=3&Size=1&LanguageId=1
38. Al-Tha'ālibī, vol. 2, 322–3. Asad, vol. 4, 512, note 13 states that she withdrew for prayer and meditation.
39. Al-'Amārī, vol. 5, 259–60, al-Zamakhsharī, vol. 2, 505 and al-Ṭabrisī www.altafsir.com/Tafasir.asp?tMadhNo=4&tTafsirNo=3&tSoraNo=19&tAyahNo=17&tDisplay=yes&UserProfile=0&LanguageId=1
40. Al-'Amārī, vol. 5, 259–60 and al-Zamakhsharī, vol. 2, 505.
41. Al-Ṭabarī, vol. 7, 5467 and 5472; and al-Zamakhsharī, vol. 2, 506.

42. Geissinger 387.
43. See Johns, 'A Humanistic Approach to *i'jāz* in the Qur'ān' 87–8. Robinson, *Christ in Christianity and Islam* 160 discusses commentary on Maryam and the '*ḥijāb*' (19:17).
44. Al-Tha'ālibī, vol. 2, 322–3, al-'Amārī, vol. 5, 260, al-Ṭabarī, vol. 7, 5468 and Quṭb, vol. 4, 2306. According to Smith and Haddad 168 and Robinson, *Christ in Christianity and Islam* 162, commentators also discuss how Jibrīl appeared in the form of a man.
45. Al-'Amārī, vol. 5, 261.
46. Bauer 23.
47. Al-Zamakhsharī, vol. 2, 507 says that it is Jibrīl, but that people also say it is 'Īsā. Al-Jalālayn 398 says that it is Jibrīl. Al-Tha'ālibī, vol. 2, 324 and al-Ṭabarī, vol. 7, 5477–9 say that it could be either, but that 'Isā is more likely. Smith and Haddad 171 also discuss commentary on this issue. Also, Abboud 76 and 187 discusses a variant reading (*man taḥtihā* instead of *min taḥtihā*) and its possible meaning. Al-Ṭabrisī says it could be either one, www.altafsir.com/Tafasir.asp?tMadhNo=4&tTafsirNo=3&tSoraNo=19&tAyahNo=21&tDisplay=yes&Page=4&Size=1&LanguageId=1
48. Al-'Amārī, vol. 5, 262.
49. Quṭb, vol. 4, 2307.
50. Asad, vol. 4, 514, note 19.
51. Al-Tha'ālibī, vol. 2, 325.
52. Al-Tha'ālibī, vol. 2, 325.
53. Al-Zamakhsharī, vol. 2, 508.
54. Al-Tha'ālibī, vol. 2, 326. See also al-Ṭabrisī: www.altafsir.com/Tafasir.asp?tMadhNo=4&tTafsirNo=3&tSoraNo=19&tAyahNo=21&tDisplay=yes&Page=5&Size=1&LanguageId=1
55. Abboud p. 87–8 and 179.
56. Khalafallāh 57–8.
57. Al-Tha'ālibī, vol. 2, 327; al-Jalālayn 400 and al-Ṭabrisī, www.altafsir.com/Tafasir.asp?tMadhNo=4&tTafsirNo=3&tSoraNo=19&tAyahNo=36&tDisplay=yes&Page=2&Size=1&LanguageId=1
58. Robinson, *Discovering the Qur'an* 235–6.
59. Al-Tha'ālibī, vol. 2, 327.
60. Booth 285.
61. Eagleton 83.

4

Evidence, Judgment and Remorse in *Sūrat Yūsuf*

I. Introduction

Throughout *Sūrat Yūsuf*, we can ascertain a focus on God, as is evident in the relevant commentaries and scholarly studies. For example, Marilyn Robinson Waldman writes about the story: 'God is ever-present in the narrative, His cosmic omnipresence thus underscored'.[1] Irfan Khan sees in it Yūsuf's message of *tawḥīd*,[2] or monotheism. Mustansir Mir, in discussing the story in connection with irony, argues that 'evil intended by human beings is turned into good by God'.[3] Philip Kennedy points to incomplete human knowledge, as opposed to God's transcendent knowledge throughout the story.[4] Muhammad Asad introduces the story of Yūsuf in the following way: 'The whole of this *sūrah* might be described as a series of variations on the theme "judgment [as to what is to happen] rests with none but God"'.[5] Similar to these scholars, and especially Asad, I will concentrate on the idea that, throughout the entire story, the narrative style works to show that God is the ultimate judge and that humans are always lacking in their ability to judge others. This chapter will develop this argument through an examination of judgment, remorse and evidence, concepts prominent in the story, as we will see. Salwa El-Awa writes about suras in general that they are 'concerned with developing a number of concepts that are vital to the Islamic message and that these concepts contribute to other contexts in the Qur'ān on the one hand, and form their own final message on the other'.[6] I will not discuss the sura's structure here, as there already exist a number of excellent studies on this topic.[7]

Similar to the above discussions on *Sūrat Āl 'Imrān* and *Sūrat Maryam*, we will focus on the different ways in which God the narrator withholds knowledge from the audience. The sura itself explicitly discusses knowledge: 'Above everyone who has knowledge there is the One who is all knowing' (12:76). First, one may look at the withholding of knowledge in the meta-text, which consists of the introduction to the story. Here, God declares that the text is clear and the best story (or one of the best stories), but these claims are difficult to understand in their precise meaning. Next, we move on to the story itself, which foregrounds the ideas of guilt, evidence and proof, in terms of determining the truth. However, knowledge is withheld from the readers in terms of evidence – human evidence such as a cup and a shirt can be manipulated, but evidence from God, even if not understood by everyone, is reliable. Finally, there emerge the issues of judgment and remorse, and once again the readers lack in knowledge and are unable to judge the characters. These deliberate narrative techniques affirm what the Qur'ān states in other places: God is omniscient, and only God can judge people. As we are faced with textual mysteries, I turn to the Qur'ānic commentaries to see how they explain or respond to these; their varied interpretations speak to the ambiguity of the text.

II. Withholding Knowledge in the Non-narrative Verses of the Sura

Sūrat Yūsuf begins with a verse that sets the tone for the rest of the story: 'Alif Lam Ra These are the verses of the Scripture that makes things clear – ' (12:1–3). The disconnected letters at the beginning show humankind its limits of knowledge and the limits of human language, and that God is the one who holds all power in general, all power over the story to come and the language in which it is told. God can even choose to use letters whose meanings are unclear. Although letters are normally used to represent sounds which in turn form words, these letters do not function in this way and, therefore, humans cannot understand their meaning.

These disconnected letters, *fawātiḥ al-suwar* or *al-muqaṭṭaʿāt*, are present at the beginning of all of the suras I analyse in this book. Some see these letters as problematic because they are difficult to interpret, but their enigma is consistent with other narrative mysteries in Qur'ānic stories. Some view the disconnected letters as part of the editorial work,[8] while most scholars, both Muslim and non-Muslim, consider them as part of revelation.[9] Muhammad Asad writes that the Companions recited and considered these letters as part of the revelation,[10] and as a demonstration of the 'incomparability' or *iʿjāz* of the Qur'ān.[11]

To some, there is an inconsistency in the presence of these letters in a book that says it 'makes things clear' (12:1). For example, James Bellamy implies that elements that mystify contradict the image of the Qur'ān as a clear book.[12] Irfan Shahīd uses a similar premise, focusing on the clarity of the Qur'ānic text. According to him, 'the Qur'ānic message is crystal clear with no ambiguity which would be difficult to understand by the Arabs in Mecca and Medina. It is utterly inconsistent with this, that the Qur'ānic Revelation would contain deliberately something that is incomprehensible as these *Fawātiḥ* . . .'[13] Both Bellamy and Shahīd base their arguments on a simplistic understanding of clarity, ambiguity, incomprehensibility and the study of literature in general. In contrast, Martin Nguyen claims that 'the Sunnī exegetical discourse [. . .] has treated the letters as an interpretative instance of open polyvalency within the Qur'an'.[14] Thus, in the Sunni exegesis, the letters do not pose a problem as a result of their mysterious nature.

The Qur'ān at times withholds information from readers in order to make certain theological points. Most of the examples discussed here are related to the narrative and involve a number of words or verses. Thus, they are unlikely to be the result of transcriptional error or misunderstanding. As discussed in the Introduction, the idea that the Qur'ān is to be seen as the word of God in and of itself requires that it cannot be fully understood by people. The Qur'ān is a lengthy book that may be clear in parts and unclear in others, clear in some ways and unclear in others, clear to some people and unclear at others. In addition, an important clue to understanding the disconnected letters, which points to their being a part of the revelation itself, consists of the fact that they occur before the mention of the book or revelation (interpreted as being the Qur'ān itself),[15] and before assertions about the authoritativeness and authenticity of the Qur'ān.[16]

Perceptively, Nguyen points out the contrast that the text itself draws between unclear letters and the idea of clarity: 'The Qur'an itself prompts this notion of obtuseness through the seeming juxtaposition of the letters with statements proclaiming the clarity of the scripture'.[17] Furthermore, the word '*tilka*', 'these', is a demonstrative pronoun with an unclear referent. Al-Ṭabrisī discusses what 'these' could be referring to: the coming verses,

Sūrat Yūsuf, or the verses that God promised to reveal in the Torah.[18] While the reader puzzles over the meaning of these letters and words, God the narrator is the One to choose what to reveal and with what words, and to decide what is clear and what is not. God says the Book is clear, and so it is clear, despite the fact that the chapter begins with disconnected letters.

The first verses of the sura are:

> 12:1 *Alif Lam Ra* These are the verses of the Scripture that makes things clear –
> 2 We have sent it down as an Arabic Qur'an so that you [people] may understand.
> 3 We tell you [Prophet] the best of stories in revealing this Qur'an to you. Before this you were one of those who knew nothing about them.

The verses start with the most general concept, letters that make up words (12:1), then gradually narrow to the Arabic Qur'ān (12:2) and, finally, focus even further on the stories in the Qur'ān, or this specific story (12:3).

As the introduction to the story continues, the second verse says: 'We have sent it down as an Arabic Qur'an so that you [people] may understand' (12:2). This verse indicates two ideas. One, the narrator assumes that the reader knows Arabic. Here, for example, al-Ṭabarī explains that the Qur'ān is in Arabic because it is the language of the people to whom it is revealed.[19] This makes one wonder what else the narrator assumes about the reader. The use of the word 'Arabic' also brings to mind the human nature of the language in use here – a book or revelation is usually written in only one language, and the narrator has chosen for it to be in Arabic, among many other options. This verse would eventually play a role in debates on the createdness or the eternality of the Qur'ān in the eighth through tenth centuries CE. The Mu'tazilites used this verse to argue for the Qur'ān's createdness, because the Qur'ān characterises itself by its language and because language is temporal. This verse is also featured in discussions connecting the message of the Qur'ān to its Arabic language in al-Shāfi'ī's *Risāla*, as well as in debates on the permissibility of using translations of the Qur'ān in various contexts.[20] This verse seems simple, but in fact holds great significance in theological discussions.

We will now move on to the third verse, by first taking note of the unusual narrative style of the story of Yūsuf when compared with most of the other stories in the Qur'ān. It is a lengthy, chronological telling of Yūsuf's life, told exclusively in one location and taking up the entire chapter. (Elsewhere, Yūsuf is briefly mentioned in verses 6:84 and 40:34.) Readers often assume that its style is completely unique amongst Qur'ānic stories. However, there exist other stories that are also told in only one location, although not as lengthy. These include the stories of Luqmān (31:13–25), *Dhū al-Qarnayn* (18:83–101) and *Aṣḥāb al-Kahf* (18:9–26).

It is tempting to assume that, because the story of Yūsuf is told in a lengthy manner and in chronological order, it would be easier to understand than other Qur'ānic stories; after all, it has more text with which to explain the story, and it does so in a linear fashion. However, it includes many puzzles that readers cannot solve within the story and, in fact, we cannot even understand why its lengthy and linear style is the way it is. As if the narrator wants to bring the narrative style to our attention, the introduction to the story states: 'We tell you [Prophet] the best of stories [*aḥsan al-qaṣaṣ*] in revealing this Qur'an to you. Before this you were one of those who knew nothing about them' (12:3). The verse does not make it clear whether this particular story is the best of stories, or all of the Qur'ānic stories collectively. The Qur'ān presents a dilemma here. If this particular story is the best of stories, why is that so? It may be because it 'is regarded as the very epitome of story telling and moral instruction', while another interpretation argues that it is the best of stories because it is about love.[21] If it is the best of stories because of its content, then why is the content never repeated elsewhere in the Qur'ān? And if this story is the best of stories because of its style – as discussed, the most noteworthy stylistic features are that it is written exclusively, in totality and linearly in one place – then why are the other Qur'ānic stories not told in the same way?[22] It could also be the best of stories because of its content and style,[23] in which case the content is the best of content, but cannot be repeated elsewhere because the style (which includes its exclusivity) dictates this, otherwise it would defy its own rubric of good style. Any of these options, as long as we single out this particular story, seems to undermine the rest of the Qur'ānic stories. If *aḥsan* conveys intensive rather than elative, meaning 'better', we have a comparative, but we do not know what is better than what. This verse, although seemingly simple, is an enigma, and neither do the commentaries help to solve the problem.

Muhammad Asad translates the verse as follows: 'In the measure that We reveal this Qur'ān unto thee, [O Prophet,] We explain it to thee in the best possible way, seeing that ere this thou wert indeed among those who are unaware [of what revelation is]'.[24] Thus, he interprets the verse as referring to the Qur'ān as a whole, and not to one particular story. He explains:

> According to Rāzī [Fakhr al-Dīn al-Rāzī, 1149–1209 CE], it may safely be assumed that the adjective 'best' refers not to the *contents* of 'that which is set forth – i.e., the particular story narrated in this *sūrah* – but rather to the *manner* in which the Qur'an (or this particular *sūrah*) is set forth'.[25]

Thus, according to some, the verse is discussing revelation in general and not singling out this particular sura.[26] Sayyid Quṭb mentions that, since the body of this sura is a story, it makes sense to mention stories at the beginning of it.[27] Interestingly, al-Tha'ālibī writes that, because this is an isolated telling of the story, unlike the other stories in the Qur'ān, and because it presents a style in which some stories are repeated while others are not, we have proof against those who claim that eloquence is in repetition, or that repetition makes a story deficient.[28]

The issue may become clearer if we compare the function of this verse to the function of repetition. As seen above, since the Qur'ānic stories sometimes repeat information, include exclusive information about a story and/or include echoes of other stories, they lead the audience to other parts of the Qur'ān to see what more there is to learn about the story which they are reading, as well as other stories that are related by echoes. In verse 12:3, comparing the stories by saying that one is better than the others leads one to compare stories and thus read more. Even when a reader – of any time-period – knows that the story is not repeated elsewhere, this verse still can fulfil the role of leading the reader to read more. While this is a possible solution to the question about the meaning of 'the best of stories', the fact remains that God asserts something that readers do not fully understand. The introduction to the story already features God's assertion that He is the one to decide if, why and what it means for something to be the best of stories, or for something to be clear.

III. Withholding Knowledge in Evidence

I will now focus on the ways in which God the narrator centres God in the concept of evidence, through various narrative techniques. In the story, people make claims and then try to prove these with the help of evidence. This contrasts with God's guiding people through 'proof' of various kinds. Evidence from God includes dreams and their correct repetition and interpretation, as well as inspiration from God, while people present shirts and bowls as evidence, which are sometimes healing and revelatory, at other times manipulated and misleading. Thus, the readers are taught that evidence from humans can sometimes be misleading, but evidence from God is always reliable.

To begin, one may consider pieces of evidence that originate from humans. The story starts with Yūsuf seeing a dream and telling his father about it. Then his brothers plot against him and one day convince their father to let them take Yūsuf out with them. Yūsuf's brothers abandon him in a well, then return to their father with a shirt 'deceptively stained with blood' (*wa-jā'ū 'alā qamīṣihi bi-damin kadhib*) as proof that Yūsuf was devoured by a wolf (12:18). Ya'qūb is not fooled by the evidence that they have manipulated.

While the shirt with the fake blood stains does not deceive Ya'qūb, a different kind of evidence appears later in the story, and this time it actually leads to the truth. Yūsuf is found and then eventually bought by a powerful man who suggests to his wife that they treat him well (12:21).[29] Once Yūsuf reaches maturity (12:22), the wife of al-'Azīz tries to seduce Yūsuf. Yūsuf rejects her advances, and as they run to the door, she rips his shirt. Her husband is at the door, and she accuses Yūsuf of attacking her and almost immediately asks for him to be punished (12:25). Yūsuf denies her accusation, and another present person explains that, if Yūsuf's shirt is torn from the front, she is telling the truth, and if it is torn from the back, he is telling the truth (12:26–7). We assume that everyone agrees to this test, and the next verse continues: 'When the husband saw that the shirt was torn at the back, he said, "This is another instance of women's treachery: your treachery is truly great"' (12:28).[30] Here, as with the blood-stained shirt that Yūsuf's brothers bring to their father (12:18), a garment serves to establish proof.[31] Just as a shirt conceals and reveals parts of the body, it conceals and reveals the truth in this story. In the earlier scene, the brothers try to manipulate Yūsuf's shirt to show something that is not the truth, but this time his shirt helps to reveal the truth.[32]

These aspects of the story constitute two examples of shirts being used as evidence, and in one case, the shirt does in fact lead to the truth. Yūsuf himself also plants false evidence. Surprisingly, Yūsuf is now in a privileged, powerful position, separated from his family. His brothers, ironically, come to him for help. They do not know that he is their brother, but Yūsuf recognises them. When they are reunited, Yūsuf plots to keep his youngest brother with him (12:58–98), by putting the king's cup in his brother's bag (12:69–72). The cup is found in his brother's bag and used as proof of the brother's guilt. In this way, Yūsuf manipulates the evidence. Thus, the reader understands that evidence can be deceiving, even when used for a good purpose, even when manipulated by a good person.

So far, the story has featured a shirt being used to make a false claim by bad people, a shirt actually revealing the truth and a cup proving a false claim by a good person and for a presumably good reason. Aside from the cup and the shirt, there are other pieces of evidence in this story, and these come from the narrator, God. First, there are the dreams in the story. In the beginning of the story, Yūsuf tells his dream to his father; his father interprets it for him, and Yūsuf sees its realisation at the end of the story. He says, '". . . Father, this is the fulfilment of that dream I had long ago. My Lord has made it come true . . ."' (12:100). Yūsuf's dream was proof of what would come to pass, and it did indeed come true. Yūsuf thus asserts God's role, and it is safe to assume that we are to believe that the dream and its interpretation came from God. Ya'qūb directly credits Yūsuf's ability to interpret dreams to God at the beginning of the story: '"This is about how your Lord will choose you, teach you to interpret dreams . . ."' (12:6). Similarly, Yūsuf's cellmates see dreams, and Yūsuf interprets them correctly (12:36 and 12:41–2).

Later, the king sees a dream, and again Yūsuf interprets it correctly. The king narrates his dream and asks for his advisors' interpretation. They tell him that they do not know how to and say, '"these are confusing dreams"' (*aḍghāthu aḥlām*, 12:44). The same phrase appears elsewhere in the Qur'ān, in the description of an accusation of the Prophet Muḥammad: 'Some say, "Muddled dreams" [*aḍghāthu aḥlām*]; others, "He has made it up"; yet others, "He is just a poet . . ."' (21:5). In both cases, what is called a dream actually represents the truth. In the story, the man who had been freed from prison overhears this conversation (implying that Yūsuf correctly interpreted his dream and that he was working for the king) and remembers Yūsuf. He claims that Yūsuf can tell them the meaning of the dream, goes to him and asks him. He is depicted as repeating the dream to Yūsuf, and thus the reader hears the dream again, thirteen words *verbatim*, only three verses later. It is described as follows: '". . . seven fat cows being eaten by seven lean ones; seven green ears of corn and [seven] others withered . . ."' (*sab'a baqarātin simānin ya'kuluhunna sab'un 'ijāfun wa sab'a sunbulātin khuḍrin wa-ukhara yābisātin* 12:43 and 12:46). In a text rather sparse in its language, one finds it striking that the dream is repeated at length. It is also remarkable that the man who was previously forgetful in mentioning Yūsuf to his master (12:42) – despite the fact that Yūsuf played such an extraordinary role in his life – relates this message in an absolutely flawless manner. The narrator shows that the dream, since it comes from God, is not manipulated, even when repeated by a person who was previously forgetful. Yūsuf interprets the dream and gives advice about how the king should deal with the coming harvests (12:47–9); this advice turns out to be useful (12:54–6). Thus, actions based on God's evidence are also fruitful. Not only is evidence from God reliable and true, but it is also not corrupted by people. This is parallel to and critical for the Qur'ānic stories, in which messengers of God convey God's message to people – and the Qur'ān itself, which is God's word delivered through Jibrīl to Muḥammad, and then from Muḥammad to others. Just as the dream is delivered faithfully, revelation from God is also delivered precisely and reliably.

The story contains a number of dreams and their correct interpretation, a gift which comes from God (12:6). Al-Ṭabarī explains that the dreams of prophets are considered *waḥī* or inspiration.[33] Dreams and the ability to interpret them are juxtaposed with the fact that what people present as evidence (such as shirts and bowls) can be manipulated. The readers thus arrive at the crux of the matter: What is reliable proof, and what is its source?

One scene that helps answer this question concerns the wife of al-'Azīz trying to seduce Yūsuf, as mentioned above. The narrator says, 'She made for him, and he would have succumbed to her if he had not seen evidence of his

Lord – We did this in order to keep evil and indecency away from him, for he was truly one of Our chosen servants' (12:24). The phrase, 'evidence of his Lord' (*burhāna rabbih*) is a puzzling one, as illustrated by the vast array of perspectives on its meaning in Qur'ānic commentary.

Al-Ṭabarī mentions a number of interpretations: Yūsuf saw the image of his father Ya'qūb biting his finger and saying no;[34] a voice called out, 'O Yūsuf, are you having an affair? If you do, you will be like a bird who tries to fly when its feathers have fallen off;'[35] a voice called and mentioned the bird without feathers, then looked like his father biting his finger; a voice called to him and said, 'Are you written amongst the prophets to act like the foolish?!' (*sufahā'*);[36] he saw Ya'qūb on the roof of the house;[37] he saw Ya'qūb hitting his chest with his hand; he saw verse 17:32 against adultery on the wall;[38] he saw three Qur'ānic verses, 82:10, 10:61 and 13:33; and he saw an image of the king. Al-Ṭabarī concludes that it could be any of these and that there is no definite proof for any of them: 'The correct thing that is said about this is what Allah Praised and Most High says, and the belief in Him, and to leave what turns away from this to the learned'.[39] Al-Tustarī says the *burhān* was Jibrīl who came, looking like Ya'qūb.[40] It is interesting that Ya'qūb lives on in many of these commentaries as a voice of wisdom within the story. Al-Zamakhsharī lists many of these ideas, while al-Tha'ālibī mentions a few.[41] Abū al-Su'ūd mentions them and argues that they are legends and untruths.[42] Al-Zamakhsharī says Yūsuf would have been inclined towards her, but did not give in to his inclination.[43] Abū al-Su'ūd and al-Tha'ālibī argue for a similar perspective,[44] with al-Tha'ālibī further explaining that God says He gave Yūsuf wisdom and knowledge, and wisdom (*ḥukm*) is to act with knowledge. Thus Yūsuf acted with what God taught him about the prohibition of *zinā* (unlawful sexual intercourse) and the prohibition of betraying the man of the house.[45] Also similar, Abū al-Su'ūd explains that the *burhān* was the strong evidence of the ugliness of *zinā* and the evil of the path to it.[46]

While God's proof was clear to Yūsuf, it is unclear to the readers and listeners of the story. Perhaps this is like the mysterious letters: They are clear to God, but unclear to the audience. What is clear is that the source of the proof is God. Presumably, God was determined to lead Yūsuf in a certain direction and, therefore, God showed him something or made him feel something to direct his actions as God wanted.

Just as God shows Yūsuf 'evidence', He shows some people 'signs' (*al-āyāt*) so that Yūsuf will be imprisoned, as Yūsuf wishes. After the women of the city show interest in him and the wife of al-'Azīz threatens him (12:31–2), Yūsuf prays:

> 12:33 Joseph said, 'My Lord! I would prefer prison to what these women are calling me to do. If You do not protect me from their treachery, I shall yield to them and do wrong',
> 34 and his Lord answered his prayer and protected him from their treachery – He is the All Hearing, the All Knowing.
> 35 In the end they thought it best, after seeing all the signs of his innocence, that they should imprison him for a while.

God responds to Yūsuf's appeal by making them (we do not know exactly who they are) decide to imprison him. This verse uses seemingly clear but in fact cryptic language. The Arabic only says that they see 'the signs' (*al-āyāt*), whereas this translation by Abdel Haleem specifies that they are 'the signs of his innocence'. Many commentators also explain that the signs were the signs of his innocence.[47] It is cryptic and ironic that they would see that he is innocent and therefore imprison him. Al-Ṭabarī argues that the proof of Yūsuf's innocence consists of the torn shirt, a scratch on his face and the women cutting their hands.[48] Tafsīr al-Jalālayn adds that they decide to imprison Yūsuf to cut off people's talk.[49] Al-Tha'ālibī explains that she told her husband that Yūsuf was disgracing her in front of people, and according to al-Tha'ālibī, this shows their tyranny to Yūsuf.[50] In this vein, Sayyid Quṭb explicates that this is an environment of palaces, authoritarian government and aristocratic circles.[51] The commentators' explanations of 'the signs' are varied and inconclusive because the Qur'ānic language here is ambiguous. What the readers do know is what God wanted them to know, 'and his Lord answered his prayer and protected him from their treachery' (12:34). Evidence from God is reliable, even if not everyone understands it.

The word 'signs' (*āyāt*) occurs three other times in this sura. The first time is in the first verse, stating that these are signs/verses of the clear Book (12:1). Next is: 'There are lessons [*āyāt*] in the story of Joseph and his brothers for all who seek them' (12:7). Once it occurs in the singular: 'and there is many a sign [*āya*] in the heavens and the earth that they pass by and give no heed to'

(12:105).[52] There are signs from God on an individual level: for Yūsuf, within the story (12:35), for all people, within the story (12:7), in this Book (12:1) and outside of the Book (12:105). It is useful to compare these 'signs' (*āyāt*) to those previously discussed in the context of *Sūrat Maryam*. There, one can find the sign that Zakariyyā asks for (19:10); 'Īsā is called a sign (19:21); prophets bow down in prostration when they hear God's signs (19:58) and people reject God's signs (19:73 and 19:77). The ideas of proof and revelation are present in the word 'sign', *āya*, in both suras. God centres Himself in both stories. This stands in opposition to human-determined evidence and proof, which at times can be manipulated and misleading in *Sūrat Yūsuf*. How can one rely on something without knowing whether it is consistently reliable, whereas God's truth is always reliable and can never be manipulated?

IV. Withholding Knowledge in Judgment and Remorse

As the narrative style in the story of Yūsuf problematises the concept of evidence, to show that God's is the only consistently truthful evidence, it also does so for the judgment of guilt and remorse. In a lengthy, moral story featuring people who commit mistakes or sins and then reform, one might expect moments of remorse and forgiveness to be prominent and even dramatised. One might also expect it to be possible to pinpoint when and how a character feels remorse. However, when examining the themes of guilt and remorse in the story of Yūsuf, we cannot do so, but instead find God at the centre. In this way, the narrator asserts that only God can judge people and that, even when God is telling the story, God is unwilling to give the readers the tools to judge the characters. This section will focus on Yūsuf's brothers, then the wife of al-'Azīz and, finally, the women of the city. It will become obvious that the reader cannot tell when or if a person is guilty or repents, and even when there is a confession, as in the case of the brothers, it is not clear that it is a confession. Furthermore, in the case of the women, the issue is also quite complicated.

One may start by looking at Yūsuf's brothers in order to examine the narrator's portrayal of guilt and remorse. In the beginning, when Yūsuf informs his father about his dream, Ya'qūb asks him not to tell his brothers about it, or else they may plot against him, as Shayṭān (Satan) is an enemy to people (12:5). Ya'qūb absolves his sons of potential blame by mentioning Shayṭān's role. In the same way, at the end of the story, Yūsuf says that 'Satan sowed discord between' him and his brothers (12:100).

Ya'qūb acts similarly at the beginning, when his sons ask him to entrust them with Yūsuf. The brothers 'said to their father, "Why do you not trust us with Joseph? We wish him well. Send him with us tomorrow and he will enjoy himself and play – we will take good care of him"' (12:11–12). In response, Ya'qūb gently mentions his fears and blames their carelessness and a wolf's instincts to hunt prey, rather than their jealousy or malice: 'He replied, "The thought of you taking him away with you worries me: I am afraid a wolf may eat him when you are not paying attention"' (12:13).[53] While Ya'qūb clearly attempts to minimise their culpability, it is unclear whether the narrator wants the readers to judge them in the same way.

After their outing, the brothers return to their father, 'weeping' (12:16). Although the narrator unambiguously explains that they present a shirt 'deceptively stained with blood' as evidence (*wa-jā'ū 'alā qamīṣihi bi-damin kadhib*, 12:18), this passage emphasises that they are weeping, *yabkūna*, and not *pretending* to weep. Does this hint at some feelings of remorse? They say, '". . . We went off racing one another, leaving Joseph behind with our things, and a wolf ate him. You will not believe us, though we are telling the truth!"' (12:17). They use the very same excuse that their father had made for them earlier (12:13). The wolf is 'symbolic and imaginary',[54] since there was never a wolf to begin with. Just as they manipulate their father and brother, they also manipulate his words and his fears, and use them against him[55] – which seems cruel. But this is complicated by their weeping; it is not obvious whether their weeping is supposed to be a demonstration of their remorse and how their lie fits with this show of emotions. The narrator is making it difficult for the reader to determine whether they harbour guilt or feelings of remorse.

The second part of this verse also requires examination. Why are they portrayed as saying '"You will not believe us, though we are telling the truth!"' (12:17)? Their words might indicate that they sense that their father does not trust them, a feeling that is evident when they try to convince their father to let them take Yūsuf out for the day. They say, '". . . Why do you not trust us with Joseph? We wish him well"' (12:11). Are these attempts to deflect blame and make Ya'qūb feel guilty for treating his children unjustly, or are they indirect confessions of their guilt? Al-Ṭabarī explains verse 12:17

thus: While it seems to mean either that they are untruthful, or that their father does not believe them even when they are truthful, the verse rather intends to convey that the father would not believe them, even if they were generally truthful.[56] This explanation, however, does not clarify why they would make such a statement if they indeed were trying to assert their veracity. Not surprisingly, Ya'qūb is not convinced by their lies, nor by the bloodstained shirt that they present to him (12:18).

Just as issues of guilt and remorse are layered in the speech of Yūsuf's brothers to Ya'qūb, they are also complicated in the portrayal of Yūsuf's brothers at the end of the story, especially if we try to identify the point(s) at which they feel remorse for their actions. When the brothers are before Yūsuf and do not recognize him, Yūsuf plots to have one of his brothers stay with him, by framing him and accusing him of stealing a bowl belonging to the king. They respond by saying that their brother Yūsuf stole, too (12:77). Is their claim true? And if it is not, why are they falsely accusing Yūsuf? Does this reflect their own guilt? Some *tafsīr* works explain that Yūsuf stole a relative's idol to break it, so that the relative would not worship it.[57] Another explanation posits that he took and buried an idol from a temple.[58] Al-Ṭabarī also mentions that once Yūsuf's brothers were eating and, when he saw liquor on the table, he poured it out.[59] A final explanation is that Yūsuf gave a goat or chicken from the house to someone in need.[60] In contrast, Sayyid Quṭb questions the veracity of their assertion and criticises those commentators who use legends to explain why Yūsuf stole, when the brothers themselves have lied before.[61] Mustansir Mir explains that they ironically accuse Yūsuf of stealing to shift blame from themselves, but instead they give Yūsuf one more reason to blame them.[62] Mir also mentions that the brothers seem to show their own guilt in stealing Yūsuf long before, 'and, in an ironical situation, they condemn themselves out of their mouths', when they tell Yūsuf that in their laws, a thief is to become a slave of the person from whom he stole (12:75).[63] The verse, in its reflection of the brothers' remorse, is puzzling. It is unclear whether they are falsely accusing Yūsuf on purpose, or whether they feel any remorse in the matter of Yūsuf, even though they promised to return their brother to Ya'qūb (12:66) and obeyed his instructions for entering the city (12:68). The fact that the narrator does not clearly state their remorse (or lack thereof) is telling; the narrator seems to be giving evidence that points in different directions so that the reader cannot come to a conclusion.

There occurs another example of mixed information regarding the brothers' remorse, when they understand that Yūsuf wants to keep their brother (12:76) and volunteer themselves instead (12:78). After possibly falsely accusing Yūsuf of theft, they are now trying to help their father and take their brother back, as they had promised. Once again, it is difficult to understand from the clues provided whether they are acting in this way because they feel remorse for their previous actions and are trying to make up for them.

Yūsuf responds: '". . . God forbid that we should take anyone other than the person on whom we found our property: that would be unjust of us"' (12:79). This is ironic, on many different levels: Yūsuf knows that his brother is not guilty, as it was him who had the king's cup falsely planted in his brother's bag – one may claim that Yūsuf steals his brother as well as the cup; meanwhile, his brothers accuse Yūsuf of previously stealing, even though they stole Yūsuf, and Yūsuf refuses to take anyone in his brother's place, as that would supposedly be unjust. The brothers face a dilemma:

> 12:80 When they lost hope of [persuading] him, they withdrew to confer with each other: the eldest of them said, 'Do you not remember that your father took a solemn pledge from you in the name of God and before that you failed in your duty with regard to Joseph? I will not leave this land until my father gives me leave or God decides for me – He is the best decider – '

It seems from this verse that at least the oldest has reformed. However, in the very next verse, he appears to assume his brother's guilt, '"so go back to your father and say, 'Your son stole. We can only tell you what we saw. How could we guard against the unforeseen?'"' (12:81). Is he unjustly assuming his brother's guilt, and if so, does this mean that he has not fully reformed? Here, Kennedy writes that the brothers are 'misguided'.[64] Once again, the narrator makes it impossible for the reader to determine the brother's guilt or remorse, with him appearing to be remorseful in one verse and then possibly not in the next.

The other brothers tell their father what happened, and he is understandably saddened. In his sadness, Yaʿqūb mentions his grief over Yūsuf:

> 12:83 Their father said, 'No! Your souls have prompted you to do wrong! But it is best to be patient: may God bring all of them back to me – He alone is the All Knowing, the All Wise',
> 84 and he turned away from them, saying, 'Alas for Joseph!' His eyes went white with grief and he was filled with sorrow.

Karen Bauer argues that Yaʿqūb manifests the tragic and the triumph in the story.[65] The phrase '"No! Your souls have prompted you to do wrong! But it is best to be patient . . ."' is exactly the same as the one that he says after being told that Yūsuf was devoured by a wolf (12:18 and 12:83). But this time, even if they are culpable, they are not as culpable as before; so is Yaʿqūb unfairly blaming them? His sons' response is strikingly unsympathetic and perhaps stems from a lack of remorse: 'They said, "By God! You will ruin your health or even die, if you do not stop thinking of Joseph"' (12:85). Yaʿqūb tells his sons: '"My sons, go and seek news of Joseph and his brother and do not despair of God's mercy – only disbelievers despair of God's mercy"' (12:87). Amazingly, Yaʿqūb himself does not despair; he does not even despair about whether there is any value in asking his sons for help in this matter. Thus, even if he thinks that they do not feel remorse, he still does not give up on them.

The brothers return to Yūsuf and ask him to have sympathy for their family and to give them '"full measure"' (12:88). They do not ask about their brother, but instead about their transaction, which may indicate a lack of care for their brother and perhaps also a lack of remorse. The scene that follows is an important one, with Yūsuf speaking first:

> 12:89 He said, 'Do you now realize what you did to Joseph and his brother when you were foolish?'
> 90 and they cried, 'Could it be that you are Joseph?' He said, 'I am Joseph. This is my brother. God has been gracious to us: God does not deny anyone who is mindful of God and steadfast in adversity the rewards of those who do good'.
> 91 They said, 'By God! God really did favour you over all of us and we were in the wrong!'
> 92 but he said, 'You will hear no reproaches today. May God forgive you: He is the Most Merciful of the merciful'.

Kennedy explains that Yūsuf asks his brothers to reflect on their moral and self-knowledge.[66] It is not obvious whether the brothers have gradually begun to feel remorseful, or whether their remorse at this point is complete. They say: ' "By God! God really did favour you over all of us and we were in the wrong!" ' (*la-khāṭiʾīna*, 12:91). However, they do not actually ask Yūsuf to forgive them, nor do they apologise to him for how they treated him. Yūsuf tells them that there will be no censure today and asks for God to forgive them: 'but he said, "You will hear no reproaches today. May God forgive you: He is the Most Merciful of the merciful" ' (12:92). Importantly, they realise their place in relation to God – God has preferred Yūsuf over them (12:91) – and that God forgives them.

The narrator repeatedly makes it impossible for the readers to understand the brothers' remorse and to pinpoint a moment or moments of remorse, and counters what could appear like moments of remorse. The narrator shows that only God knows whether a person is truly remorseful but is not willing to give the readers information to help them understand these moments of remorse. God thus displaces the reader and centres Himself in the story. At the same time, human forgiveness of each other is minimised – even when a person sins against another – and instead, once again, God becomes the main focus, with His forgiveness being what really matters.

While the brothers' remorse in their confession to Yūsuf is puzzling to the readers, so are their dealings with their father. In the next scene, Yūsuf commands some people to take his shirt to Yaʿqūb and to put it on his face so that his sight will return to him (12:93). Yaʿqūb senses the shirt and says, ' "You may think I am senile but I can smell Joseph" ' (12:94). An unidentified group of people responds: ' "By God! You are still lost in that old illusion of yours!" ' (12:95). Those who respond seem exceedingly unsympathetic. The shirt indeed returns Yaʿqūb's sight to him, and he says, ' "Did I not tell you that I have knowledge from God that you do not have?" ' (12:96). Then 'the [brothers] said, "Father, ask God to forgive our sins – we were truly in the wrong" ' (12:97). One may assume here that the speakers are the brothers. They ask Yaʿqūb to ask God to forgive them and they admit that they were wrong. Mustansir Mir interprets the brothers' repentance thus: 'Joseph's brothers realise their mistake and sincerely repent, asking their father to pray for their forgiveness . . .'[67] The father responds, ' "I shall ask my Lord to forgive you: He is the Most Forgiving, the Most Merciful"' (12:98). Again, it seems that most crucial is that God forgive them, and not people. At the same time, it is impossible for the audience or the characters to decide when, how and to what extent they feel remorse. Outside of *Sūrat Yūsuf*, there occurs a scene in which Yaʿqūb is on his deathbed, asking his sons about their faith, and they profess their belief in God (2:132–3). The reader can assume they are remorseful by this point, which is not mentioned in *Sūrat Yūsuf*.

The narrator narrates the story in such a way that the audience cannot tell when the brothers feel remorse; thus, the audience cannot judge the brothers in the story. Something similar happens with the wife of al-ʿAzīz in this context. She tries to seduce Yūsuf and then, after she hears that women are gossiping about her, she has Yūsuf appear before them in order to see their reaction of wonderment (12:30–1). Indeed, the women are amazed (12:31), and she says, '"This is the one you blamed me for. I tried to seduce him and he wanted to remain chaste, but if he does not do what I command now, he will be put in prison and degraded"' (12:32). Surprisingly, she is confessing to her misdeeds and at the same time threatening Yūsuf indirectly and in front of other people. Al-Ghazālī explains that she makes this admission because there is overwhelming evidence against her,[68] while Abū al-Suʿūd claims that she has no fear.[69] Sayyid Quṭb argues that this shows her power over Yūsuf: Shamelessly, she does not see a problem with making such a statement before the women.[70] From these explanations we may deduce that many interpreters thought of her confession as lacking remorse, if it was a confession at all. Ironically, Yūsuf himself ends up in prison after this scene: He prays to go to prison, even though he is neither morally nor legally culpable, and he is punished, even though he is the victim (12:33–4). Perhaps this also shows that all that matters is God's judgment and punishment.

The portrayal of guilt and remorse becomes further complicated later in the story, when the king realises that he could benefit from Yūsuf's skills. Yūsuf responds by telling him to question the women '*al-niswa*' who cut their hands and mentions their 'treachery', *kaydihinna* (12:50):

> 12:50 The king said, 'Bring him to me', but when the messenger came to fetch Joseph, he said, 'Go back to your master and ask him about what

> happened to those women who cut their hands – my Lord knows all about their treachery'.
> 51 The king asked the women, 'What happened when you tried to seduce Joseph?' They said, 'God forbid! We know nothing bad of him!' and the governor's wife said, 'Now the truth is out: it was I who tried to seduce him – he is an honest man'.

The king asks the women about how they tried to seduce Yūsuf, '*mā khaṭbukunna idh rāwadtunna yūsufa 'an nafishi*' (12:51). Even though only one woman tried to seduce him, they are all questioned. Similarly, Yūsuf uses the plural to refer to what the women want from him and the women's plot against him when he appeals to God to be imprisoned (*yad'ūnanī, kaydahunna*, 12:33). Along the same lines, earlier in the story, when the wife of al-'Azīz tries to seduce Yūsuf and is found guilty, the person who judges says, ' "This is another instance of women's treachery: your [plural] treachery is truly great" ' (*kaydikunna* and *kaydakunna*, 12:28).[71] Yūsuf, al-'Azīz and this speaker may mention women in plural rather than singular because they think that women in general are prone to plotting, or perhaps they are unwilling to blame the wife in particular. Another perspective consists of the narrator reflecting God's knowledge of the women in this story, that they are in fact plotting women and would have tried to seduce Yūsuf, given the opportunity, or they already tried to do so.

Further complicating things is that the root *k-y-d*, here translated by Abdel Haleem as 'treachery', is also used for God:

> 12:76 [Joseph] began by searching their bags, then his brother's, and he pulled it out from his brother's bag. In this way We devised a plan [*kidnā*] for Joseph – If God had not willed it so, he could not have detained his brother as a penalty under the king's law – We raise the rank of whoever We will. Above everyone who has knowledge there is the One who is all knowing.

Since it is used for God, we assume that it is not a morally negative root. About the word *kayd*, Merguerian and Najmabadi write:

> Depending on who engages in it and under what circumstances, it can in fact be a prophetic and divine quality, cunning verging on wit. The construction

> of *kayd* in this narrative as a negative characteristic for Zulaykha (and for all women) depends on the later commentaries that moralized the story and punished Zulaykha.[72]

Zulaykha is the name given for the wife of al-'Azīz, outside of the Qur'ān.

To further develop our understanding, we can examine the women's response when 'The king asked the women, "What happened when you tried to seduce Joseph?"' (12:51). They respond with the same words they used to express surprise when they first saw Yūsuf (12:31), '"God forbid! We know nothing bad of him!"' (*ḥāsha li-llāhi mā 'alimnā 'alayhi min sū'in* 12:51). A plural group of women answers and says that he did not do anything wrong; they do not say that they themselves did not do anything wrong. If these women were in no way guilty of trying to seduce Yūsuf, then one would expect that they would deny it when asked. And now readers may recall that Yūsuf said the women invited him to something (*yad'ūnanī*, 12:33), which commentators discuss.[73] Thus, even though it initially appears that these women are being unfairly blamed by the judge, Yūsuf and the husband, they may in fact be guilty of something. This verse is critical for our understanding of the previous issue. Our human understanding of guilt is not sufficient to fully grasp the situation, and neither do the narrator and the narrative style help, since the text does not clearly say that the women tried to seduce Yūsuf. Perhaps they did not actually try to seduce him. Maybe they just thought about it or discussed it; we do not know. The narrator is clearly withholding information from the readers and making it difficult to determine who is innocent, guilty or remorseful, thus showing that humans cannot understand each other's guilt or innocence, nor is it is their place to do so. Ironically, the readers are also being taught by the text that one cannot judge the text either – while we first judged it as unfairly blaming the women, we find that that may not be the case.

There emerges another case of the narrator withholding information when the wife of al-'Azīz says, '"Now the truth is out: it was I who tried to seduce him – he is an honest man"' (12:51). This appears to be a confession. Then somebody speaks up in the next two verses, but it is not clear who the speaker is: '[Joseph said, "This was] for my master to know that I did not betray him behind his back: God does not guide the mischief of the treacherous. I do not pretend to be blameless, for man's very soul incites him to evil unless my

Lord shows mercy: He is most forgiving, most merciful"' (12:52–3). Abdel Haleem's translation assumes that the speaker is Yūsuf talking about al-ʻAzīz, although neither name is mentioned in the Arabic and although there is no grammatical indication of the speaker's gender. Commentators provide us with two interpretations here: that Yūsuf is speaking,[74] or that the wife is.[75] Since the readers do not learn of the speaker's identity, it remains unknown who is explicating his or her intentions and temptations. Again, the readers' understanding is incomplete, as in other places in the story, because the narrator is withholding information and the readers cannot fully understand the speaker's remorse, nor do they seem to be meant to. As alluded to earlier in the discussion of the mysterious letters, this cannot simply be a transcription error; this is an elaborate feature of the text.

As I have argued here, even when God is telling the story to people, God does not provide the tools to judge the characters, withholds information and gives conflicting pieces of information. One reason why it is so difficult for the readers to understand the characters' guilt or remorse is that the narrator only tells their apparent actions and speech but lends little insight into their emotions or feelings. The narrator recreates the world of the story in the same way in which we see the world – through actions and speech – and does not give us information with which to interpret the internal. Throughout the story, God is making Himself central to the story – only God knows whether people are guilty or remorseful, and God's forgiveness is what matters, regardless of our understanding or opinion.

V. Conclusion

This chapter began with an analysis of the story of Yūsuf by looking at the introduction to the story, where we saw God's assertion of the beauty of the story and the point that it is a story in Arabic. This indicates the idea of God using a human language to tell one of the best stories. How does an omniscient being use human language to tell a story? God does so by continuously bringing the story back to God. In this analysis, we repeatedly find that human notions of remorse and evidence are fallible; what matters and what is consistently reliable is God's evidence and message, God's forgiveness and God's truth. In the story, human attempts at proving things through evidence, such as a shirt and a cup, can be manipulated. Yet, God's signs, the dreams that God inspires and their interpretation are incorruptible, even if not everyone understands them completely.

In retrospect, these points are not surprising for a Qur'ānic story: Of course, God will not give people the tools to judge each other's morality; God knows everything and is above everyone; only God can judge. Humans cannot judge the internal moral states of others based on external pieces of evidence. What matters is whether God chooses to forgive people, since only God knows if and when people are remorseful. If God says He shows to people signs or truth, He does. Just as God's word is what matters in establishing something's clarity or excellence, God's word is what matters in the story of Yūsuf, and God's word is in His book. The narrator's commentary on the story told to, we presume, Muḥammad, says, 'This account is part of what was beyond your knowledge [Muhammad]. We revealed it to you: you were not present with Joseph's brothers when they made their treacherous plans' (12:102). Through this verse, God the narrator reminds the reader that God chooses to reveal what He wills to whom He wills, in the manner that He wills.

Notes

1. Waldman 11.
2. Khan 11–13.
3. Mir, 'Irony in the Qur'an' 176. See also Mir, 'The Qur'anic Story of Joseph' 5–6 and Johns, 'She desired him and he desired her' 111.
4. Kennedy 17, 19, 23, 25, 29, 32, 34, 46, 48, 53 and 60.
5. Asad, vol. 3, 376.
6. El-Awa, *Textual Relations in the Qur'ān* 99.
7. See Cuypers, 'Semitic Rhetoric as a Key to the Question of the *naẓm* of the Qur'anic Text' 16; Rendsburg 118–20; Mir 'The Qur'anic Story of Joseph' 1–3; Robinson, *Discovering the Qur'an* 148–9; Morris 204; and Johns, 'Joseph in the Qur'ān' 31–2.
8. One perspective can be found in Abboud, referring to Gerhard Bowering: 'the disconnected letters are related to an ordering of *sūrahs*'. See Abboud 36–7 note 173. For a brief overview of several perspectives, see Ernst 56–7.
9. Shahīd, 'Fawātiḥ al-Suwar', p. 126. See also Nguyen, 'Exegesis of the *Ḥurūf al-Muqaṭṭa'a*', pp. 1–28.
10. Asad, vol. 6, p. 1133

11. Shahīd 125. See also Asad, vol. 6, 1134. He says that this is the conclusion of the grammarians, Qur'ān commentators and literary scholars al-Mubarrad (d. 898 CE), Ibn Ḥazm (d. 1064 CE), al-Zamakhsharī (d. 1144 CE), al-Rāzī (d. 925 CE), al-Bayḍāwī (d. 1286 CE), Ibn Taymiyyah (d. 1328 CE) and Ibn Kathīr (d. 1373 CE).
12. Bellamy 285.
13. Shahīd 127.
14. Nguyen 6. See also Maybudī 395–7.
15. Asad, vol. 6, 1134 and Bellamy 272.
16. Dayeh 462.
17. Nguyen 6.
18. Al-Ṭabrisī, www.altafsir.com/Tafasir.asp?tMadhNo=0&tTafsirNo=3&tSoraNo=12&tAyahNo=1&tDisplay=yes&UserProfile=0&LanguageId=1
19. Al-Ṭabarī, vol. 6, 4462. Verse 14:4 seems to support this perspective. For other perspectives, see Wheeler, 'Arab Prophets of the Qur'an and Bible' 26.
20. Zadeh 120, 61 and 75.
21. The quotation is from Johns, 'She desired him and he desired her' 111. The idea that it is the best of stories because it is about love can be found in Merguerian and Najmabadi 497–8 and Keeler 138. For another perspective, see Khan 11–12.
22. The assumption that the verse refers to the story of Yūsuf in particular as being the best of Qur'ānic stories is probably satisfying from a Western literary perspective, since this story is told in the way it should be from a traditional Western literate or chirographically biased perspective.
23. For more on this issue and its connection to the inimitability of the Qur'ān (*i'jāz al-Qur'ān*), see Abu-Zayd, 'The Dilemma of the Literary Approach to the Qur'an'.
24. Asad, vol. 3, 377.
25. Asad, vol. 3, 377 note 5.
26. Al-'Amārī, vol. 4, 250–1 and al-Ṭabrisī www.altafsir.com/Tafasir.asp?tMadhNo=0&tTafsirNo=3&tSoraNo=12&tAyahNo=1&tDisplay=yes&UserProfile=0&LanguageId=1
27. Quṭb, vol. 4, 1970.
28. Al-Tha'ālibī, vol. 2, 144.
29. See Chapter 6 on *Sūrat al-Qaṣaṣ* for more on this scene.
30. Abdel Haleem's translation indicates that the husband is speaking, although the text does not make this clear.
31. Kennedy 31.

32. Sarra Tlili, 'The Lives of Joseph – and of his Garment'. International Qur'anic Studies Association Annual Meeting, 18 November 2018 Denver, CO.
33. Al-Ṭabarī, vol. 6, 4463.
34. Al-Ṭabarī, vol. 6, 4501.
35. Al-Ṭabarī, vol. 6, 4504–5.
36. Al-Ṭabarī, vol. 6, 4505.
37. Al-Ṭabarī, vol. 6, 4506.
38. Al-Ṭabarī, vol. 6, 4510.
39. Al-Ṭabarī, vol. 6, 4511.
40. Al-Tustarī, p. 81.
41. Al-Zamakhsharī, vol. 2, 312 and al-Tha'ālibī, vol. 2, 151.
42. Al-'Amārī, vol. 4, 266–7.
43. Al-Zamakhsharī, vol. 2, 311.
44. Al-'Amārī, vol. 4, 266.
45. Al-Tha'ālibī, vol. 2, 152.
46. Al-'Amārī, vol. 4, 266. For these and some other interpretations, see also Merguerian and Najmabadi 485–508.
47. For example, al-Ghazālī 241; al-'Amārī, vol. 4, 284; Quṭb, vol. 4, 1987; al-Tha'ālibī, vol. 2, 155; al-Zamakhsharī, vol. 2, 319; and al-Ṭabrisī www.altafsir.com/Tafasir.asp?tMadhNo=0&tTafsirNo=3&tSoraNo=12&tAyahNo=35&tDisplay=yes&Page=6&Size=1&LanguageId=1
48. Al-Ṭabarī, vol. 6, 4536–7.
49. Al-Jalālayn, p. 308. Wheeler mentions that Ibn Kathīr writes that they saw signs of Yūsuf's innocence and thought that he should be imprisoned to stop people from talking about the incident. Wheeler, *Prophets in the Quran* 136.
50. Al-Tha'ālibī, vol. 2, 155.
51. Quṭb, vol. 4, 1987.
52. I have amended Abdel Haleem's translation to reflect that the word *āya* is in the singular.
53. Interestingly, some see this as a mistake on Ya'qūb's part: 'Jacob feared the wolf so it was inflicted on him. If he had feared God [instead], both the wolf and the treachery of Joseph's brothers would have been withheld from him'. Keeler 129.
54. Afsar, 'Plot Motifs in Joseph/Yūsuf Story' 188.
55. Kennedy 28.
56. Al-Ṭabarī, vol. 6, 4476–7.
57. Al-Jalālayn 315; al-Ṭabarī, vol. 6, 4596-7; al-Zamakhsharī, vol. 2, 335–6;

al-ʿAmārī, vol. 4, 298 and al-Ṭabrisī www.altafsir.com/Tafasir.asp?tMadhNo=0&tTafsirNo=3&tSoraNo=12&tAyahNo=77&tDisplay=yes&Page=2&Size=1&LanguageId=1

58. Al-Zamakhsharī, vol. 2, 335–6 and al-ʿAmārī, vol. 4, 298.
59. Al-Ṭabarī, vol. 6, 4597–8.
60. Al-Zamakhsharī, vol. 2, 335–6 and al-Ṭabrisī www.altafsir.com/Tafasir.asp?tMadhNo=0&tTafsirNo=3&tSoraNo=12&tAyahNo=77&tDisplay=yes&Page=2&Size=1&LanguageId=1
61. Quṭb, vol. 4, 2022.
62. Mir, 'Irony in the Qur'an' 182.
63. Mir, 'The Qur'anic Story of Joseph' 8.
64. Kennedy 60.
65. For the emotional plot development in the story and, in particular, Yaʿqūb's experience, see Bauer 19.
66. Kennedy 61.
67. Mir, 'The Qur'anic Story of Joseph' 10.
68. Al-Ghazālī 240.
69. Al-ʿAmārī, vol. 4, 273.
70. Quṭb, vol. 4, 1985.
71. The Arabic does not use the word 'women', although it does use the human feminine possessive suffix.
72. Merguerian and Najmabadi 502; see also 501–3.
73. Al-ʿAmārī, vol. 4, 274, al-Zamakhsharī, vol. 2, 318, Quṭb, vol. 4, 1985 and www.altafsir.com/Tafasir.asp?tMadhNo=0&tTafsirNo=3&tSoraNo=12&tAyahNo=33&tDisplay=yes&Page=5&Size=1&LanguageId=1
74. Al-Jalālayn 311 and al-Ṭabarī, vol. 6, 4565. Al-Ṭabarī further explains that this is Yūsuf speaking, in response to an angel or Jibrīl specifically (al-Ṭabarī, vol. 6, 4566–7), or in response to the wife of al-ʿAzīz, Yūsuf speaking to himself, or after God reminds him of his previous interest in her (al-Ṭabarī, vol. 6, 4568). Stern also argues that this is Yūsuf speaking. Stern 201.
75. Al-Zamakhsharī, al-Thaʿālibī, Abū al-Suʿūd and al-Ṭabrisī mention interpretations that state it could be either one (al-Zamakhsharī, vol. 2, 327–8; al-Thaʿālibī, vol. 2, 161; al-ʿAmārī, vol. 4, 285–6 and www.altafsir.com/Tafasir.asp?tMadhNo=0&tTafsirNo=3&tSoraNo=12&tAyahNo=52&tDisplay=yes&Page=2&Size=1&LanguageId=1). Muhammad Asad summarises some commentators who say it is the woman's speech, but most say it is Yūsuf's (Asad, vol. 3, 386 note 51). Maybudī says it is the woman's speech; Maybudī 332.

5

Merging Words and Making Connections in *Sūrat Ṭaha*

I. Introduction

The story of Mūsā is the most frequently mentioned one in the Qur'ān.[1] *Sūrat Ṭaha* includes a lengthy version. The sura begins with an introduction, while the majority of its text is taken up with Mūsā's story, but it also includes a short telling of the story of Ādam and a discussion of Judgment Day. My analysis below will focus on Mūsā's story in *Sūrat Ṭaha*, followed by a discussion of the rest of the sura and the connections between its various parts.

Sūrat Ṭaha includes God in at least three ways: as a character in the story, as the narrator of the story – the voice narrating the story is God's – and as the implied author of the story. For the pious reader who believes that God is the implied author of the story, that the Qur'ān is the word of God, this is a historical claim. To this role, one might also add God's role as creator of the readers in the world outside the sura. God the narrator is omniscient and reliable. However, God sometimes withholds information from the audience. God is thus an infinitely reliable narrator who reserves the right to hold back. By withholding information and using other subtle narrative techniques, God the narrator 'makes' His readers. As Wayne Booth mentions, an author '[makes] his readers by forcing them onto a level of alertness that will allow for his most subtle effects'.[2] Booth states:

> The author makes his readers. If he makes them badly – that is, if he simply waits, in all purity, for the occasional reader whose perceptions and norms happen to match his own, then his conception must be lofty indeed if we are to forgive him for his bad craftsmanship. But if he makes them well –

> that is, makes them see what they have never seen before, moves them into a new order of perception and experience altogether – he finds his reward in the peers he has created.[3]

Thus, the way to make readers well is to shape their perceptions and norms, allowing them to see what they have never seen before. This concept perfectly melds God the creator with God the narrator – God literally makes readers and gives them new perceptions and experiences, from an Islamic theological perspective, and God makes readers by making them see new things through the narrative style of the Qur'ān.[4]

In Chapter 5 on *Sūrat Ṭaha*, I explore various ways in which the narrator creates and develops consonance, through connections between characters, connections with the audience and connections between various parts of the Qur'ānic text. The creation of consonance is a phrase that I previously developed in order to discuss the Qur'ānic narrative strategy of building relationships between various elements of the text: God, the revelation and the audience. The word 'creating' brings to mind the Creator, who is the Qur'ānic narrator and author. This in and of itself argues that the Qur'ānic style goes hand-in-hand with the beliefs about God that it emphasises. We repeatedly see the narrator confirming and merging people's words in *Sūrat Ṭaha.*

Here, I will discuss examples of creating consonance through the following categories: (1) the narrator confirming God's words, (2) the narrator confirming people's words and (3) making connections through semantic echoes. In the first section, God as Creator and author shows to be true to what God the character says in a dialogue. Therefore, what God says happens. By way of narrative style, this makes a statement about beliefs: God does what God says. The second section will examine how the Creator develops the relationship between God as character and other characters in the text. This is by confirming people's words – in other words, by showing what they said in dialogue to be true in narration. In this section, I develop a new term for an aspect of Qur'ānic narrative technique: merging words. There exist a few examples of this aspect, where the dialogue merges with the narration, so that the words of a character merge with God's words. I will show how this confirms the character's words and goodness – they speak such truth that even God speaks with them. The final section employs an approach inspired by Toshihiko Izutsu, analysing the connections throughout this and other suras, which are made through semantic echoes. Hence, this chapter offers a semantic and intertextual analysis. It demonstrates that the Qur'ān constitutes an intertextual scripture that rewards the careful audience member who reads and listens carefully, who notices echoing words or phrases and then follows them to other parts of the text, compares them with each other and reflects on them. Through this type of analysis, the readers can come to a richer understanding of *Sūrat Ṭaha* and of Qur'ānic narrative style in general. Narrative choices work to further beliefs about God, and people's relationships with God.

II. Creating Consonance: The Narrator Confirming God's Words

Throughout the sura, the narrator confirms or fulfils God the character's words. There are many examples of this in the story of Mūsā in *Sūrat Ṭaha*: God as a character says something, and God the narrator shows it in the narrative; for instance, God as a character, in a dialogue, tells Mūsā and Hārūn something, and then God the narrator underpins it through narrative style.

Sūrat Ṭaha starts with the mysterious letters *ṭā hā*, followed by an introduction that is usually interpreted as being addressed to the Prophet Muḥammad. Then we jump into Mūsā's story, with: 'Has the story of Moses come to you [Prophet]?' (20:9). With the second-person address, the readers are being drawn into the story. Mūsā sees a fire and tells his family to wait for him, while he goes to see if he can find guidance there (20:10). His words are prescient, as God calls to him at the fire (20:11–12), tells him He has chosen him (20:13) and eventually says that he should go to Fir'awn because he is a tyrant (20:24). Mūsā asks God to make his task easy for him (20:25–6), expresses his reservations and asks for God's help, as well as the help of his brother, Hārūn (20:27–35).

In this lengthy dialogue between Mūsā and God, God comforts Mūsā about confronting Fir'awn: 'He said, "Do not be afraid, I am with you both, hearing and seeing everything"' (20:46). God says He is with Mūsā and Hārūn, and the narrator shows this later in the story, when Mūsā is before Fir'awn and the sorcerers, and the sorcerers cast down their staffs and ropes. The staffs and ropes seem to be moving and:

> 20:67 Moses was inwardly alarmed,
> 68 but We said, 'Do not be afraid, you have the upper hand.
> 69 Throw down what is in your right hand: it will swallow up what they have produced. They have only produced the tricks of a sorcerer, and a sorcerer will not prosper, wherever he goes'

Just like God says He would be with Mūsā, the narrator shows God as actually being there, speaking to him. In addition, as God says He hears and sees everything, the narrator shows Him hearing or seeing even what cannot be heard or seen – that is, what is in Mūsā's soul (20:67). This offers a striking comparison to the previous chapter's discussion of *Sūrat Yūsuf*, where the audience does not see what is inside people's souls. Abdel Haleem's translation uses 'inwardly' to convey the Arabic, '*fī nafsihi*', which means 'in his soul' (20:67). This also connects with and confirms the introduction to the sura, 'Whatever you may say aloud, He knows what you keep secret and what is even more hidden' (20:7). Some have interpreted this verse as addressing Prophet Muḥammad, and it is striking that God's assertion to the Prophet Muḥammad – that God knows what is secret and hidden – is demonstrated through Mūsā. We thus encounter another way in which God's words are confirmed through the narrative, and the confirmation is arguably extended from one character to another.

As God promptly fulfils His word to Mūsā, the latter fittingly obeys God with such speed that it is not even portrayed. God tells Mūsā to throw down his staff and, as result of his having done so, the sorcerers cast themselves down in prostration (20:70). The narrator does not tell us that Mūsā obeyed, but the readers know so from the consequences of his actions (the prostrating of the sorcerers). Thus, the narrator indicates the fulfilment of God the character's words (the command to Mūsā). This serves as another example of the narrator confirming God's words, even when connected to another character's actions. This can also be explained as showing God's power: God gives a command, and it is, of course, obeyed. This is similar to 'Be, and it is' – a phrase discussed at length in Chapter 2 on *Sūrat Āl 'Imrān.*

Just as the narrator fulfils God the character's words commanding Mūsā to throw down his staff, God the narrator also fulfils God the character's words about testing Mūsā's people. Mūsā and his people escape from Fir'awn, and afterwards Mūsā has another (this time very brief) conversation with God (20:83–5). Through this conversation, the reader learns that Mūsā has left his people behind (20:84). In the dialogue, God says, '"We have tested your people in your absence: the Samiri has led them astray"' (20:85). Mūsā returns to his people to find them worshipping a golden calf that they have made. The person referred to as al-Sāmirī appears only three times in the Qur'ān, always in *Sūrat Ṭaha* (20:85, 20:87 and 20:95). He misleads Mūsā's people and then receives punishment for it. Albayrak mentions the 'enigma' of al-Sāmirī's identity[5] – a character about whom information is withheld from the reader.

Mūsā confronts his people about their disbelief (20:86), and they give an odd excuse for their actions: 'They said, "We did not break our word to you deliberately. We were burdened with the weight [*ḥummilnā awzāran*] of people's jewellery, so we threw it [into the fire], and the Samiri did the same [*fakadhālika alqā al-sāmiriyyu*],"' (20:87).[6] It is unclear here what al-Sāmirī throws – the jewellery, or the idea. This is described with a verb that appears repeatedly in this story, *alqā* (20:87). If it is the idea, how lightly does al-Sāmirī throw out this idea and how casually do the people believe it? He throws, and they catch. Then they all throw their burdens into the fire.

In a flashback, Hārūn attempts to convince their people not to worship the calf, mentioning that this is a test, while using the root *f-t-n* (20:90). Hārūn's words echo God's with the root *f-t-n*. Indeed, none of this should be taken lightly. It is a weighty burden – *ḥummilnā awzāran* (20:87). The people respond to Hārūn with strong disbelief, as God indicated they would (20:85): '"We shall not give up our devotion to it until Moses returns to us"' (20:91). Their change from faith to such adamant disbelief is striking. God said the people would be tested – using the root *f-t-n* (20:85) – and they were. They fail this test, despite the miracles which they had presumably seen or at least heard about (20:56) and the blessings which they had received (20:80–1).

Not only does God say that He will test the people and the narrator shows that they clearly fail the test, but the latter also alludes to details that may explain the allure of the test. The calf that they make is not just perceived to make any sound, but it 'made a lowing sound' (*lahu khuwār*, 20:88). Abdel Haleem's translation and the Arabic original indicate that the calf was able to create a sound; al-Tha'ālibī explains that some people, including Ibn 'Abbās, said it could bellow and even walk.[7]

Mūsā asks al-Sāmirī about his actions. While the calf's sound may have been alluring, when al-Sāmirī explains himself, he says something that might further explain the animal's attraction. Many translators[8] translate the verse in the manner of M. M. Pickthall, explaining that al-Sāmirī said '. . . I perceived what they perceive not, so I seized a handful from the footsteps of the messenger, and then threw it in. Thus my soul commended to me' (*qāla baṣurtu bimā lam yabṣurū bihi faqabaḍtu qabḍatan min athari -l-rasūli fa-nabadhtuhā wa kadhālika sawwalat lī nafsī* 20:96). Some commentators explain that al-Sāmirī intends to say that he saw the messenger Jibrīl, and he took some dirt from under Jibrīl's or his horse's feet[9] and then threw this into the calf.[10] The indication is that al-Sāmirī actually saw something (whatever it was) and used it to make or animate the calf. Al-Ṭabarī includes this interpretation and also brings in another: Al-Sāmirī claims he knew something that the others did not know.[11] Accordingly, some translators translate the verse differently from the version above. M. A. S. Abdel Haleem's translation, for example, takes the word '*athar*' figuratively and interprets 'throwing' as 'throwing away', rather than throwing into something. He then interprets al-Sāmirī to be saying that he knew the teachings of the messenger and disregarded them. Abdel Haleem's translation is: 'He replied, "I saw something they did not; I took in some of the teachings of the Messenger but tossed them aside: my soul prompted me to do what I did" ' (20:96).[12] There exists a connection here with *Sūrat Yūsuf*. Albayrak observes that ' "thus my inner self suggested" echoes what is said by Jacob regarding his sons' plot against Joseph and his brother in Q.12:18, 83, and Satan's work in Q.47:25'. Albayrak also mentions that the same word is used here for what al-Sāmirī saw, '*athar*', (20:96) and for Mūsā saying that his people are 'following in my footsteps [*atharī*]' (20:84).[13] Thus, there are more intertextual connections, and Mūsā is ironically thinking that his people are following in his footsteps, when in fact they were really misled by al-Sāmirī's actions and the footsteps that he saw. As for Mūsā's people, they were certainly tested by the golden calf, its perceived remarkable physical qualities and al-Sāmirī.

While examples of the narrator confirming God's words in the story abound, there also emerges an instance that initially seems to lead us in another direction. In the first lengthy dialogue between God and Mūsā, God tells Mūsā and Hārūn to go to Fir'awn and to ' "Speak to him gently so that [*la'allahu*] he may take heed, or show respect"' (20:44). Commentators discuss this verse, particularly the word '*la'allahu*' in various ways. Does this word indicate that perhaps Fir'awn could actually be convinced? And if that is the meaning, then the fact that he is not convinced might indicate a contradiction of God's words, or a lack of omniscience in God. Muhammad Asad argues:

> Since God knows the future, the tentative form in the above phrase – 'so that he might (*la'allahu*) bethink himself', etc., – obviously does not imply any 'doubt' on God's part as to Pharoah's future reaction [. . .] it relates to the intention or hope with which the message-bearer should approach his task.[14]

In other words, people should never give up hope on – or judge – each other's faith. Al-Tustarī explains that the verse is not saying that perhaps Fir'awn will believe, since it would have said so clearly if that had been the intended meaning.[15] Al-Ṭabarī includes various opinions on '*la'alla*', stating that it can be understood as '*hal*', meaning 'will Fir'awn remember or will he fear', or '*kay*' or '*ḥattā*', 'so that'.[16]

Indeed, Fir'awn is not convinced, continuously rejects the signs and in the end receives punishment (20:78–9). God the narrator says, 'We showed Pharaoh all Our signs, but he denied them and refused [to change]' (20:56). Despite the message coming to him in gentle speech and clear signs, Fir'awn is not willing to acknowledge power being in others' hands, nor does he believe. God also says that Fir'awn '"has truly become a tyrant"' (20:24); therefore, one may argue that Fir'awn confirms God's words in that sense. Perhaps the fact that God describes Fir'awn as a tyrant is more indicative of the way in which he might respond. And we do indeed see that Fir'awn is a tyrant, as God says: He enslaves the Children of Israel; he does not recognize his people's rights to believe what they choose; and he tortures and kills them for their choice (20:71). Thus, although one may initially think that this is an example of God's word not being fulfilled in the narrative, it shows the opposite.

In the end, God tells Mūsā to leave with his people and not to fear Fir'awn: 'We revealed to Moses, "Go out at night with My servants and strike a dry path for them across the sea. Have no fear of being overtaken and do not be dismayed"' (20:77). As God says, they are not overtaken; instead, Fir'awn drowns. While Mūsā's initial dialogue with God is portrayed in thirty-nine verses, Fir'awn's death is reported in only two (20:78–9). Fir'awn drowns in the sea (*al-yamm*, 20:78), much like the golden calf is scattered into the sea (*al-yamm*, 20:97). In contrast, Mūsā, as a baby, is saved by being thrown into the sea (*al-yamm*, 20:39), and then he and his people safely cross the water (*al-baḥr*, 20:77). In Fir'awn, the change from powerful to non-existent tyrant, from life to death, is portrayed quickly and demonstrates both God's power and the power of God's word. God says Fir'awn will not be a concern for Mūsā, and the narrator shows not only Fir'awn's demise, but also his quick disappearance into inconsequence: He 'was overwhelmed by the sea' (*al-yamm*, 20:78). Sayyid Quṭb notices the concise nature of these verses and explains that no details are mentioned, so that Fir'awn remains in the reader's mind as someone very dreadful.[17] Brevity is key in the portrayal of Fir'awn's fate and helps keep God's word supreme. Here and throughout this section, when the narrator satisfies God's words, God's will is supreme and God is utterly truthful and powerful – all of these are beliefs about God explicated throughout the Qur'ān.

III. Creating Consonance: The Narrator Confirming People's Words

It goes without saying that God the narrator confirms the words of God the character in the text. Unsurprisingly, one can clearly see the narrator shaping the perceptions of the reader in this way – God does exactly what God says, and He does so promptly. This goes hand-in-hand with the theological belief in God's omnipotence and omniscience. More surprisingly, God the narrator confirms people's words through the narrative. The narrator even does this by merging characters' speeches with God's speech, as will be discussed below. The implication here for beliefs about God's nature is, once again, that God can do anything He wills, and He may desire to assert people's words, especially if these people are close to God or doing God's will. At the same time, one may look at these moments as connections being formed between God and the characters.

The first example comes at the beginning of *Sūrat Ṭaha*. As discussed above, in *Sūrat Ṭaha* Mūsā's story begins when he notices a fire and is drawn to it: 'He saw a fire and said to his people, "Stay here – I can see a fire.

Maybe I can bring you a flaming brand from it or find some guidance there"' (20:10). Mūsā mentions the possibility of finding guidance at the fire, and so he does – he finds more than just physical guidance.[18] It is worth noting that Mūsā uses the same word, perhaps, '*la'allī*', used in 20:44 and discussed above. He finds spiritual guidance there, when God summons him (20:11), inspires and guides him (20:13–23), and commands him to go to Fir'awn (20:24). Maybudī reflects:

> Fire is a mark of munificence and a proof of generosity. The Arabs would light up a fire to bring guests. But no one has ever found a banquet through a fire like Moses, and no one has seen a host from a fire like God. Moses was seeking a fire to light up a tent. He found a fire that burns spirit and heart.[19]

Maybudī here remarks on the spiritual connection that Mūsā finds, as well as the loving relationship with God. There are hints of this when Mūsā mentions the fire that he sees (20:10), using a word that comes from the root word for intimacy, '*ānastu*'.[20] The word implies that Mūsā wants to say the fire granted him comfort and intimacy. This word is distinct from the word first used to describe his seeing the fire in the third person, '*ra'ā*' (20:10). Thus, while Mūsā is described as seeing a fire, he says he feels close and drawn to it. When Mūsā goes to the fire's source, he finds closeness with God and God even tells him his life story (20:37–41), mentions showering him with love (*wa-alqaytu 'alayka maḥabbatan minnī*, 20:39), and choosing him (20:41). In addition, there is intimacy in verses 20:12–14 because God uses the first person singular.[21] Thus, Mūsā says he feels closeness from the fire and finds closeness there; he says he might find guidance there, and so he does.

Not only does Mūsā find intimacy at the fire, but God also narrates intimate and tender details to him. God mentions, 'I showered you with My love [*alqaytu 'alayka maḥabbatan minnī*] and planned that you should be reared under My watchful eye' (20:39). The word translated as 'showered' is '*alqaytu*', from the root *alqā*, which is present several times in the sura and literally means 'to throw'. The use of a verb with an immaterial object (love) is especially striking here because the same verb is used seven times in reference to a physical object in the sura (20:19, 20:20, 20:39, 20:65, 20:66, 20:69, 20:70) and possibly one other time in reference to the immaterial (al-Sāmirī's idea, discussed above, 20:87). God tells Mūsā his life story, going back to when he was an infant and when God inspired his mother to throw him in a basket in the water – ironically, in order to protect him. Then God returned Mūsā to his mother, 'so that she could rejoice and not grieve' (20:37–40). Thus, God has been watching not only over Mūsā, but also over his mother. And Mūsā does indeed use the plural, 'us', when he says to God, '"You are always watching over us"' (20:35). At the end of Mūsā's life story, God says, 'I have chosen you for Myself' (20:41), again a demonstration of Mūsā's words. When Mūsā is before Firʿawn and the sorcerers, God tells him how to proceed, and thus God is watching over Mūsā then, too (20:68–9). These examples elucidate that the narrator is not only confirming Mūsā's words, but also refining them.

Just as the narrator confirms Mūsā's expectations of the fire and what he will find there, so the narrator also confirms Mūsā's words in his conversation with God. At the beginning of the conversation, God tells Mūsā that He is God; that He chose Mūsā, so that he should worship God; that the Hour is coming; and that Mūsā should not be distracted from faith (20:12–16). Then God asks, '"Moses, what is that in your right hand?"' (20:17). Clearly, an omniscient God knows that Mūsā has his staff in his hand. Many of the surveyed commentators discuss why God asks this question. According to their interpretations, the question serves to bring attention to the miracles of the staff,[22] to prepare Mūsā for what is to come,[23] to draw Mūsā's attention to the staff and explicate its miraculous nature,[24] to show Mūsā 'the glory' of what God can create,[25] or all of the above.[26] All of these commentaries assume that God is asking this question for Mūsā's sake.

Mūsā responds to God's question: '"It is my staff," he said, "I lean on it, restrain my sheep with it, and have other uses for it"' (20:18). He answers the question not only by identifying the object in his hand, but also by describing its functions and saying that it has additional purposes, too. Mustansir Mir writes about this dialogue:

> Moses, both surprised and delighted at the honor of being God's dialogue partner, is not content to provide a brief, to-the-point answer but dwells at some length on the subject of his beloved staff [. . .] The significance of the question, of course, is that God is about to demonstrate to Moses that his

> ordinary staff will serve as a miracle-performing instrument, one that will aid him in performing his role as a prophet.[27]

Sayyid Quṭb explains that the identity of the staff is obvious, and therefore Mūsā answers the question by mentioning its uses.[28] Some commentators explain that the other uses are mundane in nature, and they list them.[29] At the same time, a few commentators seem keen to mention the special properties of the staff: it is the staff of Ādam, and it came from heaven and then was passed on through the prophets until Shu'ayb gave it to Mūsā when he married his daughter.[30] The name of the staff is Nab'a, and one of its miraculous characteristics consists of its forked branches which become candles at night. If an enemy appeared, the staff would attack them, and it could even make fruit ripen.[31] One commentator also mentions the future miracles of the staff: the staff becomes a snake; when Mūsā hits a rock with the staff, water gushes forth; and when he hits the river with it, it parts.[32]

Commentators mention the extraordinary properties of the staff that are not mentioned in the Qur'ān, and this may be a reflection of the fact that, in his wording, Mūsā leaves room for the object's potential, by saying, '"I also have other uses for it"' (20:18). He presumably means that he uses his staff for other things which he has not mentioned, but his language indicates the staff's potential, and the narrator confirms these words in the narrative. The narrator does not call the staff a staff (*'aṣā*); it is as if God does not want to simplify its identity and its potential for so much more. Maybudī implies this:

> The command came, 'Throw it down, O Moses! [20:19]. Throw down this staff concerning which you say that it is your staff'. Moses threw it down and it became a snake. When he saw that the snake aimed to come after him, he was frightened and fled. The call came, 'Take it, and fear not! [20:21]. O Moses, pick up the snake and do not fear. This is that very staff of which you spoke, claiming it was your staff. O Moses, what do you have to do with making claims?'[33]

This contrasts with the narrator later referring to the staffs (*'iṣiyyuhum*) of Fir'awn's sorcerers (20:66). Mūsā's staff becomes a snake and defies Fir'awn (20:69–70); it is thus a sign of God. This potential use and identity of the staff is arguably the most important one, and one of which Mūsā is unaware. Similarly, the most important part of Mūsā's identity consists of his potential to become a prophet, and not his identity as a person. The staff, then, can serve as a metaphor for God's power to create change and to make things do as He wills, a metaphor relevant in a story in which many transformations take place. And although Mūsā did not know all of the things his staff would do and represent, his words foreshadow them: '"I also have other uses for it"' (20:18). Thus, God shows Mūsā's words about his staff to be true throughout the story.

Just as Mūsā's words about his staff are confirmed by the story, so are his other words that he speaks. In his dialogue with God, Mūsā says: '"You are always watching over us"' (20:35), and the narrator confirms this throughout the story. God the character shows this to be true in the dialogue when He tells Mūsā the story of his birth, his upbringing in Fir'awn's household and his life until this meeting with God (20:37–41).[34] Maybudī implies that Mūsā's being tested (20:40) is also part of his being watched by God. He writes about verse 20:40:

> 'O Moses, We took you to the oven of trial and put you into self-purification so that nothing would remain in your heart but My love and nothing on your tongue but My remembrance'. [. . .] He threw him into trial mixed with gentleness, He adorned him with wounds mixed with tenderness, and He washed him with many sorts of trial. What was all this for? It was so that he would belong to Him . . .[35]

Albayrak writes about the later verse 20:84, in which Mūsā calls God '*rabbi*:' 'Since *rabb* is related to *rabbā* (to bring up, care for), His Lordship is a caring Lordship'.[36] This echoes verse 20:35, '"You are always watching over us,"' which is then fulfilled in 20:39: '"I showered you with My love and planned that you should be reared under My watchful eye"'. Thus, elsewhere, God also confirms Mūsā's words. When God repeatedly shows Mūsā's words to be true, God is simultaneously showing God's words to be true. What value is a messenger who does not speak the truth? A messenger must be truthful so that people will trust him/her and, therefore, also trust God's message and God's goodness in sending this messenger.

While the narrator shows to be true what Mūsā says about God watching him, He also shows to be true what Mūsā says about God guiding people. When Mūsā confronts Fir'awn, Fir'awn asks Mūsā about God, and Mūsā responds, '"Our Lord is He who gave everything its form, then gave it guidance"' (20:50). Commentators discuss what this verse means; one of the interpretations argues that God guides animals to food, drink, mates and (to this al-Ṭabarī adds) communal living.[37] Another interpretation posits that God gave every being creation and form, then facilitated a purpose for him or her.[38] In a later verse, to be discussed below, God confirms Mūsā's words about creating and then guiding people, by saying that God guided, *hadā*, Ādam (20:122). The story of Ādam's creation can be found in several passages within the Qur'ān, but not here; if we read the creation of Ādam elsewhere, we will find a thread that leads us back here. Thus, there occurs an intertextual connection through a reference and an exemption. By not including the creation of Ādam in this sura, one is led to wonder about and look for it elsewhere.

The root *dh-k-r* presents God's words becoming Mūsā's, and then God confirming them. First, in the beginning of the sura, God says the Qur'ān is '. . . a reminder [*tadhkirah*] for those who hold God in awe' (20:3). Then, God uses the same root in His dialogue with Mūsā, 'I am God; there is no god but Me, so worship Me and keep up the prayer so that you remember Me [*li-dhikrī*]' (20:14). Thereafter, Mūsā uses the same root in this dialogue, 'and [we] remember You [*nadhkuraka*] often' (20:34), thus confirming God's words. Afterwards, the root is issued several times, from God as a character and as narrator. God tells Mūsā and Hārūn to remember Him (*dhikrī*, 20:42), and God directs them to speak to Fir'awn, so that he might remember (*yatadhakkar*, 20:44). God refers to revelation as a reminder twice (*dhikran*, 20:99 and 20:113). Finally, the story of Ādam flows into a description of people in the afterlife: 'But whosoever turns away from the remembrance of Me [*dhikrī*], truly his shall be a miserable life, and We shall raise him blind on the Day of Resurrection' (20:124).[39] Thus, the root *dh-k-r* forms an interplay between God's and Mūsā's words, creating connections between all the various parts of the sura: the introduction, the story of Mūsā, the story of Ādam and the verses about the afterlife.

In a number of examples, God the narrator confirms the words of Mūsā, a person that God the character says He made for Himself (20:41) and is

God's messenger. There also emerges another instance, of God confirming the words of the magicians in the sura. First, the narrator seamlessly shifts from God telling Mūsā to confront Firʿawn, to Mūsā and Hārūn in dialogue with and challenging Firʿawn (20:24–57). God shows Firʿawn His signs (20:56), which Firʿawn interprets as magic, and challenges Mūsā to see who can overcome the other (20:57–8). They come together as arranged: Firʿawn's magicians throw their staffs and ropes, and they look like snakes (20:60–6). Mūsā is fearful, but God comforts him (20:67–8) and says, '"Throw down what is in your right hand: it will swallow up what they have produced. They have only produced the tricks of a sorcerer, and a sorcerer will not prosper, wherever he goes"' (20:69). As a result, the magicians prostrate themselves and declare their faith in God (20:70). Firʿawn then threatens the sorcerers:

> 20:71 Pharaoh said, 'How dare you believe in him before I have given you permission? This must be your master, the man who taught you witchcraft. I shall certainly cut off your alternate hands and feet, then crucify you on the trunks of palm trees. You will know for certain which of us has the fiercer and more lasting [*abqā*] punishment'.

The magicians respond by asserting that God's reward is more lasting, using the same word that is in Firʿawn's threat, *abqā*: '"we believe in our Lord, [hoping] He may forgive us our sins and the sorcery that you forced us to practise – God is better and more lasting [*abqā*]"' (20:73). Indeed, God confirms their words twice in later verses about the afterlife: 'This is how We reward those who go too far, and who do not believe in their Lord's revelations. The greatest and most enduring [*abqā*] punishment is in the Hereafter' (20:127) and 'do not gaze longingly at what We have given some of them to enjoy, the finery of this present life: We test them through this, but the provision of your Lord is better and more lasting [*abqā*]' (20:131). Thus, God confirms what the magicians say: that God's reward and punishment are everlasting, but not Firʿawn's.

Another way in which God the narrator confirms the characters' speeches is by merging their words with God's. A similar literary device has already been discussed in Chapter 3 on *Sūrat Maryam*. As we will see, this phenomenon happens when one person's speech in a dialogue merges into God's. The first example occurs in a dialogue between Mūsā and Firʿawn, where it is unclear whether Mūsā, God or somehow both respond to Firʿawn. At first, the dialogue moves back and forth, switching speakers with *qāla*. Firʿawn asks Mūsā a question (20:51), and Mūsā seems to be answering (20:52).[40] In the next few verses, there is a merging of Mūsā's and God's speech, bracketed at the beginning and the end by Firʿawn's questions:

> 20:51 He said, 'What about former generations?'
> 52 Moses said, 'My Lord alone has knowledge of them, all in a record; my Lord does not err or forget'.
> 53 It was He who spread out the earth for you and traced routes in it. He sent down water from the sky. With that water We bring forth every kind of plant,
> 54 so eat, and graze your cattle. There are truly signs in all this for people of understanding.
> 55 From the earth We created you, into it We shall return you, and from it We shall raise you a second time.
> 56 We showed Pharaoh all Our signs, but he denied them and refused [to change].
> 57 He said, 'Have you come to drive us from our land with your sorcery, Moses?

The beginning of verse 20:53 discusses God in the third person; hence, this can be interpreted as Mūsā's speech. However, the verse switches to the first person plural and says, 'With that water We bring forth every kind of plant' (20:53). This can be interpreted as God's speech, since God is the creator of everything. The next verse arguably could be Mūsā's speech, although 'so eat, and graze your cattle' sounds more like God's. Even in this sura there exists an instance of God's command to eat (20:81), similar to many other verses in the Qur'ān, including: 2:57, 2:60, 2:168, 2:172, 6:141, 6:142, 7:160, 23:51, 34:15 and 52:19. The next verses must be God's speech, as God is the creator and He is asserting this in the first person (20:55) and as God shows Firʿawn His signs (20:56). Mustansir Mir explains that this is a 'parenthetic observation': 'Not infrequently, dialogues contain parenthetic observations (*tadmin*) [. . .] verses [20:]53–56 constitute a *tadmin*'.[41]

This study attempts to understand the narrative force of these verses: Why is there a parenthetic observation here, in the middle of this dialogue?

What does it do for this dialogue, this story and the larger beliefs that this text aims to impart on its readers? Clearly, it is difficult to determine where Mūsā's speech ends and God's begins, because they have merged completely. How could the narrator confirm Mūsā's speech more forcefully than to have it merge with God's? We can even see these merged words as instances when characters are rewarded for their faith through the narrative style – in other words, through a narrative connection with God. At the same time, one may argue here that these instances offer a confirmation of God the character's speech. God said He was with Mūsā and Hārūn (20:46), and He shows this by way of narrative style.

One can further explore the merging of words by examining the root for knowing, *ʿ-l-m*, in the sura. First is God's introduction to the sura, asserting that God knows everything (*yaʿlam*, 20:7). Then Mūsā tells Firʿawn that only God knows the fate of previous generations (*ʿilmuhā*, 20:52). After his failed attempt to outdo Mūsā through his magicians, Firʿawn declares:

> 20:71 'This must be your master, the man who taught you [*ʿallamakumu*] witchcraft. I shall certainly cut off your alternate hands and feet, then crucify you on the trunks of palm trees. You will know for certain [*lataʿlamunna*] which of us has the fiercer and more lasting punishment'

Here, as with earlier verses, the identity of the speaker is not clear. The dialogue takes place after the episode of the golden calf, when Mūsā confronts his people and al-Sāmirī, and this is the end of Mūsā's story in this sura.

> 20:97 Moses [He] said, 'Get away from here! Your lot in this life is to say, "Do not touch me", but you have an appointment from which there is no escape. Look at your god which you have kept on worshipping – we shall grind it down and scatter it into the sea.
> 98 [People], your true god is the One God – there is no god but Him – whose knowledge embraces everything [*ʿilman*]'.
> 99 In this way We relate to you [*kadhālika naquṣṣu ʿalayka*, Prophet] stories of what happened before. We have given you a Qur'an from Us.

Verse 20:97 is presumably Mūsā's speech,[42] while verse 20:99 clearly belongs to God. However, verse 20:98 is not clearly one or the other. There are a few more references to God's knowledge (*aʿlam*, 20:104; *yaʿlam* and *ʿilman*,

20:110). A second-person addressee, often interpreted as Muḥammad, is told: '. . . [Prophet], do not rush to recite before the revelation is fully complete but say, "Lord, increase my knowledge [*'ilman*]!"' (20:114). And then emerges the idea of people learning what is the straight path (*fa-sa-ta'lamūna*, 20:135). Here, connections are made between the various parts of the sura. The story of Mūsā concludes with the end of the false god (20:97) and an affirmation of the one true God (20:98). It is noteworthy that Mūsā as character exits without any fanfare; rather, the focus is on God (20:98) and God's message (20:99).

The examples of merging speech discussed thus far involve Mūsā. However, in another instance, the narrator merges the speech of God and the sorcerers. Earlier, we examined the use of the word *abqā* in this scene. After the sorcerers see and are convinced by Mūsā's message, they submit to his faith. Fir'awn questions the sorcerers' acting without his prior permission. He provides an explanation for what happened (that Mūsā in fact taught them their sorcery and was thus able to overcome them), and even when he threatens to punish and crucify the magicians (20:71), they are still adamant in their faith. Their speech merges with God's words:

> 20:72 They said, 'We shall never prefer you to the clear sign that has come to us, nor to Him who created us. So decide whatever you will: you can only decide matters of this present life –
> 73 we believe in our Lord, [hoping] He may forgive us our sins and the sorcery that you forced us to practise – God is better and more lasting'.
> 74 Hell will be the reward of those who return to their Lord as evildoers: there they will stay, neither living nor dying.
> 75 But those who return to their Lord as believers with righteous deeds will be rewarded with the highest of ranks,
> 76 Gardens of lasting bliss graced with flowing streams, and there they will stay. Such is the reward of those who purify themselves.

While it is possible that this is entirely the sorcerers' speech, it seems to discuss their fate, implying that Fir'awn fulfilled his threat and God accepted them into heaven (20:75–6). Nowhere else is their fate clearly discussed in this iteration. In addition, verses 20:74–6 are very similar to other verses in the Qur'ān, where God discusses heaven and hell, such as 18:30–1, 85:11 and 98:8–6. Hence, these verses appear to be a very subtle and gentle way to show that the sorcerers did indeed die; yet, what is important and should remain with the readers is not that Firʿawn had them tortured and killed, but that they found faith and reward from God. The last time Firʿawn speaks in this story is before the magicians do (20:71). Thus, not only do the magicians have the last word, but they share it with God.

IV. Making Connections between Qur'ānic Verses

The story of Ādam is the only story other than Mūsā's in *Sūrat Ṭaha*, albeit much shorter than Mūsā's. The root words in the sura present at least five semantic connections between their stories. Perhaps the most striking is an end-word, with a root that occurs only twice in the sura: *a-b-y* (20:56 and 20:116). The word *abā* describes Firʿawn's rejection of the message: 'We showed Pharaoh all Our signs, but he denied them and refused [*abā*] [to change]' (20:56). Then there is Iblīs's refusal to bow to Adam when God commands him: 'When We said to the angels, 'Bow down before Adam', they did. But Iblis refused [*abā*]' (20:116). With both verses ending with this word, and the root only occurring twice in the sura, the text invites readers to compare Firʿawn and Iblīs.

When examining the root word for guidance, *h-d-y*, throughout the verses, there emerge a number of connections between the sura's various elements. First is the verse in which Mūsā sees a fire and says that he will look for guidance (*hudān* 20:10). Then, God tells Mūsā what to say to Firʿawn, and these words include: 'We have brought you a sign from your Lord. Peace be upon whoever follows the right guidance [*hudā*]' (20:47). Not only has Mūsā found guidance, but he is being commanded to spread this guidance to others. In their dialogue, Mūsā tells Firʿawn that '"Our Lord is He who gave everything its form, then gave it guidance [*hadā*]"' (20:50). This contrasts with Firʿawn, who did not guide his people (*hadā*, 20:79). Later, God addresses the Children of Israel: 'Yet I am most forgiving towards those who repent, believe, do righteous deeds, and stay on the right path [*ihtadā*]' (20:82). In the story of Ādam, the protagonist eats from the forbidden tree, and then God the narrator describes Ādam's repentance: 'later his Lord brought him close, accepted his repentance, and guided him [*hadā*]' (20:122). Ādam and his wife are commanded to leave the garden but told to follow God's guidance (*hudān* and *hudāya*, 20:123). More generally, people can find guidance by looking at the abandoned dwellings of earlier peoples (*yahdi*, 20:128). In the last verse of the sura, the narrator addresses the second person: '[Prophet], say, "We are all waiting, so you carry on waiting: you will come to learn who has followed the even path, and been rightly guided [*ihtadā*]"' (20:135).

Thus, some people offer guidance, while others do not; people can find guidance from each other, and God guides all beings. In terms of the connection between the stories of Mūsā and Ādam, both feature the same root, *h-d-y*, multiple times (20:10, 20:47, 20:50, 20:79, 20:82, 20:122 and 20:123). Some of these verses end with this root and, therefore, the word stands out to the listener and reciter of the Qur'ān. When analysing verses 20:50 and 20:122 together, one can see that the narrator shows to be true what Mūsā says – Mūsā says that God creates and guides creation, and then God creates and guides Ādam.

In contrast to the idea of guiding people, one may analyse the notion of misleading people by focussing on the root *ḍ-l-l* to find more semantic connections between Mūsā's and Ādam's stories. First, Mūsā says to Firʿawn that God does not mislead people: 'Moses said, "My Lord alone has knowledge of them, all in a record; my Lord does not err [*yaḍillu*] or forget"' (20:52). This contrasts with Firʿawn, who misleads people, as seen above: 'Pharaoh truly led his people astray [*aḍalla*]; he did not guide them' (20:79). That God does not mislead people also contrasts with al-Sāmirī, who misleads Mūsā's people: 'but God said, "We have tested your people in your absence: the Samiri has led them astray [*aḍallahum*]"' (20:85). Mūsā questions Hārūn about their people's misguidedness: 'Moses said, "When you realized they had gone astray [*ḍallū*], what prevented you, Aaron"' (20:92). Then we move to the story of Ādam. Ādam and his wife disobey God and are ordered to leave the garden; furthermore, they are told that, when they follow God's guidance, they will not be misled: 'God said, "Get out of the garden as each other's enemy." Whoever follows My guidance, when it comes to you [people], will not go astray [*yaḍillu*] nor fall into misery' (20:123). Thus, God does not mislead people, but Firʿawn and al-Sāmirī do. We also see here that God confirms Mūsā's words – both God and Mūsā say that God does not mislead people, in the two different stories (20:52 and 20:123).

There exist important connections in the idea of forgetting, indicated with the root *n-s-y*, in both stories. First, Mūsā tells Fir'awn that God never forgets (*yansā*, 20:52). Then al-Sāmirī says that the calf is also Mūsā's god, but that Mūsā forgot: '"This is your god and Moses' god, but he has forgotten [*fa-nasiya*]"' (20:88). It is a puzzling claim that a prophet who preaches belief in one God should forget who his god is; yet, they are convinced. Commentators attempt to explain the verb 'he has forgotten' (*fa-nasiya*) by debating the identity of the speaker, about whom the speaker is talking, and what he means.[43] One perspective is reflected in Abdel Haleem's translation quoted here: Al-Sāmirī says this about Mūsā, meaning that the calf is Mūsā's god, but that Mūsā forgot about it and has gone looking for his god elsewhere.[44] From another perspective, God says the same about al-Sāmirī, meaning that al-Sāmirī forgot his religion.[45] Al-Ṭabarī prefers the former explanation.[46] Quṭb explains this episode by mentioning that the people had been slaves and under the tyranny of Fir'awn for a long time.[47] Another instance of *n-s-y* in the sura occurs in the introduction to the story of Ādam, when God criticises Ādam: 'We also commanded Adam before you, but he forgot [*fa-nasiya*] and We found him lacking in constancy' (20:115). Here, then, a messenger does forget – although we do not assume that he forgot who his God is. The story ends with a verse about the afterlife: 'God will say, "This is how it is: You ignored [*fa-nasiytahā*] Our revelations when they came to you, so today you will be ignored [*tunsā*]"' (20:126 twice). This is a forceful addendum to Mūsā's words that God never forgets (*yansā*, 20:52), contrasting literal forgetting (to which Mūsā refers) and metaphorical forgetting (what God will do to disbelievers in the afterlife).

Finally, there appears the root for disobeying, *'-ṣ-y*. Here, Mūsā asks his brother if he disobeyed him in the matter of the golden calf (*a-fa-'aṣayta*, 20:93), and Ādam disobeys his Lord (*'aṣā*, 20:121). Mūsā errs in that his brother did not disobey him; God the narrator shows this in a flashback. One might argue that Mūsā is also wrong because he is falsely accusing his brother. Certainly, if a prophet can disobey God, then a brother can disobey a brother. This may seem surprising to those who assume prophetic infallibility, and it certainly opens avenues for further research.

Several other semantic connections between various elements of *Sūrat Ṭaha* are listed in Table 5.1. While not a comprehensive chart, it illustrates some of the semantic connections in the sura.

In one instance of semantic connection, a word carries both physical and

Table 5.1 Semantic connections between different parts of the Sura

Verses that Connect the Introduction to Mūsā	Verses that Connect the Introduction to Ādam	Verses that Connect Mūsā to Ādam
kh-sh-y: 20:3, 44, 77, 94	*sh-q-w*: 20:2, 20:117, 20:123	*a-b-y*: 20:56, 20:116
h-d-y: 20:10, 20:47, 20:50, 20:79, 20:82, 20:122, 20:123 × 2, 20:128, 20:135	*h-d-y*: 20:10, 20:47, 20:50, 20:79, 20:82, 20:122, 20:123 × 2, 20:128, 20:135	*h-d-y*: 20:10, 20:47, 20:50, 20:79, 20:82, 20:122, 20:123 × 2, 20:128, 20:135
ʿ-l-m: 20:7, 20:52, 20:71 × 2, 20:98, 20:104, 20:110 × 2, 20:114, 20:135		*ḍ-l-l*: 20:52, 20:79, 20:85, 20:92, 20:123
s-m-w: 20:4, 20:6, 20:8, 20:53, 20:129		*n-s-y*: 20:52, 20:88, 20:115, 20:126 × 2
		ʿ-ṣ-y: 20:93, 20:121

metaphorical meaning – that is, words derived from the root *ḥ-m-l*. There is the weight of the jewellery that the people carry and then throw into the calf (20:87), in comparison to the weight that people carry on their shoulders on Judgment Day (20:100, 20:101 and 20:111). This interacts with the idea of a burden that one carries, expressed by the root *w-z-r*. First, the root *w-z-r* refers to the helper whom Mūsā requests from God – Hārūn: 'and give me a helper [*wazīran*] from my family' (20:29). Another verse mentions the burden that Mūsā's people carry: 'They said, "We did not break our word to you deliberately. We were burdened [*ḥummilnā awzāran*] with the weight of people's jewellery, so we threw it [into the fire], and the Samiri did the same"' (20:87). There follows another verse containing both roots, about Judgment Day: 'Whoever turns away from it will bear [*yaḥmilu*] on the Day of Resurrection a heavy burden [*wizran*]' (20:100). We will encounter the *w-z-r* root once again below, in another sura.

Throughout the sura, one may also find instances of the root for sight, *b-ṣ-r*, and blindness, *ʿ-m-y*. First, Mūsā tells God that God has been watching them: '"You are always watching over us [*baṣīran*]"' (20:35). This is later followed by al-Sāmirī's explanation about what he saw and did: 'He replied, "I saw [*baṣurtu*] something they did not [*yabṣurū*] . . . "' (20:96 twice). Then the text moves on to the afterlife, where both *b-ṣ-r* and *ʿ-m-y* occur:

> 20:124 but whoever turns away from it will have a life of great hardship. We shall bring him blind [*a'mā*] to the Assembly on the Day of Resurrection
> 125 and he will say, 'Lord, why did You bring me here blind [*a'mā*]? I was sighted [*baṣīran*] before!'

Thus, the reader encounters different kinds of seeing and not seeing – God watching over people, al-Sāmirī seeing or thinking of something that others do not, and people remembering that they once had sight although they were spiritually blind – and what one does with what one sees.

Throughout the sura. the root *'-j-l* also makes an appearance. First, God asks Mūsā why he rushed to meet Him: '[God said], "Moses, what has made you come ahead of your people in such haste [*a'jalaka*]?"' (20:83). Mūsā responds with the same root: 'and he said, "They are following in my footsteps. I rushed [*'ajiltu*] to You, Lord, to please You"' (20:84). The word for the calf, *'ijl*, that his people worship uses the same root (20:88). Albayrak claims that, given the shared root between the verb for being hasty (*'ajala*) and the word meaning calf (*'ijl*), this constitutes a pun:

> Accepting the suggestion that puns work by associating words through the use of sound we see that this narrative makes us feel that there is a strong link between the rapidity of the presentation and the Israelites' haste to form the calf and worship it. The best way to show the unexpected appearance of the calf, we think, is through the wordplay of *'ajala* and *'ijl*.

Albayrak writes that al-Ṭabarī and other commentators also mention this pun.[48] There exists irony in the contrast between Mūsā's rush to please God, and his people's rush to disobey God by associating others with God. Finally, God tells the Prophet Muḥammad not to be hasty: '. . . [Prophet], do not rush [*ta'jal*] to recite before the revelation is fully complete but say, "Lord, increase my knowledge!"' (20:114). There seems to be a connection between the haste with which Mūsā wants to meet God (20:83) and the haste of Muḥammad (20:114). One might propose that some of these instances of haste come with faulty action. However, this explanation makes one wonder: Is Mūsā's rushing to meet God a mistake – perhaps in leaving his people behind spiritually, in his hasty desire for his own spiritual connection with God? Might Muḥammad's hastiness be similar? We are left not knowing what kind of moral connection we are to see in these examples of hasty action, as well as to the making and worshipping of the calf. Here, the narrator withholds information from the readers and does not allow them to judge the characters, similar to what transpires in *Sūrat Yūsuf*.

In addition to those between verses within *Sūrat Ṭaha*, there exist further semantic connections with other parts of the Qur'ān. For example, a verse in *Sūrat Ṭaha* mentions an 'Arabic Qur'ān', as does a verse discussed in Chapter 4 on *Sūrat Yūsuf*. Here, then, one encounters another connection between *Sūrat Yūsuf* and *Sūrat Ṭaha*. The Qur'ānic verses that mention an 'Arabic Qur'ān' are: 12:2, 20:113, 39:28, 41:3, 42:7 and 43:3.[49]

A more intricate connection between *Sūrat Ṭaha* and other Qur'ānic verses meets the eye: When Mūsā first talks with God, he asks God for comfort. He says, amongst other things: '"Lord, lift up my heart"' (20:25) and God responds: '". . . Moses, your request is granted"' (20:36). There is an echo of these words in *Sūrat al-Sharḥ*: 'Did We not relieve your heart for you' (94:1). Mūsā's words are '*rabbi shraḥ lī ṣadrī*' (20:25), paralleling '*alam nashraḥ laka ṣadrak*' (94:1).[50] The root *ṣ-d-r* is also present in *Sūrat al-Qaṣaṣ* (28:23 and 28:69), and the words *qalb* (28:10) and *fu'ād* (28:10), both interpreted as heart, occur in *Sūrat al-Qaṣaṣ*, as Mūsā's mother's heart is broken when separated from him and then mended again when reunited.[51] Moreover, Mūsā uses the word '*ṣadrī*' in 26:13: 'And my breast will be straitened, and my tongue will not be unfettered; so send unto Aaron'.[52] God the narrator is not only confirming the words of God the character, but also the words of Mūsā. Some interpret the second-person address in God's response (94:1) as being directed to the Prophet Muḥammad; however, as mentioned in the Introduction, one can also interpret this address as being directed at the reader. God's agreement with Mūsā is fulfilled in another sura and with another person.[53] Similarly, Mūsā in his prayer to God asks God to bless him with Hārūn and 'augment [his] strength through him' (20:31). Again, God responds in 20:36 that He will satisfy Mūsā's request, and this fulfilment happens in another sura. Mūsā uses the word '*ushdud*', 'augment', and in *Sūrat al-Qaṣaṣ*, God responds by using a verb with the same root, '*sanashuddu*' (28:35).[54]

Thus, verses 20:25 and 20:36 lead us to verse 94:1, and verses 20:31 and 20:36 lead us to verse 28:35. As a result, one can discern the movement of the narrative discourse and the story across three different suras, between the readers, the characters and the Prophet Muḥammad, and across a range of time-periods. These layers of address in Qur'ānic narrative discourse and story have already been discussed in the Introduction and Chapter 2 on *Āl 'Imrān*. The first example (20:25, 20:36 and 94:1) merges the layers with a character's request in a story being granted and alluded to in another layer of narrative discourse. With this merging of words comes also a merging of time, from Mūsā's to the Prophet's to the reader's time. This example not only illustrates God the narrator confirming God's words, but also the narrator confirming Mūsā's words; there is a merging of time and place that includes the readers of the Qur'ān.

While we have seen a number of semantic connections within the various parts of *Sūrat Ṭaha*, and between *Sūrat Ṭaha* and other parts of the Qur'ān, some roots occur only once in the Qur'ān, within the sura under discussion. These end their respective verses and thus stand out significantly. They include: 'sightless', '*zurqan*' (20:102), 'plain', '*ṣafṣafan*' (20:106), 'hill', '*amtan*' (20:107) and 'whispers', '*hamsan*' (20:108). The last three occur sequentially, one verse after another, which also draws particular attention to them. They all figure in the section concerning Judgment Day. These singular words stand alone and do not form connections through repetition, but through their uniqueness and presence in the verses about the Day of Judgment.

V. Conclusion

This chapter analysed instances of the narrator confirming God's and other people's words, the merging of speeches and making of semantic connections. When the narrator confirms God's words, the narrator shows God's word to be true, and God to be omnipotent. When the narrator confirms good people's words, God shows their words to be true, while also rewarding people. As a result, when God repeatedly shows Mūsā's words to be true, God is simultaneously affirming His messenger, as well as the trustworthiness of both message and messenger. When the narrator confirms people's words and merges them with His own, God shows that He is with people when they do good and are fulfilling His will. In those verses narrated by a speaker with unclear identity, one can see a merging and confirming of people's words, but at the same time a mystery remains. This can humble the readers, while at the same time elevating the characters. Finally, by merging the characters' speeches with God's, God rewards good people with narrative unity with God – what I call narrative *fanā'*.[55] As for the semantic connections discussed in this chapter, they themselves also constitute mergers – semantic mergers based on the roots of words. When God the narrator makes semantic connections between various parts of the sura, God is giving commentary within the text, teaching the readers how to approach the text, making them into more careful readers and rewarding them for their careful reading with more insight.

Through this type of analysis, one can arrive at a richer understanding of *Sūrat Ṭaha* and of Qur'ānic narrative style in general. Narrative choices work to further beliefs about God, as well as people's relationships with God and God's word. All these narrative choices convey God's involvement in people's lives: God is literally with people, and God speaks for, with and to them. All these examples are so subtle that the reader has to think and ask questions in order to notice them. In their entirety, these narrative techniques bring the audience closer to the text, to the characters and to God, building consonance between all of them. Disbelievers and idols rapidly drown in the sea, while messengers and believers come out of the sea safely, to enjoy everlasting narrative unity with God.

I began this chapter by discussing God in the various roles of a character, narrator and implied author of Qur'ānic stories. God is an omniscient and reliable narrator who sometimes withholds information from readers or makes them work by using subtle language. As Booth writes, 'the purposes of the individual work should dictate the standards by which it is judged';[56] similarly, the style and techniques that an author uses should be appropriate to the content of the story.[57] One obvious purpose of the Qur'ān is to establish people's belief in God. Thus, the techniques that the Qur'ān and its stories use should serve the purpose of affirming these beliefs. The methods that the narrator employs in *Sūrat Ṭaha* should advance belief, and they do indeed. When the narrator confirms God's words, He shows that God is utterly reliable; consequently, the Qur'ān is reliable, too. The audience comes to new perceptions of reality when reading the story – in particular, when reading that 'These accounts are part of what was beyond your knowledge

[Muhammad]. We revealed them to you. Neither you nor your people knew them before now, so be patient: the future belongs to those who are aware of God' (11:49).

Notes

1. Khan 5; Robinson, *Discovering the Qur'an* 158.
2. Booth 302.
3. Booth 398.
4. Auerbach makes a similar argument about the Bible; Auerbach 15.
5. Albayrak, 'The Qur'anic Narratives of the Golden Calf Episode' 53.
6. The translation by Abdel Haleem does not clearly translate '*alqā*' as 'threw'.
7. Al-Tha'ālibī, vol. 2, 356.
8. For example, Shakir, Yusuf Ali, Wahiduddin Khan, Al-Muntakhab, Progressive Muslims, Abdul Majid Daryabadi, Aisha Bewley, Ali Ünal, Muhammad Taqi Usmani, Syed Vickar Ahamed and Sahih International all translate the verse similar to www.islamawakened.com/index.php/qur-an
9. Al-Jalālayn 414, al-Tha'ālibī, vol. 2, 358, al-'Amārī, vol. 6, 39, al-Zamakhsharī, vol. 2, 550–1 and al-Ṭabrisī www.altafsir.com/Tafasir.asp?tMadhNo=4&tTafsirNo=3&tSoraNo=20&tAyahNo=96&tDisplay=yes&Page=4&Size=1&LanguageId=1
10. Quṭb, vol. 4, 2349, also says that most sources claim the verse is discussing Jibrīl and the dirt beneath his feet or his horse's feet.
11. Al-Ṭabarī, vol. 7, 5628–9.
12. Muhammad Asad, Farook Malik, Amatul Rahman Omar and Shabbir Ahmed interpret the verse in a similar manner. www.islamawakened.com/index.php/qur-an
13. Albayrak, 'The Qur'anic Narratives of the Golden Calf Episode' 65.
14. Asad, vol. 4, 528–9, note 28.
15. Al-Tustarī 103.
16. Al-Ṭabarī, vol. 7, 5592.
17. Quṭb, vol. 4, 2344.
18. Mir, *Understanding the Islamic Scripture* 161.
19. Maybudī 403.
20. Al-Ṭabarī, vol. 7, 5563 and al-Zamakhsharī, vol. 2, 531.
21. Robinson, *Discovering the Qur'an* 232.
22. Al-Jalālayn, p. 407.
23. Al-Tha'ālibī, vol. 2, p. 345 and al-Ṭabrisī www.altafsir.com/Tafasir.asp?tMadh

No=4&tTafsirNo=3&tSoraNo=20&tAyahNo=17&tDisplay=yes&Page=2&Size=1&LanguageId=1. Similar is Albayrak, 'The Qur'anic Narratives of the Golden Calf Episode' 50. He refers to Mir, 'Humor in the Qur'an' 183, 187 and 189.

24. Al-'Amārī, vol. 6, 9 and al-Ṭabrisī www.altafsir.com/Tafasir.asp?tMadhNo=4&tTafsirNo=3&tSoraNo=20&tAyahNo=17&tDisplay=yes&Page=2&Size=1&LanguageId=1
25. Al-Zamakhsharī, vol. 2, 533.
26. Al-Ṭabarī, vol. 7, 5574.
27. Mir, *Understanding the Islamic Scripture* 159–60.
28. Quṭb, vol. 4, 2332.
29. See for example al-Tustarī 102 and al-Jalālayn 407.
30. Al-Tustarī 102.
31. Al-Zamakhsharī, vol. 2, 533–4. Some of these, and others, are also in al-Ṭabrisī's commentary www.altafsir.com/Tafasir.asp?tMadhNo=4&tTafsirNo=3&tSoraNo=20&tAyahNo=17&tDisplay=yes&Page=2&Size=1&LanguageId=1
32. Al-Tustarī 102.
33. Maybudī 404.
34. Similar is 26:62–3, when Mūsā says God is with him and then God inspires him; thus, in a way He is with him.
35. Maybudī 405.
36. Albayrak, 'The Qur'anic Narratives of the Golden Calf Episode' 50.
37. Al-Jalālayn 409, al-Ṭabrisī www.altafsir.com/Tafasir.asp?tMadhNo=4&tTafsirNo=3&tSoraNo=20&tAyahNo=50&tDisplay=yes&Page=2&Size=1&LanguageId=1 and al-Ṭabarī, vol. 7, 5594-5.
38. Al-Thaʿālibī, vol. 2, 350.
39. This translation is from *The Study Quran*, accessed at www.islamawakened.com/quran/20/124/
40. Verse 20:52 says *qāla*, 'he said'; it does not say 'Mūsā said', although Abdel Haleem translates it here in this way. In Arabic, when a dialogue features a repeated *qāla*, it typically indicates a change in subject.
41. Mir, 'Dialogue in the Qur'ān' 11. For more on these verses, see Bodman 105.
42. Verse 20:97 says *qāla*, 'he said'; it does not mention Mūsā's name.
43. Al-Ṭabarī, vol. 7, 5624.
44. Al-'Amārī, vol. 6, 36, al-Ṭabarī, vol. 7, 5624 and Quṭb, vol. 4, 2347.
45. Al-Ṭabarī, vol. 7, 5624 and al-Thaʿālibī, vol. 2, 357.
46. Al-Ṭabarī, vol. 7, 5625.

47. Quṭb, vol. 4, 2346.
48. Albayrak, 'The Qur'anic Narratives of the Golden Calf Episode' 58 and 68.
49. The revelation or book – interpreted as the Qur'an – is also referred to as 'Arabic' in these verses: 13:37, 16:103, 26:195 and 46:12.
50. Robinson, *Discovering the Qur'an* 158–9.
51. For more on the use of the word '*qalb*', heart, in *Sūrat al-Qaṣaṣ*, see Bauer 23.
52. This translation is from *The Study Quran*, accessed at www.islamawakened.com/quran/26/13/
53. Giving other examples, Bauer writes about connections between various Qur'ānic stories based on their vocabulary related to emotions. Bauer 24.
54. For more on the connection between 20:31 and 28:35, see Mir, 'The Qur'an as Literature' 54. For more on the use of the word '*ṣadr*', heart, in the Qur'an, and the expansion of the heart, see: Bauer 15.
55. *Fanā'* is a Sufi concept to describe a spiritual union with God.
56. Booth 377.
57. Booth 250.

6

Sūrat al-Qaṣaṣ and its Audience

I. Introduction

Since the story of Mūsā is the one most often told in the Qur'ān, it deserves a second chapter within the context of this study. Salwa El-Awa writes that one consequence of repetition – more specifically, delayed paraphrase – is the development of concepts over a larger amount of text . . .

> . . . giving access to larger clusters of content regarding a concept or set of assumptions that is being established over wider sections of the text [. . .] there is an addition, with each paraphrase of the same topic, to the contextual information of that topic.[1]

Hence, as we will see, instances of repetition lead us to read more in other parts of the Qur'ān and, consequently, result in a deeper understanding of the story itself. In this chapter, I will focus on *Sūrat al-Qaṣaṣ* and draw a comparison with Mūsā's story in *Sūrat Ṭaha*. Whereas one can easily find merging speeches in *Sūrat Ṭaha*, these are not prominent in this iteration. Rather, *Sūrat al-Qaṣaṣ* adds new and sometimes exclusive details to the story, such as explanations of motives for actions. Although readers are given new details, they also are confronted with new mysteries. And they do not see certain elements of the story – the golden calf, for example. Moreover, there exist references to other stories. Through these narrative devices, the narrator sometimes renders the readers privileged, while balancing these details with mysteries to keep them in their place. At the same time, as with the other suras under discussion, the narrator rewards the hard-working and careful audience who reads more, understands more and consequently notices references to other stories in the Qur'ān. As has been demonstrated throughout this study, God the narrator asserts His power and place in relation to humans through the narration. According to Sayyid Quṭb, *Sūrat al-Qaṣaṣ* emphasises that there is one power in this existence, the power of God,[2] and I will examine how the narrative devices of the narrator's giving and withholding of information in the story reinforces this idea.

Underlying this analysis is an intertextual approach to the Qur'ān. In discussing such an intertextual approach, Sarra Tlili quotes Ibn Taymiyya who wrote that '"what is stated ambiguously in one place is explicated in another, and what is stated in a concise manner in one place is expounded in another"'.[3] Thus, Qur'ānic verses can be seen as explaining each other, as already shown above. Cuypers also argues that 'the whole Qur'an is considered as the literary context of a verse, according to the method of "commentary on the Qur'an by the Qur'an" (*tafsīr al-Qur'ān bi'l-Qur'ān*)'.[4] This is one reason why commentators reference other Qur'ānic verses when they comment on a particular one.

In line with Ibn Taymiyya, Salwa El-Awa employs an intertextual approach, by analysing the relation between verses when they are within the same sura, but in separate sentences.[5] She is also interested in why each verse is placed where it is, in relation to the verse before and after.[6] Analysing one sura, El-Awa explains that 'each verse can be interpreted as an item of information or as a generator of an assumption, and can be evaluated in terms of what it adds to the context whether by interaction with or by contradicting or confirming a previous item or assumption'.[7] Thus, verses can be understood with the help of other verses; without a doubt, verses do provide context with which to explicate other verses. El-Awa also shows how verses in different suras explain each other.[8] One reason for including commentators' opinions in this study lies in the fact that they can lend insight into cross-references in the Qur'ān. In addition, they provide examples of some of the ways in which the stories are interpreted, some of the questions that the stories spark for readers and some of the ways in which the stories continue to live on.

In its essence, the act of reading itself draws connections between what we read. In describing the act of reading, Roland Barthes writes that 'to read is to find meanings, and to find meanings is to name them; but these named meanings are swept toward other names; names call to each other, reassemble, and their grouping calls for further naming'.[9] Barthes is describing reading as something akin to following the threads in a spider-web. This analogy is apt for describing Qur'ānic intertextual references, as we have seen and will continue to see. As a result of Qur'ānic intertextual references, the narrator highlights for the audience that their hard work and attention, which the Qur'ān demands both overtly and subtly, are rewarded. At the same time, these allusions signal to the audience that their knowledge is never complete: There is always something more to read and to learn.

The first section of this chapter will examine the creation of consonance between the text, the narrator, the audience and even characters through the addition of new details. In the following section, I will discuss the forging of connections between Qur'ānic verses. Finally, I will analyse the withholding of knowledge through new mysteries, together with the larger concept of mysteries in the Qur'ān, and the specific terms for them. Overall, Chapter 6 argues that, through these narrative devices, God the narrator brings the audience closer to the text, to the characters and to God, while also humbling the audience and constantly bringing them back to the text. This relationship shows the readers their dependence on their Creator and on God's word, the Qur'ān. At the same time, these narrative techniques affirm in the audience the belief that God is omniscient.

II. Creating Consonance: New Details

The iteration of Mūsā's story in *Sūrat al-Qaṣaṣ* includes a number of new details; some even appear to provide explanations and motives for events mentioned in other iterations. Muhammad Asad introduces the sura by explaining that 'most of this story depicts the purely *human* aspects of his [Mūsā's] life – that is to say, the impulses, perplexities and errors which are part of the human condition'.[10] We not only see human impulses, motivations and desires, but also motivations for God's actions. The beginning of the story offers such an instance. In an explanation of events to follow, God (who here appears to be the narrator and a character in the story) explains His actions:

> 28:1 *Ta Sin Mim*
>
> 2 These are the verses of the Scripture that makes things clear:

> 3 We recount to you [Prophet] part of the story of Moses and Pharaoh, setting out the truth for people who believe.
> 4 Pharaoh made himself high and mighty in the land and divided the people into different groups: one group he oppressed, slaughtering their sons and sparing their women – he was one of those who spread corruption –
> 5 but We wished [*wa-nurīdu*] to favour those who were oppressed in the land, to make them leaders, the ones to survive,
> 6 to establish them in the land, and through them show Pharaoh, Haman, and their armies the very thing they feared.
> 7 We inspired Moses' mother, saying, 'Suckle him, and then, when you fear for his safety, put him in the river: do not be afraid, and do not grieve, for We shall return him to you and make him a messenger'.

Verse 28:3 mentions Mūsā, and verse 28:7 his mother. The implication seems to be that verses 28:4–6 are explaining God's reason for sending Mūsā to Firʿawn.[11] Could this also be the reason why he was born? According to Sayyid Quṭb, verse 28:5 emphasises that God makes known His desire.[12] The word *nurīdu* expresses what God wants. This stands in contrast to the main point in my discussion of *Sūrat Yūsuf* – that is, not being told people's points of remorse. However, while the narrator is providing readers with details about God's motives, it is unclear how much or what exactly He is explaining with these verses. Thus, while the reader is privileged with intimate knowledge about God, which constitutes a most important privilege for a believing reader, that knowledge is still limited and controlled. In this set of verses, God's opinion of Firʿawn is clear – he is an oppressor and spreads corruption. In addition, there emerges a new detail mentioning 'Haman, and their armies' (28:6). Hāmān does not figure in *Sūrat Ṭaha.*

Even though the verses do not completely explain God's motivations, the fact that this specific verse is revealing more of the narrator's motivations is clear when comparing it to other iterations of Mūsā's story. In *Sūrat Ṭaha,* the comparable introduction of the story goes as follows: 'Has the story of Moses come to you [Prophet]? He saw a fire and said to his people, "Stay here – I can see a fire. Maybe I can bring you a flaming brand from it or find some guidance there"' (20:9–10). Clearly, there is no explanation of God's motive in these verses. Another verse introducing the story in another iteration is the following: 'After these, We sent Moses to Pharaoh and his leading supporters with Our signs, but they rejected them. See the fate of those who used to spread corruption' (7:103). One may argue that the mention of 'see the fate of those who used to spread corruption' (7:103) implies that Mūsā was sent to remove this corruption and to serve as an example to others; however, verses 28:4–6 explain more of God's motivation than this verse does.

While the narrator provides some additional information about God's motivation for sending Mūsā to Fir'awn in *Sūrat al-Qaṣaṣ*, God also provides more details about Mūsā's life when he was a baby. God inspires Mūsā's mother to '"Suckle him, and then, when you fear for his safety, put him in the river: do not be afraid, and do not grieve, for We shall return him to you and make him a messenger"' (28:7). The reader is privileged with private and intimate information – a mother nursing her child and being told what to do when she fears for him. Moreover, this is information that not even Mūsā would know, since he was an infant at the time; thus, the reader is privy to more information than Mūsā himself. Despite this disclosure, the readers are never told the mother's name, nor do they know exactly how God inspired her. Commentators discuss the nature of God's inspiration to Mūsā's mother,[13] and some among them explain that God threw it into her heart or soul.[14]

While the readers are told select details about Mūsā's mother, they also receive information about Fir'awn's wife and her joyful reaction to the baby. The text says, 'and Pharaoh's wife said, "Here is a joy to behold for me and for you! Do not kill him: he may be of use to us, or we may adopt him as a son." They did not realize what they were doing' (28:9). Surely this conversation is something neither infant Mūsā, nor his mother would have known; hence, the reader is privileged with knowledge that neither of them has. With the phrase 'They did not realize what they were doing', the narrator is telling the readers something that Fir'awn and his wife do not know. The narrator is revealing to the readers some of what God knows.

Two interesting points concerning the verbs in this verse deserve attention. When Fir'awn's wife says 'Do not kill him', she uses the plural, not the singular. Abū al-Su'ūd explains that she addresses Fir'awn with the plural to honour him, so that he will help her do what she wants.[15] An alternate explanation is that Fir'awn had commanded his people to kill some of the

Banī Isrā'īl, and she was asking him to exclude this baby from those to be killed (see verses 28:4, 2:49 and 14:6; the first uses a singular verb and the latter two plural verbs). In addition, the phrase 'They did not realize what they were doing' uses a plural verb. One might assume that the verb refers to Fir'awn and his wife, but it is plural, not dual. Al-Ṭabarī, al-Zamakhsharī and Abū al-Su'ūd explain that this phrase refers to the people of Fir'awn,[16] and al-Ṭabarī argues that it could also refer to Banī Isrā'īl.[17] Perhaps the plural refers to the potential murderers of Mūsā, the group of people following Fir'awn's orders and killing other babies. Or, perhaps it refers to the three people in the scene: Fir'awn, his wife and Mūsā.

As we continue reading, we learn about Mūsā's mother's sadness, portrayed as her feeling 'a void in her heart' (28:10). Al-Ṭabarī explains that her heart was empty of anything other than Mūsā.[18] God gives her strength (privileged and private information), which one commentator explains to mean that God inspired her with patience.[19] The mother tells her daughter, of whose existence the reader learns only now, to keep track of the baby (28:11). Perhaps wanting to provide more information about her, al-Zamakhsharī adds that the sister's name is Maryam.[20] The sister keeps track of the baby, 'without them knowing'. This is the same phrase as in the scene with Fir'awn and his wife, '*wa hum lā yash'urūna*' (28:9 and 28:11). Again, the readers are told things that the characters do not know. This is followed by even more information that the characters do not know – God prevented Mūsā from feeding from wet nurses. Mūsā's sister volunteers to inform Fir'awn's family about a household in which a woman can take care of Mūsā (28:12). It is unclear whether the girl brilliantly initiates this plan herself, or whether her mother or God lead her in this direction. This scene ends with God the narrator explaining His motives once again: 'We restored him to his mother in this way, so that she might be comforted, not grieve, and know that God's promise is true, though most people do not understand' (28:13).

The lengthy telling of 28:7–13 compares to a shorter scene in *Sūrat Ṭaha* (20:38–41). In those verses, God the character tells Mūsā his life story, including God's inspiration of Mūsā's mother to put him into a chest and to put that chest into a river (20:39). The chest itself is not mentioned in the scene just examined. Both scenes include the sister's words, which vary slightly in the two versions. In 20:40, she says: '"Shall I show you someone who will nurse him?"', while in 28:12 she says, '"Shall I tell you about a household which could bring him up for you and take good care of him?"' Verses 20:38–41 end with God telling Mūsā, '"I have chosen you for Myself"' (20:41). While 20:38–41 and 28:7–13 both include privileged information about Mūsā as a baby, 28:7–13 contains even more examples of privileged information, details and motivations for characters' actions.

Sūrat al-Qaṣaṣ not only provides more knowledge about Mūsā as a baby, but it also contains details about his accidentally killing a person and the consequences of this action. However, between these scenes, there lies a temporal gap. The readers do not know what Mūsā has been doing during this time. Observing this, Sayyid Quṭb comments: 'As is the way of the Qur'ān's presentation of stories, it splits these into scenes and puts an artistic gap between them, which the imagination fills'.[21] He goes on to list a number of questions to which we do not have answers, about what happened between these two scenes.[22] The audience constantly moves between being privileged with information and being deprived of it.

The narrator clearly privileges the readers of *Sūrat al-Qaṣaṣ* when God describes Mūsā entering the city, 'unnoticed by its people' (28:15). There is an evident contrast between the fact that he is unnoticed and the fact that the readers are being given this information. When Mūsā sees two men fighting, he helps one of them – the one from 'his own people' – by hitting the other – the one from his 'enemy' (28:15). The man dies; Mūsā is remorseful and asks for forgiveness from God (28:15–16). He also makes a promise to God: '"My Lord, because of the blessings You have bestowed upon me, I shall never support those who do evil"' (28:17). This, one can assume to be a private communication with God; as seen in this sura and in *Sūrat Maryam*, God shares it with the readers. The next day, the same man asks for help, and it thus becomes clear to Mūsā that he is '"a troublemaker"' (28:18). The man in turn accuses Mūsā of trying to kill him and being a tyrant (28:19). Someone comes and warns Mūsā that '"the authorities are talking about killing you, so leave – this is my sincere advice"' (28:20). Mūsā indeed leaves the city and prays for help from God (28:21). All of these details can be compared to *Sūrat Ṭaha*, when God tells Mūsā his life story, including: '"Later you killed a man, but We saved you from distress and tried you with other tests"' (20:40). Both this and the preceding examples illustrate that not only are the readers given privileged information, but they are also more privileged in this iteration than in *Sūrat Ṭaha.*

Although *Sūrat al-Qaṣaṣ* presents a privileged iteration of the story, the readers are confronted with new mysteries here. *Sūrat al-Qaṣaṣ* describes Mūsā as entering the city (28:15), but we do not know where he was or why he is entering the city now. Had he been living elsewhere, or did he just happen to be away briefly? The narrative seems to imply that the readers do not know a certain piece of information. As is often the case, commentators notice that readers are not told certain things and, therefore, try to provide the missing details. They explain where Mūsā was and what he was doing; they give indications of the time of day[23] (during siesta time,[24] or late at night[25]). Quṭb does not approve of the commentators' additions; as mentioned above, he rather asks a number of questions and then explains that we do not know their answers.[26]

In the next scene, Mūsā leaves the city and goes to Madyan, where he eventually gets married (28:23–8).[27] This scene occurs nowhere else in the Qur'ān. We are thus privileged readers in that we are reading here exclusive information. The scene begins with Mūsā proactively trying to help people, as in the previous example:

> 28:23 When he arrived at Midian's waters, he found a group of men watering [their flocks], and beside them two women keeping their flocks back, so he said, 'What is the matter with you two?' They said, 'We cannot water [our flocks] until the shepherds take their sheep away: our father is a very old man'
>
> 24 He watered their flocks for them, withdrew into the shade, and prayed, 'My Lord, I am in dire need of whatever good thing You may send me'

As elsewhere in this and other Qur'ānic stories, a character supplicates to God. This is private information. In the next verse, one of the ladies tells Mūsā that her father would like to reward him for helping them. Mūsā goes and talks to the father, who comforts Mūsā (28:25). In the next verse, 'One of the women said, "Father, hire him: a strong, trustworthy man is the best to hire"' (28:26) and in the verse thereafter, the father tells Mūsā he would like for him to marry one of his daughters. Although the readers are privileged in learning about these events, it remains unsaid whether this all happens in answer to Mūsā's prayer (28:24). Also, the readers do not know whether the woman's words praising Mūsā (28:26) indicate that she wants to marry him. The narrator does not make this clear, since her words are immediately followed by the father's offer to Mūsā.

The commentators surveyed add a number of details to this scene. They explain that God responds to Mūsā's prayer by blessing him with the company of Shu'ayb and his children,[28] and that Mūsā was praying for food.[29] In addition, they claim that Mūsā helps the women water their flock by moving a big rock from a well. The rock was so big that normally ten (or seven) people were needed to lift it.[30] Quṭb again criticises the commentators for including all these details.[31] Some say the father's name is Shu'ayb, while others disagree: 'the identity of Moses' host has not been revealed, and I do not believe, as has been suggested by others, that he was the prophet Shu'ayb'.[32] Quṭb says that the readers are not given the name of the man who helps Mūsā, although some commentators claim that he is a relative of Shu'ayb.[33] Here, the Shu'ayb to whom al-Ghazālī and Quṭb are referring is a prophet who was sent to Madyan and who is mentioned in multiple places in the Qur'ān.[34] The commentators explain that the women return home faster than usual, so that their father asks what happened, and they tell him about Mūsā.[35] Al-Tha'ālibī explains that the Qur'ān does not include, but implies that they went home and told their father what happened; hence, he sent one of them back to invite Mūsā.[36] Several commentators give her name.[37] The commentators' insertion of details indicates that they were very much aware that information was absent and that their curiosity was piqued. They felt privileged about some details, but they wanted more.

As the commentators' insertions demonstrate, the narrator is varying the amount of details He provides. One can test this by looking at a detail that the narrator shares, even while not making clear why this detail is important enough to be included in the narration. The father tells Mūsā: '"I would like to marry you to one of these daughters of mine, on condition that you serve me for eight years: if you complete ten, it will be of your own free will"'. Mūsā agrees to the arrangement, without agreeing to either number of years (28:27–8). In fact, Mūsā says, '"Let that be the agreement between us – whichever of the two terms I fulfil, let there be no injustice to me – God is witness to what we say"' (*dhālika baynī wa-baynaka ayyamā al-ajalayni qaḍaytu fa-lā 'udwāna 'alayya wa-allāhu 'alā mā naqūlu wakīlun*, 28:28).

This is reminiscent of a verse in *Sūrat al-Kahf*, which contains a discussion about the possible number of people in the cave; here also, the readers are not actually told how many there are:

> 18:22 [Some] say, 'The sleepers were three, and their dog made four', others say, 'They were five, and the dog made six' – guessing in the dark – and some say, 'They were seven, and their dog made eight'. Say [Prophet], 'My Lord knows best how many they were'. Only a few have real knowledge about them, so do not argue, but stick to what is clear, and do not ask any of these people about them.

In Mūsā's story, why does the narrator tell us that the number of years may be eight or ten, as well as Mūsā's response, which mentions both possibilities without specifying agreement to either one? How does this further the story? Perhaps it shows the flexibility of Mūsā and his father-in-law. In terms of the relationship between the text and the reader, it shows the reader something else that they do not know – whether Mūsā stayed for eight or ten years or some other number, and if or why this is important. When consulting the commentators, one explains that Mūsā mentions eight or ten years, because there is no room for ambiguity in a contract.[38] They explain that Mūsā's words indicate that it does not constitute a problem if he stays for the longer period of time, neither is it a problem if he stays for the shorter time-span.[39] Ironically, although Quṭb criticises other commentators for adding details to the text, twice he refers to the amount of time that passes as ten years.[40] Another commentator explains that Mūsā stays for ten years.[41] In this case, then, the commentators (much like the readers) wondered how many years Mūsā stayed and tried to answer this question.

While the commentators wished to know exactly how long Mūsā stays in Madyan, the text seems to be telling and showing the readers that some things are not for them to know. When considering Mūsā's response to the contract, this point is strengthened even further. A more literal translation of his words is: '"That (is) between me and between you . . ."' (*dhālika baynī wa-baynaka*, 28:28).[42] These words emphasise to the reader that this is something between Mūsā and the man. Mūsā also adds that '"God is witness to what we say"' (28:28), which indicates that God also knows what happens in the conversation. God knows and in this case does not tell us everything – it is reminiscent of the phrase seen twice earlier, '*wa hum lā yash'urūna*' (28:9 and 28:11); in this case, we are the ones who do not know. Mūsā's words highlight the exclusive nature of the conversation. Perhaps the commentators reflect this idea by explaining that Mūsā's words indicate that the contract is between Mūsā and the man.[43]

Although Mūsā's entire time at Madyan and his marriage receive no repeated narration in the Qur'ān, his walking through the desert with his wife and then being called by God does. *Sūrat al-Qaṣaṣ* tells: 'Once Moses had fulfilled the term and was travelling with his family, he caught sight of a fire on the side of the mountain and said to his family, "Wait! I have seen a fire. I will bring you news from there, or a burning stick for you to warm yourselves"' (28:29). This compares to the following verse in *Sūrat Ṭaha*: 'He saw a fire and said to his people, "Stay here – I can see a fire. Maybe I can bring you a flaming brand from it or find some guidance there"' (20:10). The two iterations are similar, although the former mentions the context. In addition, since *Sūrat Ṭaha* mentions nothing about Mūsā meeting or marrying his wife (28:23–8), the only indication of it in *Sūrat Ṭaha* appears to be the word, '*ahlihi*', 'his people' or family (20:10). Certainly, the scene in 28:23–28 offers many more details than this.

As *Sūrat al-Qaṣaṣ* proceeds, one can find a description of the place where God and Mūsā are engaged in dialogue: 'But when he reached it, a voice called out to him from the right-hand side of the valley, from a tree on the blessed ground: "Moses, I am God, the Lord of the Worlds"' (28:30). In *Sūrat Ṭaha*, we read: 'When he came to the fire, he was called: "Moses! I am your Lord. Take off your shoes: you are in the sacred valley of Tuwa"' (20:11–12). Each description includes different details – a tree, the right side of the valley, a fire, shoes and Ṭuwā. None of these details are critical for the story, and none of them would actually help readers to identify the location in question. These examples comment on the nature of knowledge. By not conveying certain things to the readers, God the narrator and Creator tells them that they are not omniscient, only God is. God is the source of knowledge; God reveals knowledge as God wills to whomever He wills; knowledge may be found all in one location or in multiple locations; the audience may or may not understand every part of the revelation or its significance; and even if we have knowledge, it may be different from experience.[44] This last point is apparent in later verses, to be analysed below.

While the narration about the location of Mūsā's conversation with God uses details to further readers' understanding of knowledge, so does the actual conversation. As discussed above, in *Sūrat Ṭaha* God tells Mūsā to go to Firʿawn, and Mūsā responds with a request for help:

> 20:25 Moses said, 'Lord, lift up my heart
> 26 and ease my task for me.
> 27 Untie my tongue,
> 28 so that they may understand my words,
> 29 and give me a helper from my family,
> 30 my brother Aaron –
> 31 augment my strength through him.
> 32 Let him share my task
> 33 so that we can glorify You much
> 34 and remember You often:
> 35 You are always watching over us.

In the scene's iteration in *Sūrat al-Qaṣaṣ*, the readers see why Mūsā asks for these things:

> 28:33 Moses said, 'My Lord, I killed one of their men, and I fear that they may kill me.
> 34 My brother Aaron is more eloquent than I: send him with me to help me and confirm my words- I fear they may call me a liar'.
> 35 God said, 'We shall strengthen you through your brother; We shall give you both power so that they cannot touch you. With Our signs you, and those who follow you, will triumph'.

Mūsā, then, asks for the help of his brother because he has killed a man and thinks he might be killed in return, and because his brother is more eloquent than he himself. In *Sūrat Ṭaha*, he asks God to 'untie [his] tongue', and here the readers learn that, in Mūsā's opinion, Hārūn is a much better speaker than he is. Moreover, in *Sūrat Ṭaha*, Mūsā expresses his fear that Firʿawn will transgress against him (20:45). In verse 28:33, it becomes clearer what this may mean: He fears that they may kill him for his past actions. Through the new details provided in verses 28:33 and 28:34, the readers understand more about the meaning behind Mūsā's words in *Sūrat Ṭaha*.

Just as *Sūrat al-Qaṣaṣ* gives further explanation as to the motivation and meaning behind Mūsā's words in *Sūrat Ṭaha*, so the suras also shed light upon each other in another way. While Mūsā asks God for help (28:34), as discussed above, he does not use the word '*ushdud*', 'augment my strength', in *Sūrat al-Qaṣaṣ*. Mūsā uses this word in *Sūrat Ṭaha* (20:31), and God responds by employing a verb with the same root in *Sūrat al-Qaṣaṣ* (28:35), '*sa-nashuddu*', 'We shall strengthen you'. In this way, a conversation is taking place between the two characters and the two suras.[45]

The above examples elucidate that, although *Sūrat al-Qaṣaṣ* adds new information to the story of Mūsā and Firʿawn, this new information comes with its own mysteries. Mūsā's story is being recreated in various ways in *Sūrat al-Qaṣaṣ*.

III. Making Connections between Qur'ānic Verses

As evidenced in the previous example, the narrator in *Sūrat al-Qaṣaṣ* alludes to other verses in the Qur'ān. When the audience notices these references to other verses, they feel rewarded for their efforts at being attentive readers. In *Sūrat al-Qaṣaṣ*, the first allusion to another Qur'ānic story occurs in the scene of Mūsā being found as a baby. I have previously discussed this scene in Chapter 4 on *Sūrat Yūsuf* and will revisit it here. In verses 28:7–13, Firʿawn's wife tells her husband that Mūsā may be a blessing to them and that she wants to keep him as a son. This is an ironic reversal of a scene in *Sūrat Yūsuf*, in which al-ʿAzīz is talking to his wife and tells her, '"Look after him well! He may be useful to us, or we may adopt him as a son . . ."' (12:21). The reference is clear, given the same words in both stories: 'He may be useful to us, or we may adopt him as a son' (28:9 and 12:21). In addition, the narrator uses the same verb in both scenes when discussing the settlement of Mūsā (and his people) and Yūsuf in the land, '*wa-numakkina lahum*' and '*makkannā li-Yūsufa*' (28:6 and 12:21, respectively). In Mūsā's story, Mūsā ends up being a challenge for the husband and a blessing for the wife since God mentions her elsewhere as a positive example for believers (66:11). In Yūsuf's story, Yūsuf ends up being a blessing for the husband, but a challenge for the wife. In both stories, people's words partially come true. This contrasts with God's words being made true, a concept I have discussed in Chapter 5 on *Sūrat Ṭaha.*

In addition to the reversal of the stories of Mūsā and Yūsuf, one may encounter another intertextual reference in their stories. In *Sūrat al-Qaṣaṣ*, the narrator describes Mūsā as having grown up before he enters the city and accidentally kills someone (28:14–15). The first verse says: 'When Moses reached full maturity and manhood, We gave him wisdom and knowledge: this is how We reward those who do good' (28:14). *Sūrat Yūsuf* includes a very similar verse about Yūsuf: 'When he reached maturity, We gave him judgment and knowledge: this is how We reward those who do good' (12:22). In the Arabic original, the only difference between the verses occurs in the verse about Mūsā, which includes one additional word, '*wa-astawā*'. This Abdel Haleem translates as 'manhood'. (Abdel Haleem adds the name, Moses, in his translation, although it is not included in the Arabic text.) Asad mentions that verse 28:14 is 'almost entirely identical with 12:22'.[46] The surveyed commentators do not mention the allusion and instead discuss the age at which someone would be described in these terms.[47]

A reader who notices these intertextual references may think about the irony that Mūsā and Yūsuf are received in opposite ways by the families with whom they stay and that their upbringing has opposite effects on them. The audience may wonder whether Yūsuf or Mūsā served their respective families better. They may wonder about the slight difference mentioned in their growth, '*wa-astawā*'. The readers will probably sense that they have understood something that their Creator, God the narrator, has hinted at: a comparison between Mūsā and Yūsuf, as well as their stories. These will give readers a sense of accomplishment.

Here, readers can discover intertextual allusions that lead not only to a comparison between Mūsā and Yūsuf, but also a comparison of the rulers of their times. We see this allusion in the confrontation between Mūsā and Fir'awn. After Mūsā warns Fir'awn that ' "wrongdoers will never succeed" ' (28:37), Fir'awn responds arrogantly and sarcastically: 'Pharaoh said, "Counsellors, you have no other god that I know of except me. Haman, light me a fire to bake clay bricks, then build me a tall building so that I may climb up to Moses' God: I am convinced that he is lying" ' (28:38).

This verse echoes and contrasts with another in *Sūrat Yūsuf*: 'The king said, "I dreamed about seven fat cows being eaten by seven lean ones; seven green ears of corn and [seven] others withered. Counsellors, if you can interpret dreams, tell me the meaning of my dream"' (12:43). The phrase, '*yā āyyuha al-mala'u*', 'counsellors', appears in both verses. In *Sūrat al-Qaṣaṣ*, however, Firʿawn appeals to his counsellors only to assert to them that he is their god and to mock Mūsā, whereas in *Sūrat Yūsuf* the king appeals to his counsellors to ask them if they can interpret his dream. Just as he is truthful with them and sincerely seeks their help, they honestly respond that they do not know how to interpret dreams – an honesty that draws our attention, since it might have been in their interest to make up an interpretation instead (12:44). In contrast, Firʿawn misleads his people, and his counsellors do not seem to try to direct him. Firʿawn's words in *Sūrat al-Qaṣaṣ* are followed by:

> 28:39 Pharaoh and his armies behaved arrogantly in the land with no right – they thought they would not be brought back to Us –
> 40 so We seized him and his armies and threw them into the sea [*fa-nabadhnāhum fī al-yamm*]. See what became of the wrongdoers!
> 41 We made them leaders calling [others] only to the Fire: on the Day of Resurrection they will not be helped'

The fact that Firʿawn misleads his people is clear in *Sūrat al-Qaṣaṣ*, and he is thus contrasted with another type of leader through a reference echoing back to *Sūrat Yūsuf*. One may also mention here that the root *n-b-dh* is present in 28:40, when God threw Fir ʿawn and his armies in the sea, and in *Sūrat Ṭaha*, when al-Sāmirī explains that he saw something and threw it to make the calf (*fa-nabadhtuhā*, 20:96).

A third place in which the phrase, '*yā āyyuha al-mala'u*', appears in the Qur'ān is in the story of Saba' (27:29–40). In that story, Sulaymān sends a letter to Saba', the Queen of Sheba, and she uses the phrase twice, first to tell her counsellors that she received a letter, and then to ask them what she should do about it (27:29 and 27:32). Here, as with *Sūrat Yūsuf*, a message is being conveyed. Saba' reads Sulaymān's letter: '"It is from Solomon, and it says, 'In the name of God, the Lord of Mercy, the Giver of Mercy, do not put yourselves above me, and come to me in submission to God'"' (27:30–1). Similar to *Sūrat Yūsuf*, this instance reinforces the reader's faith in a message, this time presented as a quotation of Sulaymān's words. We also see that she respects her counsellors' opinions and asks them for their feedback, while her counsellors in turn respect her opinion; they inform her about the resources at their disposal and that it is her decision. Perhaps this constitutes a pattern in these stories, of leaders having counsellors with characteristics reflective of their own. Maybe this is an embodiment of another verse: 'Shall the reward of good be anything but good?' (55:60). This is, however, complicated by the fact that there are places in the Qur'ān where *mala'* do not reflect the beliefs of a prophet; for example, in the story of Nūḥ, the *mala'* reject his faith. About Nūḥ, there is a verse: 'but the prominent leaders of his people said, "We believe you are far astray"' (*qāla al-mala'u min qawmihi innā la-narāka fī ḍalālin mubīnin*, 7:60). With the word *mala'*, one phrase leads us to two other Qur'ānic stories and another verse, and it causes us to reflect on patterns, similarities and differences between them.

The readers of *Sūrat al-Qaṣaṣ* will feel rewarded when they notice another allusion in the story. This one takes place after Mūsā kills a man: 'Then a man came running from the furthest part of the city and said, "Moses, the authorities are talking about killing you, so leave – this is my sincere advice"' (28:20). The beginning of this verse clearly echoes a verse in *Sūrat Yasīn*: 'Then, from the furthest part of the city, a man came running. He said, "My people, follow the messengers"' (36:20). In both verses, the beginning is the same in Arabic, except that the word '*rajulun*', or 'man' appears in a different place; in *Sūrat al-Qaṣaṣ*, we have '*wa jā'a rajulun min āqṣa al-madīnati yas'ā qāla yā . . .*' (28:20), and in verse 36:20, '*wa jā'a min āqṣa al-madīnati rajulun yas'ā qāla yā . . .*' In both stories, the advice is sound. The attentive reader will wonder about the idea of someone coming from the outskirts of the city to warn him. Interestingly, elsewhere, after the magicians declare their faith in God, Fir'awn accuses them of coming up with a plan in the city to overthrow him (7:123). One may also think about the idea of a messenger and the soundness of the message. In his reflections on the verse in *Sūrat Yasīn*, Khaled Abou El Fadl connects it with the idea of the marginal: God's 'centrality and the marginality of all else is but a reminder that through restraint and humility we will find ourselves [. . .] the marginal is but the messenger of grace concealed in the distance between meaning and vanity'.[48] Thus, Abou El Fadl connects the idea of the marginal with the idea of God's centrality, which echoes my overall arguments in this study. Abou El Fadl's approach shows one way in which a reader can analyse the verse in *Sūrat Yasīn*, and one can reflect on if and how this connects to Mūsā's story.

Another connection is based on the root *q-ṣ-y*. In *Sūrat Maryam*, when Maryam is pregnant, 'she withdrew to a distant place' (19:22). The word for distant is '*qaṣiyyā*', the same root as used in the two verses discussed above. Again, the reader may wonder if and how this verse connects to the other two, and Abou El Fadl's reflections may apply here, too. Maryam moves to a distant place in order to bring a messenger, 'Īsā, back to the city. Through this connection, we can better understand why the narrator includes the idea of Maryam's move 'to a distant place'. This intertextual reference creates a link between different stories in the Qur'ān, resulting in a better understanding of the text as a whole.

There are only two other uses of the same root in the Qur'ān; one of them is: 'Glory to Him who made His servant travel by night from the sacred place of worship to the furthest [*al-aqṣā*] place of worship, whose surroundings We have blessed, to show him some of Our signs: He alone is the All Hearing, the All Seeing' (17:1). Here, the word clearly appears in a positive context; again, it is in association with a messenger. This time the messenger is called an '*'abd*'; in *Sūrat Maryam*, 'Īsā as a baby also calls himself an '*'abd*' (19:30). Hence, the shared roots of *q-ṣ-y* and *'-b-d* appear in both *Sūrat Maryam* and *Sūrat al-Isrā'*.

The last occurrence of the root *q-ṣ-y* does not have a positive connotation. This verse is understood to address the Prophet and his followers, about the Battle of Badr: 'Remember when you were on the near side of the valley, and they were on the far [*al-quṣwa*] side and the caravan was below you. If you had made an appointment to fight, you would have failed to keep it [but the battle took place] so that God might bring about something already ordained . . .' (8:42). In four of the five occurrences of the root *q-ṣ-y* in the Qur'ān, one can find a positive connotation and a connection between the idea of the marginal and a truthful message, messenger or blessings sent by God.

As the audience continues reading *Sūrat al-Qaṣaṣ*, they will come across another intertextual reference. Mūsā confronts Fir'awn, and Fir'awn rejects Mūsā's message: 'But when Moses came to them with Our clear signs, they said, "These are mere conjuring tricks; we never heard this from our forefathers" ' (28:36). Fir'awn claims that he never heard of Mūsā's message, and Mūsā responds: ' "My Lord knows best who comes with guidance from Him and who will have the final Home: wrongdoers will never succeed" ' (28:37). Mūsā does not tell Fir'awn that other messengers have actually been sent with the same message to Fir'awn's people. However, in another sura, the readers see this to be the case. *Sūrat Ghāfir* contains another iteration of Mūsā's story: There, Mūsā confronts Fir'awn, and Fir'awn threatens to kill Mūsā – elsewhere Mūsā fears this (40:23–6). He seeks refuge with God (40:27), and then 'a secret believer from Pharaoh's people' defends Mūsā's right to declare his belief in God (40:28). This man continues to speak, 'Joseph came to you before with clear signs, but you never ceased to doubt the message he brought you . . .' (40:34). This verse does not contain words that echo Fir'awn's earlier words. Thus, there is no aural echo that a listener can perceive. The audience may only notice the connection if they pay attention to the content of the stories and are familiar with the Qur'ān as a whole. It is, of course, insightful to know that Fir'awn is lying, and one may wonder why in *Sūrat al-Qaṣaṣ* Mūsā does not confront Fir'awn about his lie. In noticing the reference from verse 28:36 to 40:34, the reader can learn more about Mūsā and Fir'awn.

While the scene of Mūsā and Fir'awn includes references to other stories in the Qur'ān, there also exists another story in *Sūrat al-Qaṣaṣ* that contains references to other parts of the Qur'ān. In *Sūrat al-Qaṣaṣ*, Mūsā's story seems to end perhaps with verse 28:50, followed by a section on belief, reward and Judgment Day (28:51–75). Thereafter follows a story about Qārūn (28:76–82). Qārūn is a rich person who is arrogant about his wealth and gives himself credit for it. He is warned not to be arrogant; some people admire his wealth, while others know better than that (28:76–80). And then, 'We caused the earth to swallow him and his home . . .' (28:81). This turn of events resembles another story in *Sūrat al-Kahf* (18:32–42), about two men with gardens, one verdant and the other not. The owner of the lush garden is arrogant and receives a warning about his attitude; yet, he does not heed the warning and so his garden is destroyed.[49] The stories resemble each other in plot and moral, and they share a number of echoing words.

The story of Qārūn in *Sūrat al-Qaṣaṣ* also contains echoes to another verse in the Qur'ān. In *Sūrat al-Qaṣaṣ*, some people warn the admirers of Qārūn's wealth: 'but those who were given knowledge said, "Alas for you! God's reward is better for those who believe and do good deeds: only those who are steadfast will attain this"' (28:80). This verse clearly reflects another: 'but only those who are steadfast in patience, only those who are blessed with great righteousness, will attain to such goodness' (41:35). The Arabic echoes with the phrase '*wa lā yulaqqāhā illā al-ṣābirūn*' in 28:80 and '*wa mā yulaqqāhā illā al-ladhīna ṣābarū*' in 41:35. In addition, both phrases have doubled *qāfs* in '*yulaqqāhā*', which has its own reverberating quality. As I explored in Chapter 5 on *Sūrat Ṭaha*, here God the narrator confirms good people's words: The words of people in 28:80 are echoed by God in verse 41:35.

The narrator in *Sūrat al-Qaṣaṣ* shares a number of allusions with the readers, through similar plots in stories, as well as echoing words and phrases. These allusions add depth to the readers' understanding. Allusions allow the audience to feel accomplished when they notice them, while at the same time they make the audience wonder if there may exist more allusions that they could have missed. Their existence can also help explain the Qur'ān's ability to withstand repeated readings; it may take a few times for readers to notice an allusion, and even if they do, they may not fully understand its implications. Not understanding fully, they can ponder, reflect on the meaning and revisit the text repeatedly.

IV. Withholding Knowledge through New Mysteries

Intertextual references abound in *Sūrat al-Qaṣaṣ*. Just as the Qur'ānic narrator leads readers to ponder allusions to other parts of the Qur'ān, God also leads readers to ponder new details that they cannot fully understand. The narrator is careful to impart knowledge to the audience and privilege them with private information. This information, however, is balanced with details that the reader does not and cannot understand. The narrator alludes to this information, which I will refer to as mysteries, in order to remind the audience of their place – they only know things because God the narrator chooses to share them. Bodman writes that 'it may be that blanks in the story serve to encourage or require a synthetic knowledge of the Qur'ān, in which one is constantly cross-referencing the various narratives to compose the amalgamated story'.[50] However, readers do not have to 'compose' the story; it is complete even as one moves from one verse to another to better understand the verses. The story is complete, but human knowledge never is.

The first example of a mystery concerns the identity of Hāmān. There are only six references to Hāmān in the Qur'ān, and three of them occur in *Sūrat al-Qaṣaṣ*. The first reference explains: 'but We wished to favour those who were oppressed in that land, to make them leaders, the ones to survive, to establish them in the land, and through them show Pharaoh, Haman, and their armies the very thing they feared' (28:5–6). Another verse mentions Mūsā as 'a source of grief for them: Pharaoh, Haman, and their armies were wrongdoers – ' (28:8), and later, Fir'awn asks Haman: ' "Haman, light me a fire to bake clay bricks, then build me a tall building so that I may climb up to Moses' God: I am convinced that he is lying" ' (28:38). Verse 40:36 is similar to this one, with Fir'awn telling Hāmān to build him a tower.[51] The remaining two verses mentioning Hāmān list him with Fir'awn and Qārūn, as they all rejected Mūsā's message.[52] Clearly, God the narrator describes Hāmān as a 'wrongdoer' (28:8) and as someone who worked with or helped Fir'awn, or at least was given orders by Fir'awn. This is the extent of the readers' knowledge about him. We also do not know why he is mentioned in only three suras (28:6, 28:8, 28:38, 29:39, 40:24 and 40:36). We know little about Hāmān and would know nothing about him, if the narrator had so chosen.

Just as we know little about Hāmān, we also have very limited information about Qārūn, who is equally mentioned in *Sūrat al-Qaṣaṣ*. The name Qārūn appears four times in the Qur'ān; two of those times are in this very sura. Twice, it is with Fir'awn and Hāmān.[53] The other two times he is mentioned in a scene in *Sūrat al-Qaṣaṣ* (28:76–82). As discussed earlier, Qārūn is a rich person who gloats about his wealth and credits himself with it. He is warned not to be arrogant; finally, he is punished, and 'he had no army to help him against God, nor could he defend himself' (28:81). We know very little about Qārūn from the Qur'ānic text, including whether and why he is connected to Fir'awn and Hāmān. One may look at extra-Qur'ānic texts to see if there exists any mention of Hāmān and Qārūn, as other scholars have done, but pursuing this avenue of research would not advance an analysis of Qur'ānic narrative technique. Indeed, our interests here do not lie in who these people are; rather, we are interested in why the Qur'ān refers to them in the ways it does. The limited amount of information dispensed about Qārūn and Hāmān stands for the limited nature of the reader's knowledge in general.[54]

Nevertheless, some of the surveyed commentators give lengthy descriptions of who exactly Qārūn is and what happens to him.[55] They also discuss how he is related to Mūsā,[56] and they even give the names of their relatives.[57] They include quotations of his words, too.[58] Sayyid Quṭb, however, objects to these details. He lists questions about Qārūn for which we do not have answers:

> We do not need all of these narrations, nor do we need to define the time and the place. The story, as it is told in the Qur'an is sufficient [. . .] Even if it defined the time and place and clothing, there would still be things left undefined. Thus we will look at the Qur'anic portrayal, and move away from these narrations that have no benefit.[59]

Quṭb argues that, even if we were provided with many details, we would still lack others. Even though the readers are told about Mūsā's marriage and work agreement, for example, they do not know exactly how many years he stayed in Madyan. Details can never be comprehensive, and the Qur'ānic text seems to convey to its readers this message through its narrative choices. God alone has knowledge of all details and of everything, whereas the reader is always at God's mercy.

What little we know about Qārūn and Hāmān is what the Qur'ān tells us, and this deliberate conveyance of a limited amount of information appears in other parts of *Sūrat al-Qaṣaṣ* as well. Earlier, I discussed other mysteries in the story: Mūsā's entrance to the city (28:15) and then his journey to Madyan (28:22). Where was Mūsā, and why are we told that he is entering the city? Does it matter? Could this be connected to the idea of the marginal, discussed above in relation to verse 28:20? Why does Mūsā go to Madyan? The readers are given tantalising bits of information, indicating that the narrator knows something that He is not sharing.

In Madyan, we encounter another mystery. Mūsā meets the father of the women whom he helped at the well: 'When Moses came to him and told him his story, the old man said, "Do not be afraid, you are safe now from people who do wrong"' (28:25). The phrase, 'and told him his story' is especially striking in Arabic, '*wa-qaṣṣa 'alayhi al-qaṣaṣ*'. The words '*qaṣṣa*' and '*al-qaṣaṣ*' come from the same root, *q-ṣ-ṣ*, which consists of emphatic letters only and thus has a strong aural quality. Even the name of this sura derives from this phrase. The phrase clearly attracts attention, but it is unclear why the narrator wants the readers' attention. There exists another verse featuring Mūsā and this root, in the story of Mūsā and Khiḍr, which occurs in only one iteration in the Qur'ān. Before Mūsā meets Khiḍr, Mūsā is with a young man: 'Moses said, "Then that was the place we were looking for." So the two turned back, retraced their footsteps' (*qāla dhālika mā kunnā nabghi fa-irtaddā 'alā āthārihimā qaṣaṣan*, 18:64). This verse once again connects Mūsā to the root *q-ṣ-ṣ*, but why? We also find the phrase '*fa-aqṣuṣ al-qaṣaṣa*' elsewhere in the Qur'ān, although here it is addressing the Prophet Muḥammad or the reader of the Qur'ān:

> 7:176 if it had been Our will, We could have used these signs to raise him high, but instead he clung to the earth and followed his own desires – he was like a dog that pants with a lolling tongue whether you drive it away or leave it alone. Such is the image of those who reject Our signs. Tell them the story [*fa-aqṣuṣ al-qaṣaṣa*] so that they may reflect.

The only other verse in the Qur'ān that has the root *q-ṣ-ṣ* repeated twice in such close succession consists of 12:3, which I have discussed in Chapter 4 on *Sūrat Yūsuf*. In verse 18:64, one can also note the presence of the root *'-th-r*, which occurs elsewhere in Mūsā's story (20:84 and 20:96). A fruitful path for further analysis would be to explore whether the readers are to think of Mūsā as a storyteller, and whether this identity is somehow part of his role as a prophet. Is the Qur'ān drawing a parallel between a messenger and a storyteller? Or is this scene supposed to show something else?

We have seen several mysteries with which the Qur'ān confronts us, as the text does not provide the necessary context to understand more. One may ponder the mysteries in the Qur'ān more generally, questioning whether the Qur'ān itself names and discusses them. As has been discussed above, the Qur'ān presents mysteries in other stories as well. Moreover, outside of stories – for example, in some of the short Meccan suras – one encounters words, verses and images that are ambiguous. *Āl 'Imrān* contains a verse that seems to explain the nature of Qur'ānic verses and their interpretation, but carries its own ambiguities:

> 3:7 it is He who has sent this Scripture down to you [Prophet]. Some of its verses are definite in meaning [*muḥkamātun*] – these are the cornerstone of

> the Scripture – and others are ambiguous [*mutashābihātun*]. The perverse at heart eagerly pursue the ambiguities in their attempt to make trouble and to pin down a specific meaning of their own: only God knows the true meaning. Those firmly grounded in knowledge say, 'We believe in it: it is all from our Lord' – only those with real perception will take heed.

Given verse 3:7, one may suggest using the word '*mutashābihāt*' to describe Qur'ānic mysteries; however, the Qur'ān does not identify which verses are clear and which are unclear. This in itself presents another mystery. We also find the idea of '*al-ghayb*', or the unseen, in the Qur'ān. This root occurs in a number of places in the suras discussed in this book: 3:44, 3:179, 12:10, 12:15, 12:52, 12:81, 12:102, 19:61 and 19:78, and in many other places. While these concepts clearly exist in the Qur'ān, I do not use the terms '*mutashābihāt*' or '*al-ghayb*' to identify the withholding of information or mysteries in the stories, because such a usage would usurp the Qur'ānic terms. The mysteries that I discuss and those that the Qur'ān labels with '*mutashābihāt*' and '*al-ghayb*' indicate God's supreme knowledge. They appear to work like signs of God, *āyāt*; yet, again, I do not employ this term so as not to overstep the interpretive boundaries of the text. Ambiguities in the Qur'ān are part of its narrative technique and serve a purpose. This purpose can be summarised as instilling humility in the readers and opening them up to their role as receivers of a message.

While the narrator in *Sūrat al-Qaṣaṣ* presents the readers with mysteries that make them think about a message, God talks about revelation in the meta-text. It says:

> 28:44 You [Muhammad] were not present on the western side of the mountain when We gave Our command to Moses: you were not there –
> 45 We have brought into being many generations who lived long lives – you did not live among the people of Midian or recite Our Revelation to them – We have always sent messengers to people –
> 46 nor were you present on the side of Mount Sinai when We called out to Moses. But you too have been sent as an act of grace from your Lord, to give warning to a people to whom no warner has come before, so that they may take heed.

These verses resemble verse 3:44, which I have discussed in Chapter 2. The verses are addressed to the second person singular, 'you', and the translator, Abdel Haleem, and commentators interpret this as referring to the Prophet Muḥammad. Robinson writes that these are one of a group of verses 'which indicate that the speaker allegedly witnessed events that took place long ago and that he is consequently in a position to narrate what happened in the minutest detail'.[60] In these verses, Prophet Muḥammad is being told that he did not live during Mūsā's time, and that he was not a messenger to the people of Madyan. Yet, he is a messenger like other messengers, sent from God's mercy.[61] God the narrator thus makes Himself central, once again. What matters is God and the message and the messengers He chooses to send to whom He wills.

V. Conclusion

This Chapter began with a focus on the creation of consonance by means of new details. As an audience, we feel closer to the text and to the Creator of the text when we feel that exclusive details are being revealed to us. Readers also feel a connection to the characters when being invited to witness their secret prayers to God. Connections between verses cause readers to shift their gaze to compare different stories and verses to each other. These show what to focus on and thus teach how to approach the text. Finally, through the withholding of knowledge, readers realise their place of humility and turn to God and God's text. As a result of these narrative techniques, the audience learns ways of reading the Qur'ān, the nature of knowledge and one's proper place in relation to God. Through these narrative choices, the text imprints on the audience beliefs about God: God is omniscient, while people are not and cannot ever be. People learn what God wills when they turn to God and to the Qur'ān. By seeing the limits to our knowledge when compared to God's, we are also learning that there is value to knowledge. We could have remained ignorant and ignorant of our ignorance, but instead are allowed to see our lack of knowledge. Perhaps, one can even discern here the sin of disrespecting knowledge and expertise by not knowing one's standing in relation to God and others.

The narrator of the Qur'ān makes reading an active process, and this is specifically accomplished by the giving and withholding of information, by causing readers to question, ponder and even fill in details in *Sūrat al-Qaṣaṣ*. This chapter began by looking at new details that are provided in *Sūrat al-Qaṣaṣ*, but not in other iterations of Mūsā's story. It quickly became evident that many of these new details bring with them their own mysteries, and the readers are given other, new mysteries, too – information which we do not understand entirely, or are not even meant to understand. By reading and listening carefully, we hear and see references to other Qur'ānic verses. While these references are not critical for the readers' understanding, they lead to new ideas and connections to ponder. They also work to show that the audience's knowledge is incomplete. Even when we catch certain allusions, we may not understand the connections completely, and we may miss some of them. Throughout the sura, as readers, we feel rewarded for reading carefully and are given new and sometimes exclusive privileged information; yet, we are continuously put in our place by being shown that we do not know some things. Being both elevated and humbled by the text causes the readers to turn to it repeatedly, making them receptive to the revelation in a potentially never-ending cycle.

Notes

1. El-Awa, 'Repetition in the Qur'ān' 589–90. See the article for other kinds of repetition, explanations and examples.
2. Quṭb, vol. 5, 2674.
3. Tlili 46. For more on an intertextual approach to the Qur'ān, see Cuypers, *The Banquet* 26.
4. Cuypers, 'Semitic Rhetoric as a Key to the Question of the *naẓm* of the Qur'anic Text' 6.
5. El-Awa, *Textual Relations in the Qur'ān* 9 and 11.
6. El-Awa, *Textual Relations in the Qur'ān* 15.
7. El-Awa, *Textual Relations in the Qur'ān* 100.
8. For examples, see El-Awa, *Textual Relations in the Qur'ān* 157–9.
9. Barthes, *S/Z* 11.
10. Asad, vol. 4, 657.
11. Khan writes that 'while the Qur'ān says concerning Noah, Hūd, Ṣāliḥ and Lot that each of these Prophets was sent to his people (*qawm*), it nowhere says that Moses was sent to the Children of Israel or to his people. On the contrary, the

Qur'ān speaks of Moses' being sent "to Pharaoh" or "to Pharaoh and his chiefs (*al-mala'*)" or "to Pharaoh, Hāmān and Qārūn (Korah)" or "to Pharaoh and his people"'. Khan 16.

12. Quṭb, vol. 5, 2678.
13. Al-Tha'ālibī, vol. 2, 510 and al-Jalālayn 507.
14. Al-Ṭabarī, vol. 8, 6340–1.
15. Al-'Amārī, vol. 7, 4.
16. Al-Ṭabarī, vol. 8, 6346, al-Zamakhsharī, vol. 3, 167 and al-'Amārī, vol. 7, 5.
17. Al-Ṭabarī, vol. 8, 6346.
18. Al-Ṭabarī, vol. 8, 6347.
19. Al-Zamakhsharī, vol. 8, 167.
20. Al-Zamakhsharī, vol. 8, 167. I discuss the issue of Hārūn's sister's name in Chapter 3.
21. Quṭb, vol. 5, 2676–7.
22. Quṭb, vol. 5, 2681. Albayrak makes a similar observation about a different story in the Qur'ān and also includes a reference from Quṭb. See Albayrak, 'The Classical Exegetes' Analysis of the Qur'ānic Narrative 18:60–82' 290. He refers to Sayyid Quṭb, *Fī Ẓilāl al-Qur'ān* (Beirut: Dār Iḥyā' al-Turāth al-'Arabī, 1971), 5:396.
23. Al-Tha'ālibī, vol. 2, 511; al-Ṭabarī, vol. 8, 6356–7 and al-Ṭabrisī, www.altafsir.com/Tafasir.asp?tMadhNo=4&tTafsirNo=3&tSoraNo=28&tAyahNo=14&tDisplay=yes&Page=2&Size=1&LanguageId=1
24. Al-Jalālayn 508.
25. Al-'Amārī, vol. 7, 6 and al-Zamakhsharī, vol. 3, 168.
26. Quṭb, vol. 5, 2681.
27. For more on this scene, see Maybudī 483–5. See also Wheeler, *Moses in the Quran and Islamic Exegesis* 37–63.
28. Al-Tustarī 118.
29. Al-Ṭabarī, vol. 8, 6373–5 and al-Ṭabrisī, www.altafsir.com/Tafasir.asp?tMadhNo=4&tTafsirNo=3&tSoraNo=28&tAyahNo=24&tDisplay=yes&Page=2&Size=1&LanguageId=1
30. Al-Zamakhsharī, vol. 3, 170, al-Tha'ālibī, vol. 2, 513 and al-Ṭabrisī, www.altafsir.com/Tafasir.asp?tMadhNo=4&tTafsirNo=3&tSoraNo=28&tAyahNo=24&tDisplay=yes&Page=2&Size=1&LanguageId=1
31. Quṭb, vol. 5, 2687.
32. Al-Ghazālī 416. Al-Ṭabarī writes something similar, vol. 8, 6377–8; he also gives other names for the man.

33. Quṭb, vol. 5, 2687.
34. The verses are 7:85–93, 11:84–95, 15:78–9, 26:176–91 and 29:36–7.
35. Al-Jalālayn 510; al-'Amārī, vol. 7, 9 and al-Zamakhsharī, vol. 3, 171.
36. Al-Tha'ālibī, vol. 2, 513.
37. Al-'Amārī, vol. 7, 9, al-Ṭabarī, vol. 8, 6377 and al-Ṭabrisī, www.altafsir.com/Tafasir.asp?tMadhNo=4&tTafsirNo=3&tSoraNo=28&tAyahNo=27&tDisplay=yes&UserProfile=0&LanguageId=1
38. Quṭb, vol. 5, 2689.
39. Al-'Amārī, vol. 7, 11.
40. Quṭb, vol. 5, 2689.
41. Al-Tha'ālibī, vol. 2, 515.
42. This translation comes from Ahmed Ali. Abdul Majid Daryabadi and Muhammad Mahmoud Ghali also translate the phrase similarly. Translations accessed at www.islamawakened.com/index.php/qur-an
43. Al-Ṭabarī, vol. 8, 6381.
44. Ozgur Alhassen, 'You Were Not There" 82–3.
45. For more detail, see Chapter 5 on *Sūrat Ṭaha.*
46. Asad, vol. 4, 660, note 12.
47. Al-Jalālayn 508; al-Tha'ālibī, vol. 2, 511; al-'Amārī, vol. 7, 6; Quṭb, vol. 5, 2681; al-Zamakhsharī, vol. 3, 168 and al-Ṭabarī, vol. 8, 6354–5.
48. Abou El Fadl, *Conference of the Books* 190–1.
49. For more on this parable, see Afsar, 'A Literary Critical Approach to Qur'ānic Parables' 493–9.
50. Bodman 103.
51. The verse reads: 'Pharaoh said, 'Haman, build me a tall tower so that I may reach the ropes that lead' (40:36).
52. These verses are: '[Remember] Qarun and Pharaoh and Haman: Moses brought them clear signs, but they behaved arrogantly on earth. They could not escape Us' (29:39) and, 'to Pharaoh, Haman, and Korah and they said, "Sorcerer! Liar!"' (40:24). (Abdel Haleem translates the name Qārūn as 'Qarun' in the first verse and as 'Korah' in the second.)
53. See the previous note for these verses.
54. For another example in a Qur'ānic story where 'incompleteness is clearly deliberate', see Cuypers, *The Banquet* 415.
55. Al-Tha'ālibī, vol. 2, 522–5.
56. Al-Jalālayn 518, al-Ṭabarī, vol. 8, 6424–5 and al-Ṭabrisī, www.altafsir.com/

Tafasir.asp?tMadhNo=4&tTafsirNo=3&tSoraNo=28&tAyahNo=76&tDisplay=yes&Page=2&Size=1&LanguageId=1

57. Al-ʻAmārī, vol. 7, 24, al-Zamakhsharī, vol. 3, 190 and al-Ṭabarī, vol. 8, 6424-5.
58. Al-ʻAmārī, vol. 7, 24 and al-Zamakhsharī, vol. 3, 190.
59. Quṭb, vol. 5, 2710.
60. Robinson, *Discovering the Qur'an* 238.
61. Ozgur Alhassen, 'You Were Not There' 81.

7

Conclusion: Reading the Qur'ān as God's Narrative

The preceding pages have examined the Qur'ānic stories in *Sūrat Āl 'Imrān*, *Sūrat Maryam*, *Sūrat Yūsuf*, *Sūrat Ṭaha* and *Sūrat al-Qaṣaṣ* and developed a sustained discussion of the Qur'ān as an intertextual scripture that rewards the audience who reads and listens carefully, notices echoing words or phrases and then follows them to other parts of the text, comparing them with each other and reflecting on them.

Chapter 2 on *Sūrat Āl 'Imrān* 3:33–62 focused on the literary themes of knowledge, control and consonance, as a lens to scrutinise the relationship that the narrator develops between God, the readers and the text. Examining the entire story in verses 3:33–62, we find that the Qur'ānic narrative style serves to embody this image of God the narrator as being omnipotent and omniscient. Some otherwise puzzling stylistic choices can be explained based on this idea; thus, in this story style puts the audience in their place, much like it puts the narrator/God in His place.

In Chapter 3, I examined *Sūrat Maryam* 19:1–58 in terms of the structure of the story. It begins with the themes of God and family, with the theme of family becoming less prominent and the theme of God and faith eventually replacing it. Thus, God the narrator initially makes God central to the family, but eventually makes God take over the place of the family.

In Chapter 4 on *Sūrat Yūsuf*, we saw the narrative style working to show that human knowledge is always limited; the text does not allow the reader to judge the characters' guilt and remorse. One might expect moments of remorse and forgiveness to be prominent and even dramatised, or the possibility to pinpoint when and how a character feels remorse. Instead, God occupies the centre. God, the narrator, recreates the world of the story in the same way in which we see the world – through actions and speech – and does not give us information with which to interpret the internal. God makes Himself central to the story – only God knows whether people are guilty or remorseful, and God's forgiveness is what matters, regardless of our understanding or opinion.

Chapter 5 on *Sūrat Ṭaha* analysed instances of the narrator confirming God's and other people's words, merging speech and making semantic connections in the story on Mūsā. *Sūrat Ṭaha*, like all other Qur'ānic stories, includes God in at least three ways: God as a character in the story, God as the narrator of the story and God as the implied author of the story. As a result, when God repeatedly shows Mūsā's words to be true, for example, God is simultaneously affirming His messenger and the trustworthiness of both message and messenger. When the narrator confirms people's words and merges them with His own, God shows that He is with people when they do good and are fulfilling His will. By merging characters' speeches with God's, God rewards good people with narrative unity with Himself.

Mūsā also constitutes the subject of Chapter 6, but this time in the context of *Sūrat al-Qaṣaṣ*. Here, new details are added to the story, including explanations of motives for actions, as well as new mysteries and references to other stories. The narrator sometimes makes the readers into privileged readers, while balancing this privilege with mysteries to keep them in their place. At the same time, as with the other suras discussed, the narrator rewards the hard-working and attentive reader who reads more, understands more and consequently notices the allusions.

This study has developed a method of analysis for Qur'ānic stories by focusing on the overarching questions of how these stories withhold knowledge, create consonance and draw connections. God knows all and shows this to the audience by withholding knowledge from them. By withholding information and using other subtle narrative techniques, God the narrator 'makes' His readers, as Wayne Booth mentions, 'by forcing them onto a level of alertness that will allow for his most subtle effects'.[1] The audience accordingly learns about the nature of knowledge, one's proper place in relation to God and God's message, and how to read the Qur'ān. The text imprints on the audience beliefs about God: God is omniscient, while humans are not and cannot ever be. People learn what God wills when they turn to God and to the Qur'ān.

By seeing their limited knowledge when compared to God, readers also learn that there is a value to knowledge. One may simply be ignorant and, even more, ignorant of one's ignorance, but, instead, readers are made aware of their lack of knowledge. The narrator of the Qur'ān makes reading an active process: Through the alternate giving and withholding of information, readers are pushed to question, ponder and fill in details. Being elevated and humbled by the text makes readers turn to it repeatedly, thus making them receptive to the revelation in a potentially never-ending cycle. One of the effects of concealment or withholding of information in Qur'ānic stories is to keep the audience interested, to encourage them to read more of the Qur'ān and to make readers aware of and reflect upon their role as receivers of a message.

Although God asserts God's power and control through narrative technique, one can also discern the creation of consonance between God, revelation and the audience. One way in which this occurs is through the merging of speech. These mergers appear at junctures when characters are rewarded for their faith by the narrative style – through a narrative connection with God – for example, in the merging of Mūsā's and God's speech in *Sūrat Ṭaha*. By means of semantic echoes, the Qur'ān makes connections within a story, with other parts of a sura and with other suras. These semantic echoes connect verses throughout the Qur'ān in intricate webs. Echoing words and phrases in the Qur'ān carry great narrative and structural significance: They form structure within a story and connect the story to other sections of the sura. This is a narrative technique that the Qur'ān uses to develop, complicate and comment on ideas as well as stories. Moreover, similarity and variation within echoing phrases or intertextual connections is created through reference and exemption.

These allusions add depth to our understanding. They make the audience feel a sense of accomplishment when they notice them, while at the same time wondering if there could be more that they have missed. The allusions can also help to explain the Qur'ān's ability to withstand repeated readings; it may take a few cycles of reading for readers to notice an allusion, and even if they do, they may not fully understand its implications. Not understanding fully, they can ponder, reflect on the meaning and revisit the text repeatedly.

This study has demonstrated that it is acceptable for readers not to understand everything in the Qur'ānic text. In fact, this even seems to be deliberate and expected on the part of the narrator. The stories work by denying certain information to the audience, and the narrator makes it clear to the audience that, no matter what, their knowledge will always remain limited and that the little that they do know is what God the narrator sees fit to tell them. The implications of this for translation are thought-provoking: If a text tries to withhold information from readers and resists interpretation, then what is the best way to translate it?

The narratological, semantic and rhetorical approach has provided new insights into Qur'ānic stories, showing some ways in which they advance the overall metaphysical and ethical messages of the Qur'ān. This study also gives a glimpse of *tafsīr*, and of how nine different commentators at times added details to the stories. Qur'ānic stories clearly leave readers asking intriguing questions and wanting answers. Vested in the characters and their stories, the commentators thus tried to explain certain aspects in greater detail. The stories sometimes seem to violate causality in order to provoke thought and inspire comment. The very existence of the genre of *tafsīr* confirms my contention that the Qur'ān, through its style, forces the reader into a position of interpretation and inquiry – a position in which one also knows the limits of one's own interpretation.

Note

1. Booth 302.

Bibliography

I. Qur'ānic Studies

Abboud, Hosn. *Mary, Mother of Jesus and the Qur'anic Text: A Feminist Literary Study,* unpublished Ph.D. dissertation, University of Toronto, Canada, 2006.

Abdel Haleem, Muhammad, translator. *The Qur'ān: English Translation and Parallel Arabic Text.* Oxford University Press, 2010.

—. 'Qur'anic "*jihād*": A Linguistic and Contextual Analysis'. *Journal of Qur'anic Studies*, vol. 12, no. 1–2, 2010, pp. 147–66.

—. *Understanding the Qur'an: Themes and Style.* I. B. Tauris Publishers, 1999.

Abou El Fadl, Khaled. *Conference of the Books: The Search for Beauty in Islam.* University Press of America, Inc., 2001.

—. *Speaking in God's Name: Islamic Law, Authority and Women.* Oneworld Publications, 2005.

Abu-Deeb, Kamal. 'Studies in the Majāz and Metaphorical Language of the Qur'ān: Abū 'Ubayda and al-Sharīf al-Raḍī'. *Literary Structures of Religious Meaning in the Qur'an,* edited by Issa J. Boullata. Curzon, 2000, pp. 310–53.

Abu-Zayd, Nasr. 'The Dilemma of the Literary Approach to the Qur'an'. *Alif: Journal of Comparative Poetics*, no. 23, Literature and the Sacred, 2003, pp. 8–47.

— and Esther R. Nelson. *Voice of an Exile: Reflections on Islam.* Praeger, 2004.

Afsar, Ayaz. 'A Discourse and Linguistic Approach to Biblical and Qur'ānic Narrative'. *Islamic Studies*, vol. 45, no. 4, 2006, pp. 493–517.

—. 'A Literary Critical Approach to Qur'ānic Parables'. *Islamic Studies*, vol. 44, no. 4, 2005, pp. 481–501.

—. 'Plot Motifs in Joseph/Yūsuf Story: A Comparative Study of Biblical and Qur'ānic Narrative'. *Islamic Studies*, vol. 45, no. 2, 2006, pp. 167–89.

Albayrak, Ismail. 'The Classical Exegetes' Analysis of the Qur'ānic Narrative 18:60–82'. *Islamic Studies*, vol. 42, no. 2, 2003, pp. 289–315.

—. 'The Qur'anic Narratives of the Golden Calf Episode'. *Journal of Qur'anic Studies*, vol. 3, no. 1, 2001, pp. 47–69.

Algar, Hamid. 'Q. 21:78–9: A Qur'anic Basis for *Ijtihād*?'. *Journal of Qur'anic Studies*, vol. 4, no. 2, 2002, pp. 1–22.

al-'Amārī, Abū al-Su'ūd Muḥammad ibn Muḥammad. *Tafsīr Abī al-Su'ūd*. Dār al-Ḥayā' al Turāth al-'Arabī, 1994.

Asad, Muhammad, translator. *The Message of the Qur'ān*. The Book Foundation, 2003.

Ayoub, Mahmoud. 'Literary Exegesis of the Qur'ān: The Case of al-Sharīf al-Raḍī'. *Literary Structures of Religious Meaning in the Qur'an*, edited by Issa J. Boullata. Curzon, 2000, pp. 292–309.

—. *The Qur'ān and its Interpreters*. vol. 1. State University of New York Press, 1984.

Barlas, Asma. 'The Qur'an and Hermeneutics: Reading the Qur'an's Opposition to Patriarchy'. *Journal of Qur'anic Studies*, vol. 3, no. 2, 2001, pp. 15–38.

Bauer, Karen. 'Emotion in the Qur'an: An Overview'. *Journal of Qur'anic Studies*, vol. 19, no. 2, 2017, pp. 1–30.

Beaumont, Daniel. 'Hardboiled: Narrative Discourse in Early Muslim Traditions'. *Studia Islamica*, 83, 1996, pp. 5–31.

Bellamy, James A. 'The Mysterious Letters of the Koran: Old Abbreviations of the Basmalah'. *Journal of the American Oriental Society*, vol. 93, no. 3, 1973, pp. 267–85.

Ben Abdeljelil, Jameleddine. 'Ways of the Intellect: Forms of Discourse and Rationalization Processes in the Arabic-Islamic Context'. Translated by Ursula Bsees and Anthony Lowstedt, *Worldviews and Cultures: Philosophical Reflections from an Intercultural Perspective*, edited by Nicole Note, Raúl Fornet-Betancout, Diederik Aerts and Josef Estermann. Springer, 2009, pp. 11–29.

Ben Nabi, Malik. *The Qur'anic Phenomenon: An Attempt at a Theory of Understanding the Holy Qur'an*. Translated by Abu Bilal Kirkary, American Trust Publications, 1983.

Blatherwick, Helen. 'Textual Silences and Literary Choices in al-Kisā'ī's Account of the Annunciation and the Birth of Jesus'. *Arabica* vol. 66, no. 1–2, 2019, pp. 1–42.

Bodman, Whitney S. *The Poetics of Iblīs: Narrative Theology in the Qur'ān*. Harvard Theological Studies, 2011.

Boullata, Issa J. 'Sayyid Quṭb's Literary Appreciation of the Qur'ān'. *Literary Structures of Religious Meaning in the Qur'an*, edited by Issa J. Boullata. Curzon, 2000, pp. 354–71.

Cuypers, Michel. *The Banquet: A Reading of the Fifth Sura of the Qur'an*, edited by Rafael Luciani, translated by Patricia Kelly. Convivium Press, 2009.

—. 'Semitic Rhetoric as a Key to the Question of the *naẓm* of the Qur'anic Text'. *Journal of Qur'anic Studies*, vol. 13, no. 1, 2011, pp. 1–24.

Dayeh, Islam. 'Al-Ḥawāmīm: Intertextuality and Coherence in Meccan Surahs'. *The Qur'ān in Context: Historical and Literary Investigations into the Qur'ānic Milieu*, edited by Angelika Neuwirth, Nicolai Sinai and Michael Marx. Brill, 2010.

El-Awa, Salwa. 'Repetition in the Qur'ān: A Relevance Based Explanation of the Phenomenon'. *Islamic Studies*, vol. 42, no. 4, 2003, pp. 577–93.

—. *Textual Relations in the Qur'ān: Relevance, Coherence and Structure.* Routledge, 2006.

Elder, E. E. 'Parallel Passages in the Koran (The Story of Moses)'. *The Muslim World*, vol. 15, 1925, pp. 254–9.

Ernst, Carl W. *How to Read the Qur'an: A New Guide, with Select Translations.* The University of North Carolina Press, 2011.

Firestone, Reuven. 'Abraham'. *Encyclopaedia of the Qur'ān*. General Editor: Jane Dammen McAuliffe, Georgetown University. Brill Online, 2015.

Geissinger, Aisha. 'Mary in the Qur'an: Rereading Subversive Births'. *Sacred Tropes: Tanakh, New Testament, and Qur'an as Literature and Culture*, edited by Roberta Sterman Sabbath. Brill, 2009, pp. 379–92.

al-Ghazālī, Muḥammad. *A Thematic Commentary on the Qur'an*. Translated by Ashur A. Shamis, revised by Zaynab Alawiye. The International Institute of Islamic Thought, 2000.

Goldfeld, Yeshayahu. 'The Development of Theory on Qur'ānic Exegesis in Islamic Scholarship'. *Studia Islamica*, vol. 67, 1988, pp. 5–27.

Greifenhagen, F. V. 'The *qamīṣ* in *Sūrat Yūsuf*: A Prolegomenon to the Material Culture of Garments in the Formative Islamic Period'. *Journal of Qur'anic Studies*, vol. 11, no. 2, 2009, pp. 72–92.

Hasan, Ahmad. 'The Qur'ān: The Primary Source of "Fiqh" '. *Islamic Studies*, vol. 38, no. 4, 1999, pp. 475–502.

Heath, Peter. 'Creative Hermeneutics: A Comparative Analysis of Three Islamic Approaches'. *Arabica*, vol. 36, no. 2, 1989, pp. 173–210.

Hoffmann, Thomas. 'Agnostic Poetics in the Qur'ān: Self-referentialities, Refutations, and the Development of a Qur'ānic Self'. *Self-Referentiality in the Qur'ān*, edited by Stefan Wild. Harrassowitz Verlag, 2006, pp. 39–57.

Izutsu, Toshihiko. *God and Man in the Qur'an: Semantics of the Qur'anic Weltanschauung*. Islamic Book Trust, 2002.

—. *The Structure of Ethical Terms in the Quran*. ABC International Group, Inc., 2000.

Johns, A. H. 'A Humanistic Approach to *i'jāz* in the Qur'an: The Transfiguration of Language'. *Journal of Qur'anic Studies*, vol. 13, no. 1, 2011, pp. 79–99.

—. 'Joseph in the Qur'ān: Dramatic Dialogue, Human Emotion and Prophetic Wisdom'. *Islamochristiana*, vol. 7, 1981, pp. 29–55.

—. 'Narrative, Intertext and Allusion in the Qur'anic Presentation of Job'. *Journal of Qur'anic Studies*, vol. 1, no. 1, 1999, pp. 1–25.

—. 'Reflections on the Dynamics and Spirituality of *Sūrat al-Furqān*'. *Literary Structures of Religious Meaning in the Qur'an*, edited by Issa J. Boullata. Curzon, 2000, pp. 188–227.

—. '"She desired him and he desired her" (Qur'an 12:24): 'Abd al-Ra'ūf's treatment of an episode of the Joseph story in *Tarjumān al-Mustafīd*'. *Archipel*, vol. 57, 1999, pp. 109–34.

al-Jurjānī, 'Abd al-Qāhir. *Asrār al-Balāgha*. Dār al-Madanī.

Kazmi, Yedullah. 'The Qur'ān as Event and as Phenomenon'. *Islamic Studies*, vol. 41, no. 2, 2002, pp. 193–214.

Keeler, Annabel. 'Towards a Prophetology of Love: The Figure of Jacob in Sufi Commentaries on *Sūrat Yūsuf*'. *The Spirit and the Letter: Approaches to the Esoteric Interpretation of the Qur'an*, edited by Annabel Keeler and Sajjad Rizvi. Oxford University Press, 2016, pp. 125–53.

Kennedy, Philip. *Recognition in the Arabic Narrative Tradition: Discovery, Deliverance and Delusion*. Edinburgh University Press, 2016.

Kermani, Navid. 'The Aesthetic Reception of the Qur'ān as Reflected in Early Muslim History'. *Literary Structures of Religious Meaning in the Qur'an*, edited by Issa J. Boullata. Curzon, 2000, pp. 255–76.

—. 'From Revelation to Interpretation: Nasr Hamid Abū Zayd and the Literary Study of the Qur'ān'. *Modern Muslim Intellectuals and the Qur'ān*, edited by Suha Taji-Farouki. Oxford University Press, 2004.

—. *God Is Beautiful: The Aesthetic Experience of the Quran*. Polity, 2015.

Khalafallāh, Muḥammad Aḥmad. *al-Fann al-Qaṣaṣī fī al-Qur'ān al-Karīm*. Arab Diffusion Company, 1999.

Khan, Irfan Ahmad. 'The Qur'ānic View of Moses: A Messenger of God from the Children of Israel to Pharaoh'. *Islamic Studies*, vol. 45, no. 1, 2006, pp. 5–20.

Klar, M. O. *Interpreting al-Tha'labī's Tales of the Prophets: Temptation, Responsibility and Loss*. Routledge, 2009.

Laude, Patrick. 'Reading the Quran: The Lessons of the Ambassadors of Mystical

Islam'. *Sophia: The International Journal for Philosophy of Religion, Metaphysical Theology and Ethics*, vol. 46, no. 2, 2007, pp. 147–62.

Lybarger, Loren D. 'Prophetic Authority in the Qur'ānic Story of Maryam: A Literary Approach'. *The Journal of Religion,* vol. 80, no. 2, 2000, pp. 240–70.

al-Maḥallī, Jalāl al-Dīn Muḥammad bin Aḥmad and Jalāl al-Dīn 'Abd al-Raḥmān bin Abī Bakr al-Suyūṭī. *Tafsīr al-Īmamayn al-Jalālayn.* Dar El-Marefah, 2002.

Martensson, Ulrika. '"The Persuasive Proof": A Study of Aristotle's Politics and Rhetoric in the Qur'ān and in al-Ṭabarī's Commentary'. *Jerusalem Studies in Arabic and Islam*, vol. 34, pp. 363–420.

Martin, Richard C. 'Inimitability'. *Encyclopaedia of the Qur'ān.* Edited by Jane Dammen McAuliffe. Brill, 2002.

Maybudī, Rashīd al-Dīn. *Kashf al-Asrār: Unveiling of the Mysteries.* Abridged version, Royal Aal Al-Bayt Institute for Islamic Thought, Fons Vitae, translated by William C. Chittick, accessed at http://main.altafsir.com/Books/kashf.pdf

McAuliffe, Jane Dammen. 'Chosen of All Women: Mary and Fāṭima in Qur'ānic Exegesis'. *Islamochristiana,* vol. 7, 1981, pp. 19–28.

—. 'Text and Textuality: Q. 3:7 as a Point of Intersection'. *Literary Structures of Religious Meaning in the Qur'an,* edited by Issa J. Boullata. Curzon, 2000, pp. 56–76.

Merguerian, Gayane Karen and Najmabadi, Afsaneh. 'Zulaykha and Yusuf: Whose "Best Story"?'. *International Journal of Middle East Studies*, vol. 29, no. 4, 1997, pp. 485–508.

Mir, Mustansir. *Coherence in the Qur'ān.* American Trust Publications, 1986.

—. 'Dialogue in the Qur'ān'. *Religion & Literature,* vol. 24, no. 1, 1992, pp. 1–22.

—. 'Humor in the Qur'an'. *The Muslim World,* vol. 81, 1991, pp. 179–93.

—. 'Irony in the Qur'an: A Study of the Story of Joseph'. *Literary Structures of Religious Meaning in the Qur'an,* edited by Issa J. Boullata. Curzon, 2000, pp. 173–87.

—. 'The Qur'an as Literature'. *Religion & Literature,* vol. 20, no. 1, The Literature of Islam, 1988, pp. 49–64.

—. 'The Qur'anic Story of Joseph: Plot, Themes, and Characters'. *The Muslim World,* vol. 76, no. 1, pp. 1–15.

—. 'Some Aspects of Narration in the Qur'an'. *Sacred Tropes: Tanakh, New Testament, and Qur'an as Literature and Culture,* edited by Roberta Sterman Sabbath. Brill, 2009, pp. 93–106.

—. *Understanding the Islamic Scripture: A Study of Selected Passages from the Qur'ān.* Pearson Longman, 2008.

Morris, James W. 'Dramatizing the Sura of Joseph: An Introduction to the Islamic Humanities'. *Journal of Turkish Studies*, vol. 18, 1994, pp. 201–24.

Mourad, Suleiman A. 'On the Qur'ānic Stories About Mary and Jesus'. *Bulletin of the Royal Institute for Inter-Faith Studies*, vol. 1, no. 2, 1999, pp. 13–24.

Najmabadi, Afsaneh. 'Reading – And Enjoying – "Wiles of Women" Stories as a Feminist'. *Iranian Studies*, vol. 32, no. 2, The Uses of Guile: Literary and Historical Moments, 1999, pp. 203–22.

Netton, Ian Richard. 'Towards a Modern *Tafsīr* of *Sūrat al-Kahf*: Structure and Semiotics'. *Journal of Qur'anic Studies*, vol. 2, no. 1, 2000, pp. 67–87

Neuwirth, Angelika. 'The House of Abraham and The House of Amram: Genealogy, Patriarchal Authority, and Exegetical Professionalism'. *The Qur'ān in Context: Historical and Literary Investigations into the Qur'ānic Milieu*, edited by Angelika Neuwirth, Nicolai Sinai and Michael Marx. Brill, 2010.

—. 'Mary and Jesus – Counterbalancing the biblical Patriarchs. A Re-reading of *Sūrat Maryam* in *Sūrat Āl 'Imrān* (3:1-62)'. *Parole de l'Orient*, vol. 30, 2005, pp. 231–60.

—. '"Oral Scriptures" in Contact. The Qur'ānic Story of the Golden Calf and its Biblical Subtext between Narrative, Cult, and Inter-communal Debate'. *Self-Referentiality in the Qur'ān*, edited by Stefan Wild. Harrassowitz Verlag, 2006, pp. 71–92.

—. 'Orientalism in Oriental Studies? Qur'anic Studies as a Case in Point'. *Journal of Qur'anic Studies*, vol. 9, no. 2, 2007, pp. 115–27.

—. 'Qur'an and History – a Disputed Relationship. Some Reflections on Qur'anic History and History in the Qur'an'. *Journal of Qur'anic Studies*, vol. 5, no. 1, 2003, pp. 1–18.

—. 'Referentiality and Textuality in *Sūrat al-Ḥijr*: Some Observations on the Qur'ānic "Canonical Process" and the Emergence of a Community'. *Literary Structures of Religious Meaning in the Qur'an*, edited by Issa J. Boullata. Curzon, 2000, pp. 143–72.

—. *Scripture, Poetry, and the Making of a Community: Reading the Qur'an as a Literary Text*. Oxford University Press, 2014.

—. 'Two Views of History and Human Future: Qur'anic and Biblical Renderings of Divine Promises'. *Journal of Qur'anic Studies*, vol. 10, no. 1, 2008, pp. 1–20.

Newby, Gordon D. 'The Drowned Son: Midrash and Midrash Making in the Qur'an and *Tafsīr*'. *Studies in Islamic and Judaic Traditions*, edited by William M. Brinner and Stephen D. Ricks. Scholars Press, 1986.

Nguyen, Martin. 'Exegesis of the *Ḥurūf al-Muqaṭṭa'a*: Polyvalency in Sunnī

Traditions of Qur'anic Interpretation'. *Journal of Qur'anic Studies*, vol. 14, no. 2, 2012, pp. 1–28.

Ozgur Alhassen, Leyla. 'A Narratological Analysis of the Story of Ibrāhīm in the Qur'ān: Faith, Family, Parents and Ancestors'. *Religion and Literature*, vol. 49, no. 3, 2019.

—. 'A Structural Analysis of *Sūrat Maryam* Q. 19:1-58'. *Journal of Qur'anic Studies*, vol. 18, no. 1, 2016, pp. 92–116.

—. '"You Were Not There": The Creation of Humility and Knowledge in Qur'ānic Stories: A Rhetorical and Narratological Analysis'. *Comparative Islamic Studies*, vol. 11, no. 1, 2015 [2017], pp. 65–94.

Quṭb, Sayyid. *Fī Ẓilāl al-Qur'ān*. Dar al-Shorouk, 2007.

Rendsburg, Gary A. 'Literary Structures in the Qur'anic and Biblical Stories of Joseph'. *The Muslim World*, vol. 78, no. 2, pp. 118–20.

Reynolds, Gabriel Said. *The Qur'ān and Its Biblical Subtext*. Routledge, 2010.

Riddell, Peter G. 'The Transmission of Narrative-Based Exegesis in Islam: al-Baghawī's Use of Stories in his Commentary on the Qur'ān, and a Malay Descendent'. *Islam: Essays on Scripture, Thought and Society: A Festschrift in Honor of Anthony H. Johns*, edited by Peter G. Riddell and Tony Street. Brill, 1997.

Rippin, Andrew. '"Desiring the Face of God": The Qur'ānic Symbolism of Personal Responsibility'. *Literary Structures of Religious Meaning in the Qur'an*, edited by Issa J. Boullata. Curzon, 2000, pp. 117–24.

—. Review of *Studien zur Komposition der mekkanischen Suren* by Angelika Neuwirth. *Bulletin of the School of Oriental and African Studies, University of London*, vol. 45, no. 1, 1982, pp. 149–50.

Robinson, Neal. *Christ in Christianity and Islam*. State University of New York Press, 1991.

—. *Discovering the Qur'an: A Contemporary Approach to a Veiled Text*. 2nd ed. Georgetown University Press, 2003.

Robson, James. 'Stories of Jesus and Mary'. *The Muslim World*, vol. 40, no. 4, 1950, pp. 236–43.

Rubin, Uri. 'Traditions in Transformation: The Ark of the Covenant and the Golden Calf in Biblical and Islamic Historiography'. *Oriens*, vol. 36, 2001, pp. 196–214.

Ruf, Frederick J. 'The Consequences of Genre: Narrative, Lyric, and Dramatic Intelligibility'. *Journal of the American Academy of Religion*, vol. 62, no. 3, 1994, pp. 799–818.

Sakaedani, Haruko. 'The Correlation between Definite Noun Phrases and Verb

Forms in Qur'anic Narrative Texts'. *Journal of Qur'anic Studies*, vol. 6, no. 2, 2004, pp. 56–68.

Saleh, Walid. *The Formation of the Classical Tafsīr Tradition: The Qur'ān Commentary of al-Tha'labī (d. 427/1035).* Brill, 2004.

—. '"What if you refuse, when ordered to fight?" King Saul (Ṭālūt) in the Qur'ān and Post-Quranic Literature'. *Saul in Story and Tradition*, edited by Carl S. Ehrlich. Mohr Siebeck, 2006.

Sells, Michael. *Approaching the Qur'ān: The Early Revelations.* White Cloud Press, 1999.

—. 'A Literary Approach to the Hymnic Sūras of the Qur'ān: Spirit, Gender, and Aural Intertextuality'. *Literary Structures of Religious Meaning in the Qur'an*, edited by Issa J. Boullata. Curzon, 2000, pp. 3–25.

Shahīd, Irfan. 'Fawātiḥ al-Suwar: The Mysterious Letters of the Qur'ān'. *Literary Structures of Religious Meaning in the Qur'an*, edited by Issa J. Boullata. Curzon, 2000, pp. 125–42.

Silvers, Laury. '"In the Book We Have Left out Nothing": The Ethical Problem of the Existence of Verse 4:34 in the Qur'an'. *Comparative Islamic Studies*, vol. 2, no. 2, 2008, pp. 171–80.

Smith, Jane I. and Haddad, Yvonne Y. 'The Virgin Mary in Islamic Tradition and Commentary'. *The Muslim World*, vol. 79, no. 3–4, pp. 161–87.

Stern, M. S. 'Muhammad and Joseph: A Study of Koranic Narrative'. *Journal of Near Eastern Studies*, vol. 44, no. 3, 1985, pp. 193–204.

Stewart, Devin J. 'Divine Epithets and the Dibacchius: Clausulae and Qur'anic Rhythm'. *Journal of Qur'anic Studies*, vol. 15, no. 2, 2013, pp. 22–64.

Stowasser, Barbara Freyer. *Women in the Qur'an, Traditions, and Interpretation.* Oxford University Press, 1994.

Syamsuddin, Sahiron. '*Muḥkam* and *Mutashābih*: An Analytical Study of al-Ṭabarī's and al-Zamakhsharī's Interpretations of Q.3:7'. *Journal of Qur'anic Studies*, vol. 1, no. 1, 1999, pp. 63–79.

al-Ṭabarī, Abū Ja'far Muḥammad ibn Jarīr. *Jāmi' al-Bayān 'an Ta'wīl al-Qur'an.* Dār al-Salām, 2007.

al-Ṭabrisī, Abū 'Alī al-Faḍl ibn al-Ḥasan. *Majma' al-Bayān fī Tafsīr al-Qur'an.* Accessed at www.altafsir.com/Tafasir.asp?tMadhNo=4&tTafsirNo=3&tSoraNo=28&tAyahNo=14&tDisplay=yes&Page=2&Size=1&LanguageId=1

Taji-Farouki, Suha, ed. *Modern Muslim Intellectuals and the Qur'ān.* Oxford University Press, 2004.

Tlili, Sarra. *Animals in the Qur'an.* Cambridge University Press, 2012.

al-Tha'ālibī, Abū Zayd 'Abd al-Rahmān b. Muḥammad b. Makhlūf. *al-Jawāhir al-Ḥisān*. Dār al-Kutub al-'Ilmiyya, 1996.

Toorawa, Shawkat M. '*Sūrat Maryam* (Q. 19): Lexicon, Lexical Echoes, English Translation'. *Journal of Qur'ānic Studies*, vol. 13, no. 1, 2011, pp. 25–78.

Tottoli, Roberto. 'About Qur'anic Narratives: A Review Article Koraniceskie skazanija (Qur'anic narratives) by Gianni Capra; M. B. Piotrovskij'. *Oriente Moderno*, vol. 72, no. 7–12, 1992, pp. 87–91.

—. *Biblical Prophets in the Qur'ān and Muslim Literature*. Translated by Michael Robertson. Curzon Press, 2002.

al-Tustarī, Abī Muḥammad Sahl bin 'Abd Allah. *Tafsīr al-Tustarī*. Dār al-Kutub al-'Ilmiyyah, 2002.

Wahyudi, Jarot. 'Literary Interpretation of the Qur'ān: "Fawāṣil al-Āyāt," "Qasam" and "Istifhām," Three Examples from Bint al-Shāṭi''s Tafsīr'. *Islamic Studies*, vol. 37, no. 1, 1998, pp. 19–28.

Waldman, Marilyn R. 'New Approaches to "Biblical" Materials in the Qur'ān'. *The Muslim World*, vol. 75, no. 1, pp. 1–13.

Ward Gwynne, Rosalind. *Logic, Rhetoric, and Legal Reasoning in the Qur'ān: God's arguments*. Routledge/Curzon, 2004.

Welch, Alford T. 'Formulaic Features of the Punishment-Stories'. *Literary Structures of Religious Meaning in the Qur'an*, edited by Issa J. Boullata. Curzon, 2000, pp. 77–116.

—. Review of *Studien zur Komposition der mekkanischen Suren* by Angelika Neuwirth. *Journal of the American Oriental Society*, vol. 103, no. 4, 1983, pp. 764–67.

Wheeler, Brannon. 'Arab Prophets of the Qur'an and Bible'. *Journal of Qur'anic Studies*, vol. 8, no. 2, 2006, pp. 24–57.

—. *Moses in the Quran and Islamic Exegesis*. Routledge/Curzon, 2002.

—. 'Moses or Alexander? Early Islamic Exegesis of Qur'ān 18:60-65'. *Journal of Near Eastern Studies*, vol. 57, no. 3, 1998, pp. 191–215.

—. *Prophets in the Quran: An Introduction to the Quran and Muslim Exegesis*. Continuum, 2002.

Wolf, C. Umhau. 'Moses in Christian and Islamic Tradition'. *Journal of Bible and Religion*, vol. 27, no. 2, 1959, pp. 102–8.

Yazicioglu, Isra. *Understanding the Qur'anic Miracle Stories in the Modern Age*. The Pennsylvania State University Press, 2013.

Zadeh, Travis. *The Vernacular Qur'an: Translation and the Rise of Persian Exegesis*. Oxford University Press, 2012.

Zahniser, A. H. Mathias. 'Major Transitions and Thematic Borders in Two Long

Sūras: *al-Baqara* and *al-Nisā*". *Literary Structures of Religious Meaning in the Qur'an*, edited by Issa J. Boullata. Curzon, 2000, pp. 26–55.
—. 'The Word of God and the Apostleship of 'Isa: A Narrative Analysis of Al 'Imrān (3):33–62'. *Journal of Semitic Studies*, vol. 36, 1991, p. 77–112.
al-Zamakhsharī, Abū al-Qāsim Maḥmūd ibn 'Umar. *Al-Kashshāf.* Dār El-Fikr, 2006.
Zebiri, Kate. 'Towards a Rhetorical Criticism of the Qur'ān'. *Journal of Qur'anic Studies*, vol. 5, no. 2, 2003, pp. 95–120.
Zubir, Badri Najib. 'Departure from Communicative Norms in the Qur'an: Insights from al-Jurjānī and al-Zamakhsharī'. *Journal of Qur'anic Studies*, vol. 2, no. 2, 2000, pp. 69–81.

II. Biblical Hermeneutics

Alter, Robert. *The Art of Biblical Narrative*. Basic Books, 1981.
—. 'Sodom as Nexus: The Web of Design in Biblical Narrative'. *Tikkun Magazine*, vol. 1, no. 1, pp. 30–8.
Bal, Mieke. *Death and Dissymmetry: The Politics of Coherence in the Book of Judges*. University of Chicago Press, 1988.
Rosenberg, Joel. 'Biblical Narrative'. *Back to the Sources: Reading the Classical Jewish Texts*, edited by Barry W. Holtz. Summit Books, 1984.
Stern, David. *Midrash and Theory: Ancient Jewish Exegesis and Contemporary Literary Studies*. Northwestern University Press, 1996.
Sternberg, Meir. *The Poetics of Biblical Narrative: Ideological Literature and the Drama of Reading*. Indiana University Press, 1985.

III. Literary and Orality Theory

Auerbach, Erich. *Mimesis: The Representation of Reality in Western Literature - New and Expanded Edition.* Princeton University Press, 2013.
Austin, J. L. *How To Do Things With Words: The William James Lectures Delivered At Harvard University in 1955.* Oxford University Press, 1975.
Bal, Mieke. *Narratology: Introduction to the Theory of Narrative*. 3rd ed. University of Toronto Press, 2009.
Barthes, Roland. 'Mythologies'. *Literary Theory: An Anthology*, edited by Julie Rivkin and Michael Ryan. Blackwell Publishing, 2004, pp. 81–9.
—. *S/Z: An Essay*. Translated by Richard Miller. The Noonday Press, 1974.
Benjamin, Walter. *Illuminations: Essays and Reflections*, edited by Hannah Arendt, translated by Harry Zohn. Schocken Books, 1969.

Booth, Wayne C. *The Rhetoric of Fiction*. 2nd ed. University of Chicago Press, 1983.

Brooks, Peter. *Reading for the Plot: Design and Intention in Narrative*. Harvard University Press, 1984.

Chatman, Seymour. *Story and Discourse: Narrative Structure in Fiction and Film*. Cornell University Press, 1978.

Eagleton, Terry. *Literary Theory: An Introduction*. Basil Blackwell, 1983.

Genette, Gerard. *Narrative Discourse: An Essay in Method*. Translated by Jane E. Lewin Cornell University Press, 1980.

Goody, Jack. *The Domestication of the Savage Mind*. Cambridge University Press, 1977.

Lord, Albert B. *The Singer of Tales*. Harvard University Press, 1960.

Ong, Walter J. *Orality and Literacy: The Technologizing of the Word*. Routledge, 1988.

Saussure, Ferdinand de. 'Course in General Linguistics'. *Literary Theory: An Anthology*, edited by Julie Rivkin and Michael Ryan, Blackwell, 2004, pp. 59–71.

White, Hayden. *The Content of the Form: Narrative Discourse and Historical Representation*. The Johns Hopkins University Press, 1987.

Index